PRAIRIE PILOT
LADY LUCK WAS ON MY SIDE

THE STORIES OF WALTER D. WILLIAMS
Compiled and Edited by Deana J. Driver

DriverWorks
Ink
www.driverworks.ca

The short stories in this book are the memories and opinions of the late Walter Williams, and should be considered in the context of the era in which he lived and worked.

Library and Archives Canada Cataloguing in Publication
WILLIAMS, WALTER D., 1911-1979
PRAIRIE PILOT: LADY LUCK WAS ON MY SIDE: The Stories of Walter D. Williams
/ Compiled and Edited by Deana J. Driver
Includes bibliographical references and index.
ISBN 978-0-9810394-2-8
1. Williams, Walter D., 1911-1979--Anecdotes. 2. Bush flying--Prairie Provinces--Anecdotes. 3. Bush pilots--Canada--Biography.
I. Driver, Deana, 1956- II. Title.
TL540.W5615A3 2008   629.13092   C2008-904899-7

Editing and book design – Deana Driver
Front cover photo – Walter Williams with CF-EVO, 1950
Back cover photo - CF-EVO in flight
Photos courtesy – Dave and Miriam Williams, Faye Climenhaga
2008 photos of Kerrobert – Deana Driver

Printed and bound in Canada.

Published by
DriverWorks Ink
Saskatchewan, Canada
www.driverworks.ca
110 McCarthy Blvd. N., Regina, SK S4R 6A4
(306) 545-5293

Index

Introduction ∘   9

Preface ∘   17

Foreword ∘   21

The Beginning ∘   24
Solo Flight ∘   26
First Passengers ∘   28
Early Flight In EGF ∘   29
Joe Kreiser – Altario Fence ∘ ∘ ∘ ∘ ∘ ∘ ∘ ∘ ∘ ∘ ∘ ∘ ∘ ∘   31
Rough Landings – Tight Takeoffs ∘ ∘ ∘ ∘ ∘ ∘ ∘ ∘ ∘   33
Plane Repair – Flight To La Ronge ∘ ∘ ∘ ∘ ∘ ∘ ∘ ∘   36

Good Deeds, Good Work ∘ ∘ ∘ ∘ ∘ ∘ ∘ ∘ ∘ ∘ ∘ ∘ ∘ ∘ ∘   39
Hospital Trips – Biggar – Major ∘ ∘ ∘ ∘ ∘ ∘ ∘ ∘ ∘ ∘   40
Andy Meier – Home In The Dark ∘ ∘ ∘ ∘ ∘ ∘ ∘ ∘ ∘   42
Ephriam L. Read – To Saskatoon ∘ ∘ ∘ ∘ ∘ ∘ ∘ ∘   43
Mike Balanoff – Veterinarian ∘ ∘ ∘ ∘ ∘ ∘ ∘ ∘ ∘ ∘ ∘   44
Mrs. Crawford – Out Late ∘ ∘ ∘ ∘ ∘ ∘ ∘ ∘ ∘ ∘ ∘ ∘ ∘   45
Plane Wreck ∘   46
Harold Kellough – Bill Tocker ∘ ∘ ∘ ∘ ∘ ∘ ∘ ∘ ∘ ∘   55
Plane Repaired ∘   58
Ready For Flight Again ∘ ∘ ∘ ∘ ∘ ∘ ∘ ∘ ∘ ∘ ∘ ∘ ∘ ∘ ∘ ∘   63
Large Truck Transmission ∘ ∘ ∘ ∘ ∘ ∘ ∘ ∘ ∘ ∘ ∘ ∘ ∘   66
Mail – Groceries – Medicine ∘ ∘ ∘ ∘ ∘ ∘ ∘ ∘ ∘ ∘ ∘   67
Mrs. May - Vanscoy ∘ ∘ ∘ ∘ ∘ ∘ ∘ ∘ ∘ ∘ ∘ ∘ ∘ ∘ ∘ ∘ ∘ ∘   68
Doc James – No Winter Roads ∘ ∘ ∘ ∘ ∘ ∘ ∘ ∘ ∘ ∘   69
Wrecked Ryan ∘   72
Sask Tel And Sask Power Flights ∘ ∘ ∘ ∘ ∘ ∘ ∘ ∘   74
Police Flights ∘   76

Train Wreck East Of Biggar ○ ○ ○ ○ ○ ○ ○ ○ ○ ○ ○ ○ ○ ○ ○ ○ ○ ○ 82
Dr. Eyde – Macklin ○ 85
Mrs. Russel Bielby – To Biggar ○ ○ ○ ○ ○ ○ ○ ○ ○ ○ ○ ○ ○ ○ ○ 86

Winter In The Air ○ 87
First Winter – Drunk Passenger ○ ○ ○ ○ ○ ○ ○ ○ ○ ○ ○ ○ ○ ○ 88
Sharing The Big Day ○ 90
Alsask – Injured Boy ○ 92
First Forced Landing ○ 94
Mother With Sick Child – Major ○ ○ ○ ○ ○ ○ ○ ○ ○ ○ ○ ○ ○ ○ 95
Dad Rising Early For Me ○ ○ ○ ○ ○ ○ ○ ○ ○ ○ ○ ○ ○ ○ ○ ○ ○ ○ 98
Blood Poisoning – Greene Elevator ○ ○ ○ ○ ○ ○ ○ ○ ○ ○ ○ ○ 99
Howard Carter – Out Of Propane ○ ○ ○ ○ ○ ○ ○ ○ ○ ○ ○ ○ ○ 100
Warm Winter Days – Sticky Snow ○ ○ ○ ○ ○ ○ ○ ○ ○ ○ ○ ○ ○ 101
R.M. Mariposa – Books To Audit ○ ○ ○ ○ ○ ○ ○ ○ ○ ○ ○ ○ ○ 103
Trips For Two Sick Women ○ ○ ○ ○ ○ ○ ○ ○ ○ ○ ○ ○ ○ ○ ○ ○ 105
Sebastian Schell – On A Suitcase ○ ○ ○ ○ ○ ○ ○ ○ ○ ○ ○ ○ 107
Ralph Wright – To Saskatoon ○ ○ ○ ○ ○ ○ ○ ○ ○ ○ ○ ○ ○ ○ ○ 108
Flew Baby To Lloydminster ○ ○ ○ ○ ○ ○ ○ ○ ○ ○ ○ ○ ○ ○ ○ ○ 109
Mechanic's Wife And Baby ○ ○ ○ ○ ○ ○ ○ ○ ○ ○ ○ ○ ○ ○ ○ ○ 110
Mrs. Murray Lowe – To Dodsland ○ ○ ○ ○ ○ ○ ○ ○ ○ ○ ○ ○ 111
John Vaber ○ 113
Forced Landing – Jack Allen ○ ○ ○ ○ ○ ○ ○ ○ ○ ○ ○ ○ ○ ○ ○ 115
Dr. Dicola – Veterinarian ○ ○ ○ ○ ○ ○ ○ ○ ○ ○ ○ ○ ○ ○ ○ ○ ○ 117
Percy Klaen ○ 118
Cutter Near Tramping Lake ○ ○ ○ ○ ○ ○ ○ ○ ○ ○ ○ ○ ○ ○ ○ ○ 119
Corpse – Consort To Castor ○ ○ ○ ○ ○ ○ ○ ○ ○ ○ ○ ○ ○ ○ ○ ○ 120
Prince Albert – Radio ○ ○ ○ ○ ○ ○ ○ ○ ○ ○ ○ ○ ○ ○ ○ ○ ○ ○ ○ 124
Meadow Lake – Lake Landing ○ ○ ○ ○ ○ ○ ○ ○ ○ ○ ○ ○ ○ ○ 126
Doc Jones – Upset CPR Snowplow ○ ○ ○ ○ ○ ○ ○ ○ ○ ○ ○ 128
Jim Charteris – Damage – Repair ○ ○ ○ ○ ○ ○ ○ ○ ○ ○ ○ ○ 130
Wilkie – Flying Santa Claus ○ ○ ○ ○ ○ ○ ○ ○ ○ ○ ○ ○ ○ ○ ○ 133
'Lady' To North Battleford ○ ○ ○ ○ ○ ○ ○ ○ ○ ○ ○ ○ ○ ○ ○ ○ 134
Lady From Chicago – Father Dying ○ ○ ○ ○ ○ ○ ○ ○ ○ ○ 136
Taxi Services ○ 137
Kelfield Agent's Wife ○ ○ ○ ○ ○ ○ ○ ○ ○ ○ ○ ○ ○ ○ ○ ○ ○ ○ ○ 139
Lady To Wilkie Hospital ○ ○ ○ ○ ○ ○ ○ ○ ○ ○ ○ ○ ○ ○ ○ ○ ○ 140

Merle Kirk – Swan River ◦ ◦ ◦ ◦ ◦ ◦ ◦ ◦ ◦ ◦ ◦ ◦ ◦ ◦ ◦ ◦ ◦ ◦ ◦ 142
Trip Home From Swift Current ◦ ◦ ◦ ◦ ◦ ◦ ◦ ◦ ◦ ◦ ◦ ◦ ◦ ◦ ◦ 144
Snowbanks Bare Ground ◦ ◦ ◦ ◦ ◦ ◦ ◦ ◦ ◦ ◦ ◦ ◦ ◦ ◦ ◦ ◦ ◦ 147
Schoolteacher – A Load Of Books ◦ ◦ ◦ ◦ ◦ ◦ ◦ ◦ ◦ ◦ ◦ ◦ ◦ 148
Snow Or No Snow ◦ 150

Fun and Foolishness ◦ ◦ ◦ ◦ ◦ ◦ ◦ ◦ ◦ ◦ ◦ ◦ ◦ ◦ ◦ ◦ ◦ ◦ ◦ 152
First Flight To Pick Up Dave ◦ ◦ ◦ ◦ ◦ ◦ ◦ ◦ ◦ ◦ ◦ ◦ ◦ ◦ ◦ 153
Local Barnstorming And Gift Rides ◦ ◦ ◦ ◦ ◦ ◦ ◦ ◦ ◦ ◦ ◦ ◦ 155
Dave And Alan – Banff Mountains ◦ ◦ ◦ ◦ ◦ ◦ ◦ ◦ ◦ ◦ ◦ ◦ 159
Coyote Hunting ◦ 162
Baldy Bell – Barnstorming ◦ ◦ ◦ ◦ ◦ ◦ ◦ ◦ ◦ ◦ ◦ ◦ ◦ ◦ ◦ ◦ 165
Denzil Girl To Prelate ◦ ◦ ◦ ◦ ◦ ◦ ◦ ◦ ◦ ◦ ◦ ◦ ◦ ◦ ◦ ◦ ◦ 166
Meadow Lake Trip – Bush Fire ◦ ◦ ◦ ◦ ◦ ◦ ◦ ◦ ◦ ◦ ◦ ◦ ◦ ◦ 168
Brenda – Biggar – Right Wheel ◦ ◦ ◦ ◦ ◦ ◦ ◦ ◦ ◦ ◦ ◦ ◦ ◦ 169
Winnipeg Flood – Arnold Cornish ◦ ◦ ◦ ◦ ◦ ◦ ◦ ◦ ◦ ◦ ◦ ◦ 170
Doug Herriott – Harris – Deer ◦ ◦ ◦ ◦ ◦ ◦ ◦ ◦ ◦ ◦ ◦ ◦ ◦ ◦ 173
Trip To Calgary – Dad – Los Angeles ◦ ◦ ◦ ◦ ◦ ◦ ◦ ◦ ◦ ◦ ◦ 174
Trip From Calgary – Fog Layers ◦ ◦ ◦ ◦ ◦ ◦ ◦ ◦ ◦ ◦ ◦ ◦ ◦ 176
Return To Calgary – Death Close ◦ ◦ ◦ ◦ ◦ ◦ ◦ ◦ ◦ ◦ ◦ ◦ 179
Green Lake – Fishing ◦ ◦ ◦ ◦ ◦ ◦ ◦ ◦ ◦ ◦ ◦ ◦ ◦ ◦ ◦ ◦ ◦ ◦ 181
Humourous Flights ◦ ◦ ◦ ◦ ◦ ◦ ◦ ◦ ◦ ◦ ◦ ◦ ◦ ◦ ◦ ◦ ◦ ◦ ◦ 183
Precision Drilling – Provost – Czar. ◦ ◦ ◦ ◦ ◦ ◦ ◦ ◦ ◦ ◦ ◦ 187
John Herron Flew To Saskatoon ◦ ◦ ◦ ◦ ◦ ◦ ◦ ◦ ◦ ◦ ◦ ◦ ◦ 189
Wedding Cake Takes A Trip ◦ ◦ ◦ ◦ ◦ ◦ ◦ ◦ ◦ ◦ ◦ ◦ ◦ ◦ ◦ 190
Picked Up Marion ◦ 192
Regina – Barely Cleared Runway ◦ ◦ ◦ ◦ ◦ ◦ ◦ ◦ ◦ ◦ ◦ ◦ 194
Dan Boice's Party ◦ 196
Jack MacNeill – North Battleford ◦ ◦ ◦ ◦ ◦ ◦ ◦ ◦ ◦ ◦ ◦ ◦ 199
Hughenden – Chicken Dinner ◦ ◦ ◦ ◦ ◦ ◦ ◦ ◦ ◦ ◦ ◦ ◦ ◦ ◦ 201
Mother – Red Deer – Thanksgiving ◦ ◦ ◦ ◦ ◦ ◦ ◦ ◦ ◦ ◦ ◦ 203
Dr. Palmer – Unity ◦ ◦ ◦ ◦ ◦ ◦ ◦ ◦ ◦ ◦ ◦ ◦ ◦ ◦ ◦ ◦ ◦ ◦ ◦ 204
Lac La Ronge – Dave And I ◦ ◦ ◦ ◦ ◦ ◦ ◦ ◦ ◦ ◦ ◦ ◦ ◦ ◦ ◦ 206
Jim Fisk – Gull Lake ◦ ◦ ◦ ◦ ◦ ◦ ◦ ◦ ◦ ◦ ◦ ◦ ◦ ◦ ◦ ◦ ◦ ◦ 208
Dick Pittaway – Flew Close By ◦ ◦ ◦ ◦ ◦ ◦ ◦ ◦ ◦ ◦ ◦ ◦ ◦ 210
Peter Foulger – Home Movies ◦ ◦ ◦ ◦ ◦ ◦ ◦ ◦ ◦ ◦ ◦ ◦ ◦ ◦ 213

Near The End Of The Road ○ ○ ○ ○ ○ ○ ○ ○ ○ ○ ○ ○ ○ ○ ○ ○ ○   215
A Tribute To Harold Patterson ○ ○ ○ ○ ○ ○ ○ ○ ○ ○ ○ ○ ○ ○ ○ ○   216
Selling Aviation ○   218
Satellite Flying School ○ ○ ○ ○ ○ ○ ○ ○ ○ ○ ○ ○ ○ ○ ○ ○ ○ ○ ○   220
Jim Young – Compeer, Alta. ○ ○ ○ ○ ○ ○ ○ ○ ○ ○ ○ ○ ○ ○ ○ ○ ○   224
Ed Hopkins – Near Wilkie. ○ ○ ○ ○ ○ ○ ○ ○ ○ ○ ○ ○ ○ ○ ○ ○ ○   227
Going To Sleep In Flight ○ ○ ○ ○ ○ ○ ○ ○ ○ ○ ○ ○ ○ ○ ○ ○ ○ ○   230
Bill Hellofs – Cattle Buying ○ ○ ○ ○ ○ ○ ○ ○ ○ ○ ○ ○ ○ ○ ○ ○   233
Air In My Hair ○   235
Acknowledgements ○   239

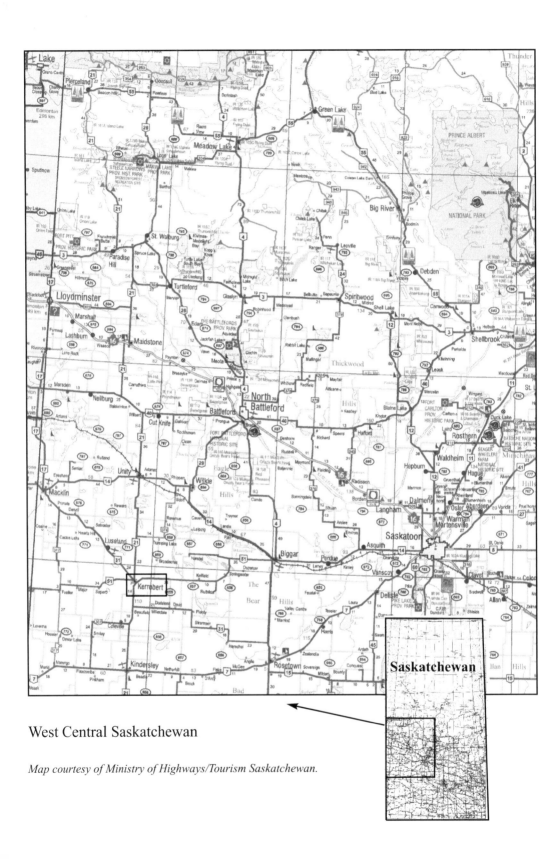

West Central Saskatchewan

Map courtesy of Ministry of Highways/Tourism Saskatchewan.

Introduction

Walter David Williams, the author of the stories in this book, was born on September 9, 1911, about 10 months after the wedding of his parents, Blake and Marion (nee Lockerbie) Williams. By the time he was 11, Walter had three siblings Katherine (Katie/Kay Cameron), Marion (Drummond) and Grace (Bomersine). The family farmed in the Revenue area of west central Saskatchewan until Walter was eight, when Blake and Marion sold the farm to Kasper Herle and moved the family into Kerrobert, a quiet little Canadian Pacific Railway town about 40 kilometres south of Revenue that now primarily serves the oil and agriculture industries.

Kerrobert's pioneer Immigration Hall was being taken apart in three sections at that time, so Blake Williams bought the centre section and moved it to the uphill side of Pacific Avenue onto a basement foundation to become the Williams family's home. Blake added a fieldstone veranda to three sides of the house and a fieldstone staircase on the front. He built a second floor inside the large structure and dug a root cellar below the front veranda. A mahogany staircase and railing joined the main floor to the second level and a large box for bedding had a permanent spot at the top of the stairs near the bedrooms and bathroom. Memorable fixtures of the house were a fireplace and piano, a variety of seating areas, shelves full of books, a plate rail near the ceiling all around the large dining area, and plenty of plants to create a homey atmosphere.

The Williams family hired a local woman to help with the laundry and housework. She used a hand-cranked wringer washer and clothes were hung outside on the iron clothes rack to dry. In winter, the washing was done indoors and the porch was covered with damp clothing.

These were the days of large phone boxes with ear pieces and families making their own entertainment such as playing cards and other games in their homes or with neighbours, or enjoying community dances and local sporting events such as hockey games and summer fairs. From the late 1940s on, radio dramas and movies at the Masonic Lodge hall were a popular pastime.

Walter Williams lived in the family home on Pacific Avenue for all but a few of the 50 or so years he lived in Kerrobert. The house is still in use today by the Hansen family. While the porch was renovated years ago to create an enclosed family room, the home's original mahogany staircase is still there along with the original claw foot bathtub.

In his early years, Walter was involved with Boy Scouts and various sports at school including wrestling. For men of that generation, being a tough guy was important. Showing a softer side was considered unmanly, and Walter was no exception to this rule. He had his share of fights with the boys in the neighbourhood and learned how to stick up for himself at an early age. Occasionally, though, Walter let a glimpse of his softer side show. He shared his family's love of music, playing cornet and joining with others to sing and play for family gatherings and community events. Blake Williams sang tenor in the United Church choir and Walter inherited his father's singing voice.

Soon after moving into Kerrobert, Walter's father opened a McCormick-Dearing dealership which became an International Harvester shop during the Second World War. The small shop near the old livery stable alongside the railroad tracks sold Imperial Oil products and IHC farm machinery and trucks. As a young man, Blake had jumped into a boxing ring occasionally to fight any challengers and earn a little extra money, so he knew how to take care of any trouble in the shop or elsewhere for that matter, but collecting on debts owed to the shop was sometimes an onerous task, especially during the Dirty Thirties.

Walter and his friend Oscar Neubaeur, who worked at the dealership for more than 30 years, at one point spent three years tending cattle at Turtleford, about 225 kilometres north of Kerrobert, to collect on a farmer's debt. The cattle had been given to Blake as payment of a machinery bill owed, so someone had to make sure the animals survived long enough to be sold.

While in Turtleford, Walter played cornet in the local band and gave free wrestling lessons to any of the local boys who asked for them. By 1936, Walter and Oscar were able to close down their Turtleford extension and come home.

Walter had quit high school in Grade 11 to work in his father's business. He also took on other work to help make ends meet during the Great Depression, including driving truck for the local creamery. That job helped him in later years to effectively navigate his airplane to numerous farms in the region.

After high school, Walter rekindled a relationship he had during his high school years with a local girl named Frances Jean Allcock. Jean was a year younger than Walter and taught school in the Kelfield and Ivy school districts, staying with farm families in the area. On one occasion, Walter walked the 30 or so kilometres from Kerrobert to visit Jean and walked home that same day. Walter and Jean had a sporadic long-distance relationship for about 10 years before marrying on February 15, 1939.

It was obvious from the beginning, to almost everyone except perhaps the bride and groom, that their marriage was not the best idea. Although they had seemed to get along just fine during their courtship, living with one another just didn't work out. Jean was constantly full of laughter and enthusiasm while Walter in those days was more serious about everyday life. As a young married man, he was more sombre and sullen and had a tendency to be grumpy. While Jean yearned for constant adventure and new experiences, Walter was not yet ready to share such a life with her. As Jean's sister Ferne Vincent explained, "Jean was a high-spirited girl. They had nothing in common."

The couple moved into a small house in Kerrobert that was a wedding gift from one of Jean's uncles. Their son David (Dave) was born the following year, in June 1940. Walter and Jean shared a love for their son, but little else. Jean moved out of their home when Dave was two years old and took teaching jobs in teacherages away from Kerrobert. Young Dave lived in Kerrobert for the next four years, being cared for by Walter and Walter's mother Marion.

After the 1942 Japanese attack on Pearl Harbour, Walter and his father stayed up all night to decide that their best service to Canada during the Second World War would be to maintain farm equipment and literally help to feed the Allied cause rather than to go overseas to fight. Walter had always been a risk-taker, like his father before him. "Walt never did anything halfway," his son Dave explained. Everyone was sure that Walter would not return alive if he ever went overseas to war.

The wartime work for the shop was very demanding in terms of the hours that Walter worked to keep the machinery in the region running. Ships carrying machinery parts from England were being torpedoed during the war, so Walter had to manufacture his own parts, such as brass bushings, on his lathe in the shop. He also did a considerable amount of blacksmithing work. He fixed everything from shot guns and seeding and cultivator equipment to pencil sharpeners and crank pins for a locomotive. Walter smoked heavily to stay awake for many hours and those who knew him well remember his fondness for his pipe and smelly cigars.

Their hard work during the war allowed their machinery business to prosper during difficult times. In October 1945, Blake and Walter built a new 7,000-square-foot (650-sq-metre) shop to go along with their new business name – B. Williams & Son IHC. It was one of the biggest shops in the surrounding area and boasted a concrete floor, a 14-foot ceiling and steam heat throughout that came from an old Case tractor boiler.

"Dad hauled the boiler in on his 1½-ton DS-30 International truck, which we teetered around on dirt roads way overloaded, entirely illegal nowadays," said Dave. "B. Williams & Son always tested their limits."

The large shop still sits on Railway Avenue as a Kerrobert landmark, about a block south of the site of the original shop, which was torn down in 1966. The former home of B. Williams & Son IHC is now the home of KEP Industries Ltd., suppliers of agricultural and industrial products

For fun after the war, and possibly to ease the pain of a broken marriage for which he blamed himself, Walter Williams purchased a Harley Davidson motorcycle to rip around the countryside. He paid Kreiser's Garage in Altario the sum of $325 for the bike.

In 1946, Jean moved north to Meadow Lake, Sask., taking Dave with her. (Jean taught school in Meadow Lake for the next 13 years before moving to Alberta for two years and then to finish her career in St. Walburg, Sask.) When Jean left for Meadow Lake, Walter moved back in with his parents and rented out their marital home to IHC employees and others for the next many years.

Dave visited his father and grandparents occasionally on weekends and holidays, and lived in Kerrobert for a few years during Grades 7 to 9. He returned to Meadow Lake partway through Grade 10, though, preferring his mother's kindness to his father's *terseness. Walter and Jean kept in contact throughout Dave's growing-up years, particularly through Walter's various trips between Meadow Lake and Kerrobert.*

Walter Williams was a hard worker who was supportive of his community, and those characteristics endeared him to many of his neighbours. He took courses through a mechanics school in Edmonton, Alta., and became one of the most capable mechanics and welders in the Kerrobert area, which helped the IHC dealership keep its customer base.

In the course of making long automobile trips back and forth to Meadow Lake to visit his son, Walter reactivated the flying bug he caught as a boy and began to take flying lessons. He earned his Private Pilot Licence in 1947 and on September 17, 1948, purchased a lightweight 65-horsepower Aeronca Chief airplane, Model No. 11-AC, from Harold F. Mitchinson of Saskatoon (a pilot and a survivor of the battle at Dunkirk) for the modest price of $2,300. The plane's serial number was 1849, but airplanes are known by their alphanumeric registration numbers, and this one was called CF–EVO. The CF portion is to designate Canadian planes and the last three letters are for that specific aircraft.

Over the next 15 years, the yellow 'EVO'[1] with orange lettering and a dark blue teardrop painted on each side of the plane's body would become Walter's best friend. It would see him through many fascinating and daring adventures, which are the subject of this book.

Aside from his activities in the air, Walter Williams contributed in many other ways to his local community. He ran the movies that showed in the town's hall during the Second World War and was a member of the town council, in charge of the water system. He became an expert at thawing frozen water mains with his electric welding generator. He was a Past Master of the Kerrobert Lodge No. 90 A.F. & A.M. and a 3rd Degree Member of the Scottish Rite. He was a Past Patron of the Order of the Eastern Star, Chapter No. 137 at Kerrobert and was behind the construction of the Kerrobert Airport and flight school, as described in the coming pages. Walter enjoyed trap shooting clay pigeons for fun and supported all variety of events that occurred in small prairie towns in those days including hockey games and community dances.

When Blake Williams died in 1951, Walter's life became much

---

[1] *EVO - Pronounced E.V.O. (ee-vee-oh)*

more complicated. His father's death forced Walter to move out from behind his welder's mask to handle things in the front office, and Walter wasn't very comfortable in this new role. Walter Williams was a great welder, a great mechanic and a skilled pilot, but he was not the best businessman, and the business was already heavily in debt to local investors when Walter had to take control. Walter also lacked the customer relations skills that help keep a business afloat, and he was inept at collecting debts.

One of the other complicating factors was that Walter loved his airplane more than he loved managing the business. Walter put most of his spare money into maintenance and gas for his airplane, which was more fulfilling to him in many ways than his IHC business. Even though he had competent staff working for him and he worked all night himself to get repair jobs done after flying his plane all day long, the business suffered and Walter was constantly worried about its future.

In March 1961, Walter's mother Marion died of cancer and a month later, one of Walter's closest friends died in an accident. Shortly after those two events, Walter realized that he had lost his zest for flying and, in 1963, he sold his beloved EVO.

He managed to keep the business afloat until 1970, when the downsizing of International Harvester Company Ltd. cost Walter Williams dearly in the loss of his franchise. His debt load was overwhelming and a year later, he lost all his property, including his marital house and the family home toward his debts. He declared bankruptcy and moved to Dinsmore and then Tisdale to work for other IHC dealerships.

Walter's life took a decided upturn in March 1973 when he married Romona Underwood, a woman he had gotten to know more than two decades earlier when she worked for Dr. Lorne McConnell, Saskatoon's first neurosurgeon. By 1973, Rev. Lillian Romona Underwood was a United Church minister who had spent 14 years as a missionary in Korea and three years as a hospital chaplain for out-of-town United Church patients in Saskatoon. She and Walter had been dating intermittently for at least 14 years prior to their marriage, spending time with each other whenever Romona was home on leave from her missionary work and once she returned to

Canada. Walter's son Dave recalls going along on several outings with Walter and Romona in the early years of their relationship to act as a 'chaperone.'

Walter and Jean finally divorced each other in the early 1970s after decades apart, which made way for Walter's marriage to Romona. Jean and Walter had not divorced previously because adultery was the only allowable reason for divorce in Canada at that time, and Jean also did not want her son growing up in the 1940s and 1950s with the stigma of having divorced parents. Divorce was "not proper," she had said. Permanent marriage breakdown became a ground for divorce in Canada in 1968.[2]

All along, Romona had used her pastoral gifts as a minister to help mend fences between Walter and Jean and other members of Walter's family. Walter and Romona lived in Saskatoon after their marriage and, by all accounts, they enjoyed being together. They liked to go trailer camping and fishing, and everyone enjoyed the couple's presence at family gatherings.

For his 60th birthday, Walter received a replica St. George's Cross medal from Dave for being 'the bravest man' his son had ever known (see Preface). Also, when he was 65, Walter joined his son in doing some climbing and exploring of Canada's geography that many younger men would have found daunting.

In 1974, Jean Williams moved from her home in Saskatchewan to Revelstoke, B.C., to be near her son Dave and his wife Miriam (Chase), who married in June 1975.

In June 1979, Romona Underwood Williams retired from full-time ministry to enjoy her retirement years with Walter. However, her plans changed drastically later that year when Walter died suddenly, at the age of 68.

In her January 1980 letter to friends, Romona wrote: "On December 4th, while installing an automatic door in our new garage as a surprise for me, Walter had a cardiac arrest and had died by the time I went to find out why he had not come in ... I am thankful for the years we had as friends, as husband and wife, and for the faith in eternal life, which we shared. Attending church has been hard, for it is one of the many precious memories I have – his strong voice singing and his teasing words, 'It's nice when they come to the

[2] *Government of Canada* **Divorce Law in Canada** *paper, prepared by Kristen Douglas. (http://dsp-psd.tpsgc.gc.ca)*

note you're on.' I grieve that I must go ahead without him but am thankful he was not left an invalid."

In 1986, Romona received an Honorary Doctor of Divinity, becoming Rev. Dr. Lillian Romona Underwood Williams. A unit of the United Church Women's group at St. Paul's United Church in Kindersley is named after her, honouring her work as a missionary.

On April 13, 2000, Frances Jean Williams died in Revelstoke at the age of 88. She enjoyed spending every summer during her 30-plus teaching years and retirement at her Greig Lake cabin near Meadow Lake. She had also been involved in her local United Church and community choirs over the years. Jean was survived by her son David (Miriam) Williams and five siblings: Esmond (Helen) Allcock, Gwendolyne (Bill) Low, Bruce (Mary) Allcock, Ferne Vincent, and Douglas (Marg) Allcock. She was predeceased by her brother Steele Allcock in 1941 and sister Sylvia Weeks in 1996.

On March 29, 2006, Romona Underwood Williams died in Saskatoon at age 92. She was survived by her adopted daughters Joye (Barc) Binnie of Saskatoon and Gwen (Garry) Greenshields of Prince Albert and their families as well as Walter's family: his son David (Miriam) Williams of Revelstoke, B.C.; stepdaughter Elizabeth (Keith) Hollingsworth and family of Alberta; nieces and nephews: Alan (Marilyn) Cameron and Merle Lembicz of Lacombe, Alta.; Gerald (Marilyn) Bomersine of Okotoks, Alta.; Brenda (Court) Lawrence of Ottawa, Ont.; Faye (Glen) Cleminhaga of Kindersley, Sask. and their families.

Before Romona died, she asked that Walter's short stories of his times as an early prairie pilot be published. These stories, typed by him in script font on an old manual typewriter during the course of more than 25 years, were to be shared as a testament to that era and to the man and his community.

Prairie Pilot: Lady Luck was on My Side *is the fulfillment of Romona's wish.*

— Deana Driver

— Deana Driver (dee-na) is a journalist/author/editor/publisher in Saskatchewan.

Preface

The Bravest Man I Ever Knew

This book is a selection of the memoirs of Saskatchewan pioneer air pilot Walter Williams of Kerrobert. Walter's mercy flights pre-dated those of the Saskatchewan Air Ambulance Service[3] and the Canadian Armed Forces Search and Rescue Service.[4]

Walter and his father Blake had the farm machine garage of B. Williams & Son, I.H.C., in Kerrobert. The business closed in bankruptcy in 1971 after Walter had used much of its proceeds to keep flying his airplane, an Aeronca Chief 11-AC; CF-EVO, bright yellow with blue trim and orange registration letters on both sides and top of wings. The plane had a 65-horsepower, four-cylinder Continental engine.

I remember the first time he and I saw the plane. It had Christian gospel messages neatly lettered all over it. Its owner at that time was a flying missionary/pastor. This was hardly appropriate for my father then, so the messages were cleaned off before the deal was closed. (As a sign painter, I know that a brisk application of paint thinner and horse-rub alcohol would do that, but don't drink the mixture! One of Dad's early passengers did that and he was raving blind on his way to hospital and then to the cemetery. To safely haul this man in his small, two-seat airplane with dual controls,[5] Dad applied 'safety harnesses' by tying up the man's hands and feet like an Egyptian mummy with the tie-down ropes he used for EVO so the man couldn't reach the controls or interfere with them.)

On the night of Pearl Harbour, Blake and Walter decided their war effort would be to help the Allied Forces get enough food by supplying and repairing farm machinery. So Dad stayed home with

[3] *While Saskatchewan's Air Ambulance Service began in 1946, it was based out of Regina with a Saskatoon base added in 1953. (Encyclopedia of Saskatchewan)*
[4] *The Canadian Armed Forces began its search and rescue operations after the Second World War. (www.warmuseum.ca) Walter was not a member of the Armed Forces.*
[5] *EVO had two control wheels (similar to automobile steering wheels) side by side, one in front of the pilot and one in front of the passenger. The wheels had the same functions and were made for training sessions and emergencies. Walter's son Dave recalls grabbing the wheel once when he was about 12 years old to steer the plane away from some oncoming trees, then waking his father who had fallen asleep at the controls.*

my Mom and me, bereaving Canada of another courageous war legend like Billy Bishop, Billy Barker, Wop May or Buzz Beurling. I'm glad, or all I would have in memory of my father would be letters, photos, medals and a worthy name in Canadian history.

Walt's exploits to help people during Saskatchewan winters, with skis on the Aeronca, deserved a knighthood but he was always in trouble with the (federal) Department of Transport (D.O.T.). The RCMP used his services then, whereas helicopters would be available for them now. One time, EVO was damaged when it hit a barbed wire farm fence in the snow. Dad used the fence wire to tie the ski undercart back together so he could deliver a maternity case to hospital in time to report and fly home.

Word got out to the D.O.T. They telegraphed Dad, telling him to report to them at Winnipeg. The country was winter-locked, so Dad flew the plane there. The D.O.T. threw the book at him and phoned Cpl. Bert Fisk in Kerrobert to say they had Williams and were there any charges waiting for him. Cpl. Fisk replied, "Send him home! We need him here!"

It cost Dad many thousands of dollars to make all the repairs ordered on EVO by the D.O.T. before he could fly it out of Winnipeg and home to Kerrobert. Dad never got along with the system. I inherited that trait from him.

In 1971, B. Williams & Son closed out with a bankruptcy total of about one and one-half million dollars. Few Master-ranked Free Masons go to prison, and I'm glad Dad was spared from that. His involvement with the Masons marked him as one of 'the Good Guys.' The way I witnessed Dad stand up to evil and defend the weak and needy, he had earned in my sight the Red Cross of Saint George emblazoned across his chest!

After he went broke, on his 60th birthday night (in September 1976), he was working for other I.H.C. dealers near Kerrobert, pumping gas, selling parts and doing chores. I needed a birthday gift for him and knew his heart was broken over me, his not-so-great son who had gone off to his own life rather than help with the family business.

I walked into a cheap used-goods store in Drumheller, Alta., and saw a Victoria Cross (the supreme British war medal) pinned upon a corkboard with all the costume jewellery, geegaws[6] and other trinkets

---

[6] *Geegaws – Flashy trinkets.*

in the shop. My old Army blood froze.[7] Obviously, an old soldier had died and his family, cleaning out his home, didn't know what this was and sold it! I bought the medal for $30, the cost of a tank of gas to get home to Revelstoke, B.C., in those days.

The real VCs are inscribed on the back, but this one wasn't. I had a disposable Victoria Cross. (Imitations of the Victoria Cross are made for people to purchase if they choose to replace lost or stolen VCs or to keep their original in a safe place such as a bank safety deposit box. This way, if the holder went drinking with his pals and lost the medal, the real one would be in a bank box somewhere safe.)

I bought a case for the medal at a jewelry store and wrote a 'Citation for Walter Williams and all his life at Kerrobert with CF-EVO.' Dad had gone fishing on his birthday that year at Jackfish Lake, where he used to take me in EVO. I found him there, and we walked out to a sunlit little bay where we used to shut off the boat motor and eat our lunch. I wished Dad a happy birthday and gave him the medal.

The citation had the desired effect. I wasn't the King of England, but I knew I was the most important man on earth to him – his son. We had a real sob session there, washing away many bad times and memories. The words embossed on the medal – 'FOR VALOUR' in big, bold capitals – said it all from me to him, for all the kinds of courage he had shown me. I always told my Scouts and Cadets that it is no disgrace for a man to weep. What is important is what he weeps about. I am thankful to one anonymous old veteran, the only reason I could have for holding an imitation VC in my hand, so I could give it to the bravest man I ever knew, and I did.

In the brutal times of the 1930s Depression, Walter Williams resolved to be a good man and a strong man. He was obsessed with courage, and that is how he grew up as a child of Saskatchewan pioneers in the Kerrobert and Tramping Lake District. In marriage to him, my poor love angel mother was helpless to his moods, so she packed me up and took me with her to teach around the province. Ten years later, I knew how she felt when I left Dad at Kerrobert to grow up my way.

Later, in Rev. Romona Underwood (a United Church minister) of Saskatoon, he found a wife who could abide him; and she was the

---

[7] *Dave Williams was in the Canadian Armed Forces for about six years before going back to Kerrobert for a time to work with his father and then moving to B.C. to become a sign painter, pilot and diver.*

love of his life until Dad fell dead with a ruptured heart in 1979. We buried him beside friends in a Saskatoon cemetery. I put a picture of CF-EVO on his tombstone, with its snow skis just clearing a barbed wire fence in takeoff.[8]

On Judgment Day, I think Dad will get over the wire, too, and to his reward in heaven. Mom is there, too, 22 years later. There, everything must be understood and forgiven, for it to be heaven.

– Dave Williams, Revelstoke, B.C.

---

[8] *Dave drew EVO just getting over a collapsed fence in the snow, "a hazard Dad always had to watch for. Dad flew at night and in bad weather, and flew past more hazards than we knew about."*

Foreword

These stories are written to record reflections of experiences in my active flying time of 16 years from 1946 to 1963. There were many other experiences, but all through those years, I broke many of the rules in The Book and bent most of the rest of them.

I came off with a lucky and good average, considering the chances taken in situations which each time seemed to require such measures. Most of these situations developed from requirements of other people (many times, complete strangers) who were in one kind of trouble or other, and an 'airplane' was the only answer. Circumstances like weather, short fields, darkness, ground or snow conditions were often disregarded in the interest of those whom I felt obligated to help because it was in my power to do so.

These rustling of the leaves of memory are in my own language, completely bereft of refinements and niceties of professional writers.

One of my rewards for these efforts was in 'selling' aviation, particularly to people who had always been terrified of flying but necessity had required that I fly them somewhere. Casual, quiet and kindly explanation, pointing out that aviation is practical, that this-or-that many thousand persons are in the air at any moment of the day or night often changed their attitude from fear to one of confidence and trust.

My earliest contact with an airplane was the arrival of a First World War 'Jenny' (short for JN-4) on rough rocky ground over the hill behind the water tower in our home town of Kerrobert, Saskatchewan. I was just a kid then, and the pilot asked me to hold a wing for him so he could make a short turn to avoid something. He was barnstorming, after his time in Service, and had put his savings into the 'Jenny.'

Next was a plane, open cockpit, from Cherry Airways of Saskatoon. I would have been 14 or 15 by then. Our dad bought rides for the whole family and my youngest sister, Grace, went along with me for our turn. We were last. Next day, at the next barnstorming stop, this plane was grounded because the engine was 'missing' so badly.

Next, several years later, was a Stinson called 'Lady Wildfire' (advertising a coal of that name) from Prince Albert. Cecil Hellofs and I paid an extra dollar each for 'stunts.' All we got was a couple of good stall turns, but I can recall thinking I'd have to live the rest of my life without a stomach. Mine was still way 'up there.'

A few years passed and it was a nice winter day. A little Piper Cub landed and taxied up beside a house on the edge of town. I looked it over carefully and decided that aviation was at last coming nearer to my ambitions in that style of plane.

More years passed, through marriage and the birth of son David in 1940. Separation finally placed him at Meadow Lake. In those days, Meadow Lake was not too easily accessible, especially in wintertime. By Easter of 1946, after having a particularly difficult trip there and finding to my surprise that David was ill and confined to bed, I fought my way back to Saskatoon by car. I then took my first flying lesson in an Aeronca Champion from Harold Mitchinson of Mitchinson Flying Service (in Saskatoon).

Subsequent lessons had to be worked in, coincidental with trips of a business nature to Saskatoon, and subject to the availability of a plane and favourable weather. By June or July of 1947, I had obtained my Private Pilot Licence.

Renting the Piper Cub EGF for over a year gave me some flying experience, but it was always based from Saskatoon and by that time I was ready to mortgage the rest of my life to have a little plane at home. This came to pass when Mitch sold me a little second-hand 65 HP Aeronca Chief side-by-side two-seater, wheel control, in September 1948. That was the start of so many experiences which have enriched my life, for better and for worse, in so many ways.

This was in the period before high wide roads, more efficient snowplowing, increased horsepower and bigger and better development in vehicles. My flying years were the last of the era requiring rural air service of an emergency nature. Prior to 'my day,' these emergencies had to be handled with a team of horses, a snowplane,[9] snowplows or whatever, which were prolonged and rough, and some of the patients didn't survive the trip. Many of these men fattened their egos by calling them 'mercy' trips, but I could never speak of my efforts in that way, knowing that they were appreciated, known, and my satisfaction of accomplishment, giving and helping, filled my heart.[10]

I have dedicated this work to you, Dave, in the hope that you will better understand your dad, and perhaps know the better why you are yourself. I am very proud of you, Dave, and hope that in some way, I have helped you to be the unusual and fine person you are. Some of these experiences you shared in, others you didn't, but you know they really happened and in them you may find part of yourself, as you are.

Second dedication goes to my wife Romona, who was the receptionist in Dr. L.H. McConnell's office, where I obtained my first and subsequent medicals. Romona was the first one who had a ride with me right after I got my licence. Blind faith? Well, whatever it was, she's still with me, and I'm sure you're glad for that, and unselfish enough to share.

Flying put Technicolor into my life. Deleting these experiences would be tantamount to diminishing my life and memories from colour TV back to black-and-white.

– Walter D. Williams
(likely written in the late 1970s)

---

[9] Snowplane – A lightly-built plane on skis that does not fly. It has a 'pusher' airplane motor on the back of it and a caged propeller behind the engine.

[10] Many pilots after the Second World War offered flight taxi services, searches or other work to assist police so they could build air time towards becoming a commercial pilot or earn money for expensive aviation fuel, said Dave Williams. Walter kept a supply of aviation fuel at his Kerrobert hangar but used automotive gasoline when necessary.

The Beginning

When Walter Williams became a pilot, there was no electricity yet for yardlights on farms. His small plane had no lights like bigger commercial aircraft had and no radio for the first while that he owned it because radio was in its infancy. He purchased a simple radio a couple years after he began flying, which then allowed him to land at the larger airports of Saskatoon and North Battleford.

He was prohibited from flying at night because he wasn't routinely landing at a lit airstrip, but that didn't stop him. "When we would get home after dark, he would land the airplane blind with no lights, special instruments or radio," said his son Dave. "He considered the altimeter, but really used the night lights of Kerrobert as trigonometric beacons, like a ship's captain. We would power stall gently down in the dark until the undercart touched on."

Using a compass and his own intuition, Walter flew according to landmarks and made his way from one location to another by looking at a roadmap or following roads, highways, fences or railroad tracks. His previous job of driving a cream truck in the country surrounding Kerrobert helped him find his way to farms in the area. He also followed directions given by farmers when they phoned his shop for assistance.

"Walter educated himself about his flying," explained Dave. "He knew where everything was and had an inarguable sense of direction on the prairie, as if he was a human compass. Of all the pilots I've known, Walt Williams seemed to have the inherent navigational instincts of a Canada goose and, with that, a proclivity for flying in bad weather."

EVO was a dependable, lightweight plane with wider seats at 40 inches (one metre) than most other two-seaters had, and an engine that at 65 horsepower was much smaller than those in today's cars. On wheels in warm weather and skis in the winter, EVO required only about 35 yards (32 metres) of runway area in good conditions to get the engine revved to 40 miles per hour (65 km per hour) so the plane could lift off. Walter took advantage of many cow pastures and fields to complete this task. EVO weighed 920 pounds empty and Walter often had to use his own muscle power to physically turn the back end of the plane so EVO faced in the right direction for takeoff. This is a common method of turning small planes, but doing so in the middle of a bumpy fence-lined pasture added more challenges to that job. Walter also spent many hours digging EVO out of the snow by hand or pushing and pulling to get the plane out of a hole in a field.

EVO had a wingspan of 36-feet-two-inches (11 metres), and was about 21 feet (6 m) long. Walter travelled at a cruising speed of about 70 mph (112 km/h). With both the nose tank and reserve tank behind the seat full, Walter could fly EVO for about four hours in good weather before needing to refuel.

During the spring and summer, Walter protected his plane from the constant threat of prairie fires by cultivating furrows around it. At times, he pulled the plane across the railroad tracks and into the B. Williams & Son shop to protect it from harsh weather but he soon built a hangar for the plane on the west side of the air strip nearer to the shop, about one mile (1.6 km) from the Williams home.

Solo Flight

Beginning my flying lessons, I was nearly 35 years old. It took me a lot longer to complete the course than, say, a 17-year-old Saskatoon boy who could come out for a daily lesson if he wanted to and other circumstances permitted. Therefore, we found that we were way in to 1947, I had bought more hours than most other students and I still had not soloed.

Mitch took me aside, explained this situation and suggested that I solo. I told him that my lessons had been so scattered I didn't feel I had the concentration of crash courses. He said the kids were soloing at eight-and-a-half to nine hours and here I was at 10-and-a-half hours and hadn't soloed. I mentioned the age gap, my being twice the age of the kids and perhaps more cautious. At last he said, "Get in and I'll check you out." (Almost all of my instruction had been given by various other instructors.) This was about 40 minutes before official darkness in summertime.

The check-out flight seemed to go alright. After we'd landed, Mitch got out, left me in the back seat of EGF[11] and told me to get going. "Make one landing only and then taxi over to the hangar – and remember, one flight only." I felt like I'd been thrown into deep water without knowing how to swim. Well, here goes, I thought.

I set the trim[12] and gave 'er the gas. Takeoff was quicker without the added weight of an instructor along, and I was in the air. Boy, I felt lonesome! Made the circuit (before the days of radio), and my let-down path took me right over what they used to call 'The Hudson Bay Slough.' It was a very smooth evening but in passing over this body of water, daytime heat escaping and rising from the water caused turbulence which threw me around a bit and by the time I touched down, I must have looked like a dancing clown. Felt like one, too.

Got her straightened out right side up and landed crazily, feeling that my hair was on sideways. My, it felt really good to be back on

[11] *The Piper Cub EGF had one seat behind the other, unlike the Aeronca Chief EVO, which had pilot and passenger seats beside each other.*
[12] *Set the trim – A specific part that is adjusted to assist in straight and level flight.*

the ground, right side up, stopped and safe. No damage done. I taxied over to where Mitch was, near the buildings, shut it off, and tremulously got out of the plane. Mitch (tongue-in-cheek, no doubt) kindly said I'd done fine and I got a pat on the back (for not busting up his plane, I bet).

(One thing, now amusing, was the time after I had soloed when I mentioned that I was having trouble due to my own uncertain timing of availability, getting an appointment for a pilot's physical examination with Dr. L.H. McConnell, whom Mitch had recommended. Mitch really raised the roof and immediately made an appointment suitable to my erratic timing. I should have had this examination before taking any training at all and here I was, having made my solo flight without having accomplished this very necessary requirement. I guess he got in touch with Romona (who was running McConnell's office) and due to Mitch's urgency of this requirement in his business, I had an almost immediate appointment. Well, I was a pretty strong and healthy animal at that time and very soon had passed my aviation physical examination. Then L.H. wanted to talk all day about his flying days.)

I had made that trip to Saskatoon on Old Smokey, the motorcycle, and on my way back home the old motorcycle seemed to be about two or three feet above the ground – I was so elated that I had made one flight – ALONE. Before getting to Biggar, my battery weakened and I sneaked into Biggar with practically no lights, rented a hotel bed for four hours or so, and at daylight continued on to Kerrobert, feeling like a different man. Boy, what a solo flight can do for a fella – especially his first!

I made several more check-out flights with an instructor to make sure I was capable of flying alone. After that it was, "Go five or seven miles this way or that way and practice spins, etc."

Finally, the great day arrived for taking the Private Pilot's test, with Department of Transport (D.O.T.) officials observing. We had to demonstrate spins, pass over the designated landing area at 1,500 feet, shut down the engine to "idle" and soar and glide to a landing as close to an old rubber boot or dark rag, and come to a power-off landing as close as we could to the target without using brakes. A fellow from Dundurn, taking his test at the same time, with a lot more ego than mine, cut me off the first try, so I went through procedures again and came pretty close to the old gum boot on the field. I passed!

Of course, this had to be in addition to a written exam, carefully supervised by a D.O.T. official, which I happened to pass, too. So, now I was eligible for a Private Pilot's Licence.

Mitch subsequently rented EGF to me at the same time as he refused others. I appreciated this very much and it made me especially respectful of his trust in me. I didn't let him down, and he eventually sold me EVO and then I had a plane of my own!

First Passengers

In 1947, when I received my Private Pilot's Licence, I was burning to fly. I invited Romona and her assistant Marie to go for a ride with me in EGF, the Piper Cub I'd trained in. They graciously accepted and I gave them both a "flip." It wasn't their first, but to me it was a big deal.

Romona went for another flight with me later and her father was upset that I looped the plane with her in it. I don't think he ever forgave me for doing that! However, nobody got hurt and everybody except Mr. Underwood had a good time.

Early Flight In EGF

Before buying EVO, I had to rent an aircraft to make flights and Mitch always let me have the Piper Cub J-3, the plane in which I learned to fly. I know he rented it to me while refusing others. I was burning inside to get more hours of flight logged so I spent dollars buying 'time,' instead of spending time foolishly some other ways.

Morley Nord and I had driven to Saskatoon, and instead of driving home right away, we went to the airport and Mitch said I could fly EGF out to Kerrobert and fly it back the next morning. Seventy-two-miles-an-hour wasn't very fast but it was all airtime, which seemed important to me. Morley was all for it, so away we went.

The air wasn't too clear that day but we made out OK. Alan Earl knew of our intentions and started for Kerrobert in the car Ashdown's Furniture furnished him for roadwork, about the same time as we took off. We landed in a little field next to the highway at the Isadore Meyer farm, just out of Kerrobert. We no sooner got to the highway when along came Alan, and he drove us into town.

I left EGF in the field overnight and in the morning, when I was ready to take the plane back to Saskatoon and pick up my truck, my mother was willing to go along for the ride. Only thing wrong was that it was a foggy morning, but I could see where the sun was through the fog and thought it wouldn't take very long to fly up through the relatively thin ground. So my trusting mother and I took off and, using the sun and the time of day as a guide, we got above the fog and headed in the general direction of Saskatoon.

We seemed to fly a long time over the fog, but finally there was a clear spot. We descended and found the name 'Valley Centre' on a grain elevator. We were at least 10 miles (16 km) off course. Turning left and following the railway, we soon came to Asquith, about 25 miles west of Saskatoon. The fog was burning off by this time and we had an easy time finding the airport at Saskatoon.

I recall that a rotary snowplow was throwing out a great plume of snow, right near the airport.

Mother was taking it quite well in the rear seat, although her feet were getting cold. Approaching the open landing area, I went into a left side-slip, missed the fence, and we were safely on the ground. When we taxied in, I was greeted with the remark that we had come in 'just like old timers.'

Everything was fine, I paid my bill and Mother and I drove home in the truck. By the time we got back to Kerrobert, Mother had had quite a day and so had I. I didn't have very many hours in my log book at that time.

Joe Kreiser – Altario Fence

One nice Sunday in the late fall of 1948, John Herron and I flew out west to Altario to visit Joe Kreiser. Joe was a good friend, ran a garage and blind-dogged a few machine deals for us in his area. He had once owned Old Smokey, the motorcycle I rode for 3½ years. We got along well and thought we'd fly out and give him a flight.

Altario is in very hilly country, which makes it difficult to land or take off anywhere near the hamlet. There was one little field nearby where a Piper Cub had landed a couple of times, but it sure was a short one. Using it cornerwise added a few yards, but I was a pretty green pilot at that time. Also, it was a calm day, I was on wheels and a light snow covered the field – factors which had the effect of making the distance about half as sufficient as without these detriments.

However, after John, about 120 pounds, and I landed, 240-pound Joe got in and I started the takeoff, heading for the far corner. The combination of snow resistance on the wheels and calm air were, I suppose, the most contributory factors outside of my own indiscretion, and it was soon apparent that we were not going to make it. I chopped the throttle, put on full brakes, but the tires just slid over the warm snow. When it became a certainty we were going to hit the fence, I cut the ignition.

Well, we hit the corner of the fence alright. The engine cowling was bent up somewhat. The right front wheel had hit a post or something and the main axle broke away from the oleo[13] and stabilizer strut. We were broken down. It was only a quarter mile to Joe's garage, so we propped up the right side of the plane, removed the broken parts and headed for the shop. There, I fashioned bits and pieces and welded them together, until we thought we could fly the thing home and later on to Saskatoon for proper repair.

It was getting pretty dark by the time we had everything together and we got EVO out on to a roadway. There was quite a hill not far to the south, the direction of our takeoff. Joe went ahead over the hill

---

[13] *Oleo – A shock absorber.*

to stop any traffic, to avoid a collision. Allowing enough time, John and I let all the horses out of the barn[14] and took off in the dark, over the hill, and we were off on our first flight in darkness for either of us.

We had contacted Fred Lalear, who was our truck driver, so that he would be able to shine the truck lights on the runway at home. He must have thought we were too late to get off at Altario, so was on the road to Altario to pick us up. We knew the lights on the old DS-30 truck, and saw Fred coming west towards us on the highway. We dropped altitude to a point where we'd just miss the roof of the truck with our wheels and met him at low altitude. We had no lights and it was really a dirty trick to play on Fred as he nearly died of fright.

We doodled around long enough for Fred to get back to the home field and get into position with his lights shining down the runway. Again we nearly took off his roof but made a dandy landing. Fred sure cussed us out for the scare we'd given him, and all I said was, "But Fred, after all, you were going the wrong way!"

Following that, I had to make up a plausible report to the dear old Department of Transport, get clearance to ferry the plane to a repair shop in Saskatoon, go through red tape after red tape, and finally get official clearance to continue flying the plane. Actually, I stopped flying only as long as it took to have the repairs made.

---

[14] *Horse out of the barn – Powered up the plane to its full horsepower.*

Rough Landings – Tight Takeoffs

In the fall of 1948, some guy came along, a traveller or teacher, I forget now, but he was in the Kerrobert area and had a crush on a girl on a farm near Mossbank, Sask. He sure wanted to see her on the weekend and have dinner with her folks. Would I fly him? I don't know what made me take it on, but I did after he told me there was an emergency landing area near where he wanted to visit.

We took off and he talked just about all of the time. I thought I had enough loose screws but he sure had me beat. It had to be an early takeoff if we were to have lunch there, let them visit a bit, and get home again. Looking at the map, I planned to go to the Mossbank place, fly a bit out of my way coming back to gas at Moose Jaw, and fly home from there. The weather was fine.

He seemed to know the country down there and pointed out the place where planes landed in the past – just a flat place near a dry lake bottom. Hills and 40-wire telephone lines didn't lighten my heart, as I still hadn't built up much flying time and he was a heavy guy. When I got near the ground, I noticed it was rough and would be bouncy. As I touched down, I was trying to lose speed when all at once the plane swung around in a circle – a ground loop, and I hadn't done a thing to cause it. The right wing nearly hit the ground.

We did stop and, slightly nervous, I looked around for the cause. In those days, the tail wheel on those light planes was about twice the size of a doughnut (later I installed a larger Maule wheel[15] with a pneumatic tire), and there was a light spring attached to each side of a crossbar, to help keep the wheel centrally directed. The right spring was gone, which allowed the remaining left spring to pull the tail wheel to steer the tail assembly to the right. This swung the plane to the left so fast the plane could have suffered severe damage. The passenger was a bit scared, but took it pretty well.

At the farm, following a meal, the girl's father and I went through his shop and junk pile to find something I could use for a repair

---

[15] *A Maule wheel tire has one bracket on it rather than one on both sides.*

measure. We found an old bedspring assembly in the junk, and I took one of the small springs from the end of it. Some wire, to adjust length to match the left spring, and the wheel regained its proper position. I didn't like to trust a rusty old bedspring, but had to make the best of it.

On takeoff, the wind direction made it necessary to cross a 40-wire phone line between two hills. I don't think we touched the top row of wires but we must have been close. Turning, we headed straight for Moose Jaw, the course taking us right across Johnson Lake. This lake looks like a shallow alkali thing, with a sodium sulphate plant at Chaplin, near the north shore. I held my breath a bit as we crossed it and it seemed to be pretty large about the time we were halfway across, but EVO kept plugging away and the lake finally fell away behind us.

Gassing at Moose Jaw, I told the fellow to get in – we're goin' home. I sure learned some early lessons that day about knocking around the country in a light plane.

Other experiences, on other flights, rush up from my memory:

A traveller for a flour company had a brainwave one day. If the weather was good 'tomorrow,' (it was winter), could I fly him to a number of places in one day – just one round trip taking in all these points. They were in the Loverna, Hemaruka and Esther part of the country, not too kind to aircraft ground requirements. Looking over the deal, I said I thought we could make it, so we made a deal. These were all the calls he was to make by car for the whole week, and if we could pull it off, he'd have the rest of the week for his own purposes. He caught a lot of heck from his company afterwards but that was a part of his affair, not mine. We made all the calls, as he didn't spend much time with any one storekeeper in the hamlets.

There was one spot I got into that was soft and small with little or no wind to shorten the takeoff. I managed to clear the fence and continuing a short way further, flew right past a schoolhouse. The thing I'll never forget is seeing the ink wells on the school desks as we flew past the windows.

Another winter, I got a call from a bulldozer operator in the Broadacres area, in a field just across the road from the original John Park farm. The call came just at dusk and there was no room to help me see my way. I had been doing a lot of flying for the company he worked for, so I said I'd try to get him to Kerrobert – just stand by and wait. I found his outfit, landed in the dark. He came puffing and wading through the snow and got in. Now for a blind takeoff – it was slightly uphill and I remember seeing a fence go by – real close. Then I started down the road at the west side of Broadacres. Another unforgettable memory was seeing a table all set for supper as we flew past the window in the dark.

Plane Repair – Flight To La Ronge

One summer day, John Herron asked if I'd like to have the plane washed. I said yes and suggested that he take our DS-30 1½-ton truck down to the hangar to stand on while he washed the wings. I explicitly told him to not back the truck to the plane, but to park the truck and carefully roll the plane up to it.

He took the truck down but was soon back, on foot. He couldn't have looked worse or more downhearted. He told me that he had done the opposite to that which I had advised and backed the truck to the plane, bumped into it, breaking a couple of structural members of the fuselage, as well as tearing some of the fabric.

Well, he was punishing himself already and had been such good help in so many ways in the past that there was nothing I could do but consider that possibly I could have done something like that myself. I think he would have felt better if I had bawled him out, but I didn't. We drove to the hangar in the pickup truck, pushed the plane back into the hangar and drove both trucks uptown.

I phoned Bob Graham of Saskatoon, who worked for Mitchinson, explained the damage and arranged a time to have the repair work done. When that time arrived, I flew EVO into Saskatoon and we put 'er 'way back in the corner of the hangar, where Bob repaired it. This would be before 1951 because our father was still with us at that time.

This job took several days of whatever Bob's time he could spend on it and before he had finished, a fellow (we will call Tom) came along and wondered if I would be interested in the both of us flying to Lac La Ronge. He had friends there who were on government work re: fishing, etc. This would be over the weekend. I phoned my Dad to see how things were getting along at home, telling him about the La Ronge idea. He said, "Sure, go ahead if you want to."

After paying for the plane repair, I thought I would have enough money with me to pay my share of the trip since Tom said we could stay with his friends up there. So we gassed and took off with only a highway map to follow, which was pretty sketchy in that northern country those days. It was an adventure of a different nature and in a part of Saskatchewan I'd only heard about.

There was still good light when we landed on their earliest airstrip at Lac La Ronge, which was only cleared bush and very sandy. A big truck had got stuck right in the middle of the runway, and left a big wide hole. We skirted that and got on, parked, and tied down.

We caught a ride, or walked, into La Ronge – three miles. The highway cut across one corner of the runway. Met Tom's friends and settled in with them. The next day we were all day on their government boat and had a pretty good time. About noon, we went into a rocky bay where the water was shallow and we could see the fish swimming around. Threw out a hook, caught one and threw it onto the rock bank. Twenty minutes later, we were eating the fried fillets. Also, I was interested in the northern orchids which grew out of the cracks in the rock. At this place there was only rock – no soil!

Next morning, I paid the local taxi $3 to take us three miles out to the airport, remarking that it must be hard to make a living in Lac La Ronge. Paid inflated prices for airplane gas. Then I made a test flight alone around the big runway hole and to feel the wind, etc. and landed again. We loaded up and made final takeoff for home.

Approaching Prince Albert in the evening, I decided that we'd not make Saskatoon before dark so it would be a case of staying at P.A. overnight. We'd make the rest of the way in the morning. When I cut the engine to idling, it nearly stopped due to icing in the carburetor intake and I realized that this can happen in the summertime as well as in winter. Pulled on the carb heat and nursed the engine into continued operation.

Got a taxi downtown – I paid – and got a hotel room. We washed and shaved and I told Tom that I had less than a dollar left in my pocket after paying all the expenses so far. The hotel room was not paid for. He went to his pocket and came up with less than a dollar.

Well, what now?! I called two or three numbers of people I knew in P.A. with no answer, so went down to the desk and talked the men there into cashing a cheque for $10. This paid for the room and the taxi out to the airport in the morning. We flew to Saskatoon in the early morning. Tom got out and I flew home on the last of my gas.

In 1977, I met Tom at Beaver Lumber in Saskatoon, a doctor so successful he makes appointments only with the ritzy, but he didn't offer to pay his share of that Lac La Ronge trip. But it's a great satisfaction to know what he is and what I think I am. I don't want his money now – it wouldn't smell very nice. He can be happy with what he has – I'm happy with what I've done.

Good Deeds, Good Work

Walter Williams flew his plane year-round as a hobby but when the weather turned bad, he was called on to move people and goods around the area. "He flew when the roads were closed and things were tough. He would be flying every day and then there would be times when he wouldn't be up for two or three weeks," said Walter's brother-in-law Esmond Allcock.

"He would fly when he wasn't supposed to," added Esmond. "If you wanted him, he'd go. He liked the limelight a little, too, but he earned it. He paid his dues."

"When I was a kid, if you saw a plane, you thought of Walter Williams because Walter was the only one that had a plane. He was a local hero around here," said Richard Anderson, a family friend. "When I was little, my three-wheeler would break and Walter would take it into the back. Walt would always tell me it was 25 cents to fix it, and then he'd laugh. He never charged us kids."

Walter used his own judgment as well when it came to charging for his flying services. At times, he would charge based on the cost of fuel and his time away from his business. Other times, if it was a family member he was taxiing around or someone whom he knew did not have much money, the charge was minimal or non-existent. "Some of it was chargeable and some of it he'd do because it had to be done," said Esmond.

Walter Williams willingly took chances in all sorts of weather conditions to fly out to farms to deliver groceries as well as medicines for people or their animals. Usually in the course of agreeing to make the flight, he asked questions about the job ahead of time but many times he minded his own business and started the flight without knowing the full story.

Hospital Trips – Biggar – Major

Many of the flights were made to take people to or from the Biggar Hospital. Most of these would be from the Kelfield area, where it became common to use Gordon Kelly's field near the house for pickup or drop, although there were more trips made right to the farm of the passenger.

Major and Tramping Lake were other points from which many calls were made. These short hops averaged about seven dollars each. One day, along with other flights, I flew to Major seven times, landing this-side or that-side or to a nearby farm, to suit the convenience of the passenger. Every landing field and wind direction made for great variety in that department.

One of these trips, that day, resulted when a man from north of Major drove his team and sleigh-box out to the field where I had landed to let out a passenger and take one on. His 18-month-old son had eczema almost all over his little body and they wanted him in Kerrobert Hospital if I could arrange it. This man was mightily pleased when I told him to drive home while I went to Kerrobert and back, and he would have just enough time to get his wife and baby ready and I'd land right at the farm. The boy surely was a sick little fellow and the hospital told me later that it was a good thing I'd brought him in THAT day – not the next, as they barely saved him.

John and Paul Urbinsky farmed northeast of Major and one winter day, I had a call to pick up John's wife and little boy as soon as possible. I told them to get ready – I was on my way. The men had been grinding feed for the livestock and what with the noise of tractor and grinder, didn't notice what had happened to the little boy, who had been playing around the yard. They finally did hear a noise and, on looking around, found that the dog had the boy down and was CHEWING his face. Well, THAT boy was in the hospital in a matter of minutes. The trip would have taken the rest of the day by any other means due to deep, deep snow and blocked roads.

Another really nice winter morning, I had just returned to home base with Mary Henning and her daughter Anne. Anne had had knee trouble for some time, and the doctor wanted to see it. They had been trying to doctor it by phone up to that time. When I taxied up to the hangar, George Cunnings was there to inform me that one of the Carter men out near Kelfield had been seriously cut by a circular saw and would I go for him – NOW! George took Mary and Anne to the hospital and I hit right out for Carter's farm. There he was with a big white cloth wrapped around his hand, waiting in the open field. I was stopped about two minutes, he said, "Dodsland," and away we went to Dodsland Hospital. Again, the patient was in the hospital within minutes of injury. I recall that landing...

I had a long list of flights to make that day and also I didn't want Carter to have to walk any further than necessary, so I chose to land in a small space between Bill Hoffmeyer's barn and the main road out to the highway on the west border of Dodsland. The space was small, so I side-slipped just over the telephone and power lines and Bill's fence and slammed 'er on. I had to zigzag to lose speed, ending in a near ground loop to the left. It was a tight turn and the right ski rode up on the snowdrift next to the fence, which let the right wing miss the fence – only barely – it swept right over it. I remember Carter saying, "I'd say we just made it – we missed both the barn and the fence!" We stopped alongside the fence next to the village, about 1½ blocks from the hospital. We walked in.

To get out of that field (it was a very fine morning with little breeze, to make a shorter takeoff), I raced around in a tight circle to gain a few miles per hour, then aimed for the space between the barn and the fence. I had all the horses out of the barn (65-horsepower), and lifted just in time to miss some piles of stuff behind the barn. Beyond that was dropping ground to a lower level, which allowed me to nose 'er down and get a bit more speed, and I was away again, scot-free. A few minutes later, I was on the snow again, making another call. Flights like this were just part of the day's routine those days.

Andy Meier – Home In The Dark

One early spring evening while I still had skis on EVO, a fellow came into the shop asking if I could fly him home that night, somewhere south of Tramping Lake. His name was Andy Meier. I don't remember what year it was, but it was early in my time with EVO. He knew where the home farm was but I didn't, and time being after dark didn't strengthen my enthusiasm. But his story about being away from home so long – the Army or something – and he surely wanted to get home that night. The spring breakup was in effect and snow patches were diminishing in size every day, but the temperature was below the freezing point at that moment so the snow would be OK for skis. Asked why he'd waited until dark drew the reply that he'd just got into town, whether by bus, car or train, I don't recall.

I said, "Well, if you can pick out the home farm and indicate a clear field, we'll try 'er." So away we went in the dark and headed out in the general direction of his destination. Finally he said, "There it is!" He pointed to a nearby field, claiming that it was clear of fences, power lines, etc. I flew around several times to find a place in the dark where there would be enough snow for me to land him, and get off again myself. He must have been crazy and I knew I was, but believe it or not, we landed and he got out safe and sound (except in the head).

After that, I backtracked in the dark and managed to get into the air again and fly back to the home field. All the while, I cussed myself for the foolhardiness of this venture. Eventually EVO was put to bed in the hangar – everything fine and nobody hurt. Reflecting now, I realize that this was only one of many incidents which should have reduced my future to zero.

Ephriam L. Read – To Saskatoon

On one of my business flights to Saskatoon, Eph Read went along. He was as calm about flying as anyone I ever flew – I think – partly because we were mutually trusting friends, and I'd done so many flights successfully (he wasn't acquainted with all the risks I took). It was a nice day and before we got to Saskatoon, had attained a one-mile altitude, so he could realize how little everything looked from a mile up (1.6 km). Landed at Saskatoon, we taxied downtown, each did his business and we flew home again. Eph was quite pleased, and for him it was free.

Later, a year or two, on skis, March 1952, I made a short flight to his farm because the roads were pretty tough at that time. Ken Barkley (brother-in-law of Dick Pittaway later) went along with me. Ken was with IH Motor Trucks and we wanted to sell Eph a small truck. Well, with business talk and watching Tobie (the dog) do all his tricks, it was darned good and dark when we walked out to the plane to fly home. We could see the Kerrobert lights OK, only we weren't there.

With the extended stay, EVO was a little cranky about starting but we got 'er goin', warmed 'er up and since I knew it was a safe field, we just ran 'er off. After seven or eight miles, we felt our way onto the home field and landed OK.

Mike Balanoff – Veterinarian

Mike Balanoff farmed southeast of Major, was a veterinarian and liked it when one of our hardware men, Walt Herity, called him 'Doc' all the time. To everyone else, he was just Mike. Not a big man, my most honest opinion was that he must have been a pretty rough doc for livestock and I had many a look at his rusty instruments, which he called 'tools.' How he got so many calls was something I couldn't divine but he was kind of old – a legend in his community – which was considerable in size, as witnessed by the length of flights I made with him. Also, vets were hard to come by in those days.

Mike was a game old guy, accepted everything I suggested, whether sensible or safe or not. My biggest worry was the big bag of 'tools' he always lugged around, about the same weight as he was himself. This was partly compensated by his not being a big heavy man and many were the times when I lugged my insides out, assisting him with an animal.

One flight from his farm to the Kindersley area, the Kindersley Dairy in fact, was made in very dim weather on skis. We flew low, crossing fences and the edges of fields at a kind of guess-angle. I was lucky and hit the Kerrobert-Kindersley highway about a mile from the Dairy. On the way, we saw a coyote and I suggested we 'buzz' it. Mike was game and we did it, nearly scaring the coyote out of his skin. This was unusual and, for Mike, a talking point in his future.

He was a tough old guy, from an older school than mine, Russia, I think, and exhibited complete faith in anything I suggested. I responded with unstinting assistance in whatever unsavoury efforts were required in his work with sick animals. Sometimes it was pretty demanding in strength and tolerance but he was the vet, eh? – and my trusting customer.

Mike and I were always friends – I made many flights for him – some tough, some easy – and whether he is still with the living or dead, he still thinks well of yours truly.

Mrs. Crawford – Out Late

One trip I made to Swift Current on skis, I had company in the person of Mrs. Alex Crawford, who had previously said that she would appreciate a visit to a friend in that town – a Mrs. McAvoy. I think Al Smith was to make some small repair to my plane and promised that I could get back home the same day. Well, as was Al's usual, he finished the job so near dark that a person had to fly home in the dark or stay overnight.

I contacted Mrs. Crawford and she said she would go whenever I decided to, even if it meant flying home in the dark, so I said, "Get out here – we're goin'." She's a very jolly person and thought it a great joke all the way home, in the dark for 130 miles. I told her it was nothing new for me and my only worry was that the police could turn me in for flying after limits.

We approached Kerrobert with considerable altitude so we could glide in quietly and lessen the chances of being caught out late. Imagine my surprise and Mrs. Crawford's great mirth when, as we approached the hangar, an extra car was there – Bert Fisk – R.C.M.P! Bert didn't turn me in and Mrs. Crawford is still laughing at that turn of events. Bert even drove her home!

Plane Wreck

One winter afternoon, I was canvassing farmers for machine sales, landing at each one's farm. With most country roads closed or in real tough shape, these people welcomed a visitor, especially by air. It looked good for the neighbours to see EVO parked at their farm. I was doing pretty well and had written up quite a few orders for spring business, but I was worried about the weather. I kept running into little wet fogs which would ice up the wings' edges a bit, and the weather was so mild I wore only a jumbo sweater. Had I been wiser, I would have gone home and stayed there.

Finally, and while there was plenty of time left in the afternoon, I phoned a good friend, Kasper Herle, who was farming my dad's homestead on a partnership basis. Kasper hoped eventually to buy the farm. There was a hockey match in Kerrobert that night, and it was agreed that I'd pick him up and we'd go to the match. I'd fly him home the next morning.

Well, I picked him up OK and soon after takeoff, began to have fog trouble. The distance was only 32 road miles (50 km), or about 18 to 20 air miles, but that's a lot of fog. It varied from more and less and more and less, until we reached an area near Kerrobert where one could see his way only if he flew no higher than the telephone line. Icing of the plane became more rapid and though we were only about five or so miles from home, our time was down to a minute or so. In avoiding the telephone line at a correction line about three miles north of the home field, I lost sight of the telephone line. Then we were down to pure luck, iced up, and not even able to distinguish ground level. Full throttle barely kept the plane off the ground, and I knew I'd really had it this time. We had come through a coulee and missed Gordon Cassidy's trees and then lost our guide line.

Everything was iced up and I could see out only through an open slide-window at my side but that was where we'd been, not where we were going. Finally there was a big bump. Throttle still wide open, there was a slight pause – then CRASH! Afterwards, I guessed that we must have stalled onto the snow field in about flight attitude, bounced almost straight into the air and then fell down for a crashing bump a few yards further. There happened to be a wheat stook right where the prop struck it, and there was little left of the prop but the hub, for something like 2200 revolutions per minute.[16]

Everybody asked, "Weren't you scared?" My honest reply was that I was too busy and concerned for that but the sudden silence and stillness, sudden lack of motion, was one of the greatest shocks of my life – that sudden change, in less time than NOW.

I don't think I was knocked out, but knew I had broken my face on the full-back control wheel, because when I opened both eyes, I saw two of everything. This was due to diplopia (or double vision, like if I looked at a fence post, I saw two – one above the other). I had a nose bleed like nobody else ever had, I thought – there was a pencil-sized stream of blood reaching, unbroken, to the snow.

I got an answer from Kasper, assurance that all that had happened to him was that he had been hit in the eye by the other control wheel at his side of the cabin. I had lost my felt hat, but had a tea cozy fur hat behind the seat, so I put that on. I could get my door open, but after unsnapping Kasper's safety belt, found we couldn't open his door. The landing gear on his side was broken down, and the right wing was half buried in the snow, with the wooden wing span broken 5½ feet from the tip. So I got out and Kasper came out my side and I was greatly relieved to find that neither of us had injury to arms or legs – we could WALK!

There was about half of a large Kleenex carton in the plane, so I retrieved that and we both used it to mop and wipe blood. I had the worst time of mopping with my greater injuries. Had to keep one eye closed so I could see only one of anything. Kasper had an overcoat, but I wasn't clothed any better than a jumbo sweater, and it was getting colder. Soon it was dark.

I turned my good cheek around to find the current direction of the breeze, and wrongly guessed which side of the trail to town we had landed on. If I could find that trail, there was a slight chance that we could catch a ride with someone going to the game, but we walked away from the trail instead of towards it.

We wandered off into the increasing darkness (nobody knew

[16] *2200 revolutions - Turning full-speed after the propeller was gone.*

about us or where we were – we were strictly on our own). We were only 300 feet from a coulee and a fence was there, too (we'd have been luckier just hitting the fence.). I'm sure we crossed that coulee twice, hearing dog barks occasionally, but just kept wandering on.

Finally, Kasper played out – he had been following in my tracks all the way but said he could not go any further. I tried to encourage him by suggesting a rest, but he said no – no further for him. Well, I thought then that our only chance for survival was to keep walking in a circle until morning.

All of a sudden, a light (dim) appeared over Kasper's shoulder. Like a drowning person grasping a straw in mid-ocean, I turned him around and said excitedly, "There's a LIGHT, Kasper, let's hurry – the light may not last long." He replied that he was played out, so I said, "Well, I'll leave you tracks," and took off. Poor Kasper followed closely behind!

This turned out to be a light from a farmhouse window – the farm having been vacant for 25 years – until three days before. What luck! We found the back door, explained to the man that we were half covered with blood from facial injuries, and to forewarn any other people in the house. He finally went into the kitchen. What a sight we must have been! The family consisted of Ed Gust, his wife, a boy and two girls. Mrs. Gust was all for heating water to wash the blood off of us but I assured her that the doc would not appreciate that, preferring to treat injuries without the intervention of non-sterile attempts.

The fog was so thick and wet that Ed could hardly find the barn, even with a lantern, but he did. He harnessed up a team, hooked them to a sleigh-box, tied the lantern to the end of the sleigh tongue and away we went into the foggy night, to find Kerrobert, only three miles away.

The only protection Ed could give us in that sleigh-box was a binder canvas, and I got pretty cold on the way to town. There was only a doubtfully-findable track where Ed had moved out to the farm three days before, but the horses must have found it and stayed on it, because we finally did reach Kerrobert, at a very slow walk of the horses. The fog there was so thick that you had to be right under a street light to see it.

Having not heard from me, Oscar Neubauer and a young lad were waiting at the shop, not knowing what to expect, and by this time it was well after eight o'clock – nearly nine. When we walked in the door, Kasper had a lot of cuts around his right eye, having shattered a 1/8" spectacle lens on the control wheel. My right cheek was open, eye socket broken in three places so that the eye was lowered and sunken back into my head. My nose was broken, the right side of my palate lowered, and all right side upper teeth waving this way or that. Oscar claimed he saw my teeth through the opening in my cheek, but I think he was excited. He called Doc James, who came from the hockey game, and from the same game he brought his 'operating room nurse.'

We were taken to the hospital, where we were examined. Kasper was attended to in the case room, had no broken bones but took 31 stitches around the right eye, three of which were applied to the eyelid, and the eyeball wasn't even scratched! Kasper was not full of that kind of courage but, heels in the base of the case-room table and a firm grip on the handles, managed it while Doc James sewed his eyelid together. It did help that James told him that one twitch could mean a damaged eyeball.

My injuries were more extensive. This was the only time I was injured in my years of flying – due to flying, that is. My right cheek was split open (the control wheel was sure bent all to heck where my face hit it), cheekbone broken, right eye socket broken in three places, right side of nose broken, and right side of my palate was caved downwards, and all my upper teeth on the right side could wave back and forth if I could stand it.

I ended up on the operating table, and James was trying to help me undress. I asked why all the help and he said, "Well, you may be in shock, y'know." I laughed and said I could run downtown and back if necessary, and finished undressing myself. Well, five X-rays later revealed that I was a hurt boy and was put to bed for the rest of the night, right beside Kasper! I was given a tetanus shot and another to make me sleep, but I was too busy to sleep, what with worrying about the next day being payday for six men, and blood and juice coming out all over the place.

James had sewed up my split cheek (and he was the neatest sewer I ever saw – he had sewed me up on other occasions and in time I couldn't find the place). The nurses were very solicitous, and I kept getting messages from people who came to the hospital to see how it was with me – all good, and appreciated.

The night finally passed, the right side of my face swelled up like half of a football, and my right eye was two inches deep in the swelling. I could see with my left eye, but the right one was a total loss at that time. I couldn't eat, so the girls gave me some thick soup and a straw and I got that down. It felt good.

Next morning Doc James came in and said he could handle Kasper on the local scene, but recommended Saskatoon, Regina or Edmonton for me, because they all had specialists and facilities beyond the capabilities of Kerrobert Hospital. This was in the days of the 1918 Kerrobert Hospital – not the new one that was built since then. I looked at him with my one good eye and pleaded, "Can't YOU fix me up, Doc?" He assured me that he wanted the best for me, and these other places had better means.

I said, well, Saskatoon was my 'big town,' so away he went. In 10 minutes or less he returned, saying all was arranged, and the ambulance plane would be in Kerrobert in about an hour to pick me up. Arrangements made, I had to hurry into my clothes (have some better ones brought from home), arrange power-of-attorney for Morley Nord to run the business and pay the men in my absence, and get one of my men to have me waiting for the ambulance plane when it arrived. It took some hustling, but I didn't want anyone waiting for ME!

In the middle of that night in the hospital, say two or three in the morning, Kasper whispered, "Valder, I don't think I'll fly any more!" I said that was nonsense – we'd get ourselves fixed up, fix the plane, and fly again. (Three years later to the day – February 27th – I called at his farm on a nice day, and after talking in the house for an hour, flew him for an hour, buzzing all the neighbours, just to show them that we didn't quit easy, and to give Kasper a new dignity among his friends. It was his last flight, and years later Oscar Neubaeur and I went to Unity to his funeral – in no way connected with our accident.)

I had a bit of static with the nurse on the ambulance plane, pretty new on the job, coming originally from Biggar. She insisted that the rules demanded that all head injuries were to be taken in on a stretcher. I said I'd walk to Saskatoon rather than lie down on a stretcher. It was my FACE that was injured, not by HEAD. I'd answer any riddle she could think up. Art Davis, an old friend, was the pilot, and he told her they had a 'toughy' on their hands, and let me sit beside him in the front seat of the Cessna '95. There wasn't enough room for my hat, due to the close slope of the windshield, so I took it off. The disgruntled nurse sat in a rear seat, I made out a cheque for the trip, and she gave me the receipt.

Art radioed ahead and said I wanted a taxi, not an ambulance, since the taxi was a lot cheaper. Finally the nurse and I were getting along pretty well. I showed her my wreck and she showed me her home farm.

At the hospital (City), I cleared 'Admittance' and was told by an elderly nurse that if I wasn't taken to my bed in a wheelchair, she could lose her job, so I sat in the damn thing and let her wheel me. I felt like a cheater and a sissy.

I was put in the 'McConnell Ward,' along with 13 other fellows with back operations and broken heads. Mine, according to an elderly nurse who visited every patient once a day, was the oldest and hardest bed in the institution, but I was walking around most of the time anyway and spent no more than six hours a night lying on that thing.

McConnells, now – there was L.H. the father, and Fred the son. Fred would stick a thumb into my injured area, twist and squeeze (trying to make me flinch, I think), and then ask innocently, "Does that hurt?" I'd assure him that it did, and more than once thought of strangling him.

There was so much swelling, they spent several days trying to reduce it, with nice girls putting on hot compresses and medications. The right eye, buried in all that swelling, gathered pus and matter, which never seemed to be taken into consideration. One girl, who said she liked men who smoked cigars, spent an hour one day cleaning out that eye, and earned my appreciation and admiration, because nobody had told her to do it and it was a great relief to me.

Finally, they put me on the operating list for next morning, and really put my lights out for that operation. All they did that time was to wire my bottom and top teeth together, so that the lower teeth were to hold the loose bank of upper teeth up, and after healing, I could chew, but nothing was done about the cheek bone and eye socket.

The night before the second operation, a couple of doctors came in to show me a skull with red marks all places where I was broken. It didn't really 'make my day,' but I had a good sleep anyway. I was told afterwards that at one time when I was being wired up, my tongue fell back into my throat and choked me. They put an ordinary store string through a hole in the tip of my tongue and let it hang out between my front teeth to hold my tongue forward. The only man in Saskatoon at that time who was licensed to wire people's teeth together was a gink[17] I'll call Smith. A month or more later, when he removed the wires (and not too gently, me being a big strong boy and all that, and he chipped my teeth in the process at that), wanted his $80 'in cash.' I shelled it out, and he was right if he thought I was disgusted.

He told me that he had finished my wiring job on his knees, looking up, because they had turned me face down on the operating table. However, I was finally free to get my teeth apart, and eat solid food again. While wired up, I'd had to get along by sucking soup through a glass tube, which I carried like a pen or pencil. (Some soup was made pretty thick, to accommodate the situation.) This is a good way to lose weight, too.

The second operation, when they wired up my cheek and eye socket, had to be done practically 'now,' because the string was not there to keep my tongue from choking me again. Oh, the three docs gave me a 'local,' which was only skin deep, and helped a little while they re-opened my eye and made a big slash over the zygomatic arch (the bone at the front of one's temple) which was broken apart to 3/8 of an inch, and had to be wired together. I was given no anaesthetic, nor strapped down, but just lay on the slanting operating table.

They rolled up a big chest and table of saws, knives, and electric drills, and at all times one doc held a hand on my chest. I felt the cutting and the blood running. Instead of using an electric drill, they used a little finger drill in the bone. It seemed to take a long time. The stainless steel wire was ready.

They chewed the rag all the time, and I took all they handed out. When they stuck an ice pick into my cheekbone and lifted to close the zygomatic arch and tighten the wire, I felt the most excruciating pain

---

[17] *Gink – Slang for a foolish, odd person.(www.thefreedictionary.com)*

of my whole life. I thought I just couldn't stand it – but I did – didn't make a sound, flinch or faint, and I learned about pain – it can be unbearable, but with each passing minute, it dulls to a tolerable level.

With my good eye on the wall clock, that operation lasted one hour and five minutes. Now, about that string –

When I began to waken after the first operation and returned to my bed, I was on my side, with a nurse's hand on my upper arm. She talked soothingly when I stirred, purring like a kitten. When I could finally make things out with my good eye, I deduced that my sore tongue was caused by the long string, hanging out in two lengths from my front teeth. I made writing signs, so the nurse gave me a little pad and pencil. I asked about the string and was told the reason for it, assured that the intern would remove it – soon. Well, it wasn't very soon and then the guy came along, and instead of cutting one piece off short and pulling on the other one, the darned fool just pulled on one long one and the other long piece was pulled, dry, through the hole in my tongue. Boy, I could cheerfully have killed that guy right then. Talk about a sore tongue – I sure had one then.

I wandered all over that hospital, all day and part of each night. I remember standing at the doorway of the iron lung, where some poor soul was inside with advanced polio. This machine made as much noise as a threshing machine and I recall trying to figure how to make a quieter one for over an hour. I guess they got tired of my restlessness and wandering, so turned me loose in a couple of weeks. I went home in a mid-March bus – front seat, and was just about played out when I got home. But I was back at the office the next morning, facial stitches waving in the wind, and talking through wired teeth.

I have been a happier man since that 1952 accident, mainly because I had learned to 'count my blessings.' Good luck so far exceeded bad luck, and flowers, visits and expressions of friends surely helped out. So many flowers came that I soon asked the nurses to just bring me the card and give the flowers to someone who had none. One man sent a card, saying that he'd finally paid the old bill he'd owed me for a long time – I got a kick out of that one.

Recovery of cutting and wiring didn't take too long, but my right eye, in an enlarged socket, put the eyeball lower and further back in my head. Muscle adjustments had to slowly adjust the right eye to the left one. I was free of double vision for straight ahead, to the left, or lower spectrum was not too bad, but upper or right-side vision resulted in diplopia. It was 2½ years before I was cleared for flying again, physically, and repairing the plane was another story I shall write about later. (I think this one is long enough as it is.)

I think the greatest strength and thrill came when Romona managed to get her Aunt Bertha into my corner of the ward in her wheelchair. It took special effort and Aunt Bertha and I enjoyed each other, and had a good friendship.

Harold Kellough – Bill Tocker

It was duck hunting season and I was worried about all the dry grass surrounding the hangar. One morning, we left Oscar Neubauer in charge of the shop and Harold Patterson and Jack Fairbairn and I went down to the airport to burn a fire-guard around the hangar. We were just finished and ready to return to the shop at a quarter to twelve noon when we heard and saw a small plane streaking in fast. "Boy, that one's really goin'. Wonder what it is."

Turned out to be a 125-HP Piper, and I think they increased their speed past cruising by descending from altitude with power on. They spotted the hangar and landing strip, made a vertical 180-degree turn and pounced on the strip as smooth as glass, taxied in fast, stopped and jumped out, all smiles. They surely knew how to fly and throw that little plane around. These affable gentlemen approached us with their hands out for a shake and introduced themselves.

They exuded the impression that they were having the time of their lives – came from Prince Rupert, B.C. Harold Kellough was engineer for QCA (Queen Charlotte Airways) at the QCA seaplane base. He had flown for them but was now staying at their base, maintaining and repairing their aircraft. Bill Tocker owned a 180 Cessna and was working for a fisheries plant at Prince Rupert, perhaps in charge of personnel, and a real bullwhip type. Harold had a soft side, as it turned out, but Bill was hard and tough. He went along with Harold's soft side, though.

Harold, though very thorough and competent, did not have such (quite) quick reflexes as hard and tough Bill, and I later heard of Bill's miraculous flights in his Cessna 180. Part of Bill's work was to spot areas in the sea where there were schools of fish in plenty, for the trawlers to 'work.' He would radio and the trawlers would move in and make the best haul they could – sometimes sardines – sometimes salmon. Then he would put the boots to the people in the plant, to increase the canning efficiency and production.

These two were very good friends, at the peak of their prime – a 'die-for-each-other – you-lie-and-I'll swear-it's-true' association, capable of pulling off any stunt you see on TV or movies, no matter how impossible or dangerous. They were real men, of knowledge and action. Bill was single at that time while Harold had a wife who was a wonderful person (I never met her but other people told me of her), with four young sons. Harold was my choice of the two, but Bill sure came through, too, true and blue.

It was noon, so Harold Patterson and Jack Fairbairn jumped into the back of my pickup and we drove Harold Kellough and Bill Tocker uptown to a restaurant. After lunch, they came to the shop and explained that Floyd Glass Jr. (now Athabasca Airways – Prince Albert and Lac La Ronge) was to meet them at Kerrobert, and they'd all go duck hunting.

Floyd had met these two when he flew for QCA previously. Floyd was born and raised in Kerrobert and was my wrestling partner in our younger days. The Glass family moved to Prince Albert where Floyd Sr. farmed and ran a dairy, as he had done at Kerrobert for many years. Floyd Jr. began his career in flying there, and now in 1978 is still operating his airways, successfully and well-organized. Floyd did not show up for the hunting, and by phone our new friends learned that business pressure (Floyd was then manager of Saskatchewan Government Airways at Prince Albert), prevented him from keeping the rendezvous. Floyd did come down just before Harold and Bill left for home, for about an hour, and they had a short visit after all.

So, it meant that I loaned Harold and Bill my pickup truck, binoculars, etc, and let them live in my vacant house in Kerrobert (due to my separation), while they spotted ducks and geese, and conducted a fairly successful shooting season. At our home, they used our bathtub and had a few meals, courtesy of our mother. Guess they had a good time, because they came back another year, but that's another story in itself.

My wrecked EVO was in the hangar, and Harold asked why I didn't have it repaired. I said I'd have to slowly recover from my injuries before I could pass an aviation medical, be at the mercy of the pirate plane-fixers in our area, and was not ready to accommodate the pirates. Anyway, I couldn't pass a medical for some time yet.

When they finally had to leave for home (I think they had a total of two weeks away from home each) we were fast friends, and I really hated to see them leave. They said they'd be back next year. I assured them I'd be on hand (God willing) and do anything to help them have a good time, and if they came, it would 'make' my year. I gassed them up and away they went – I stood there on the field and watched them go and long after they passed out of sight. I really liked those guys.

There's another story here and I'll try to relate it...

Harold and Bill had acquired the Piper as salvage along the B.C. Coast. The former owner had encountered weather trouble, crashed and made it to the rocky shore. He just left the wreck there and never went back. He must have been pretty scared, because the boys found his dirty underwear on the rocks nearby. Harold and Bill went through the proper channels, salvaged the wreck, and Harold rebuilt it. Looked and ran like new, and after they returned from Saskatchewan with it, sold it for something like $5,000, which was a pretty good price in those days. The tide had a rise and fall of 22 feet at the point of salvage, which did not make salvaging easier.

Plane Repaired

The visit from Prince Rupert the next year was quite a deal. Harold and Bill flew out in a little 65-HP Aeronca Chief, the very same plane as my wrecked EVO. Harold had bought it from a fellow who had landed, on wheels, on the seaplane dock. He put on full brakes, the wheels slid on a large icy patch, then stopped sliding when he hit the dry concrete; and here they were in the rebuilt plane, on the prairies, having crossed over and among the Rocky Mountains.

They were the same two happy fellows, but said that five more fellows were coming by car. Bill's boss, owner of the canning factory and fleet, a cook and two dogs, foreman of the plant, etc. This firm had a Japanese boat builder who had built three real heavy punts, which they previously shipped out to me, and I had them stored in our warehouse. I said they could use the house, which I was reluctant to rent due to sentiment, and Harold and Bill settled in right away, prior to the arrival of the rest of the gang.

Harold said I hadn't done anything to have my wreck repaired, and I told him I didn't think I could pass a 'madical' yet, and was just waiting. He said, well, let's fix 'er up while I'm here. He said his mother and sister were living in Winnipeg and he and Bill would like to fly there to see them. I said, "OK, we'll haul the wings and fuselage up to the shop, you list everything you think you'll need, and when you land at Winnipeg, go to McDonald Aircraft Supply and order anything you'll need, ship it C.O.D. via CPR and maybe it will all be here when you get back."

At the shop, we had both wings and the fuselage for his estimates. He listed everything he would need and they took off for Winnipeg.

Meanwhile, as I hadn't flown a plane for two years, he took me for a flight in his Aeronca. He wanted me to make the whole flight – takeoff, landing and all. Of course, he had in both controls in case I'd lost my touch. Well, I took off, made a flight 'around,' and made a perfect landing. Harold was so pleased, he patted me on the back and said I could fly his plane anytime! I sat in the command seat, on the left. This made me feel pretty good, and gave him confidence in rebuilding my plane.

Arriving at Winnipeg, Harold, who knew some of the D.O.T. officials, went to the department offices to acquaint them of the intended repair job at Kerrobert. He ran into a little trouble and static because the head man had been transferred and was packing to leave. This was the man Harold most depended upon. So it would be a whole new ball game. But he went to McDonald's, got out his list and placed the order – marked RUSH – and then went visiting his folks.

McDonald's filled the order and shipped it forthwith, according to instructions and order – they, too, knew Harold. Before the boys returned from Winnipeg, the carload of friends arrived at Kerrobert and I put them up in my empty house. When the boys returned from Winnipeg, the McDonald order had not arrived, which disturbed us very much. Harold began, in his time he could spare from joining the others in duck hunting, to tear the wreck apart, and I started to work on CPR to find out where was the order of materials.

It turned out that the order was in Saskatoon, boxcar # so-and-so, but due to the weekend, etc., could not be touched until a certain time after the weekend according to rules all over the place. Harold was on limited time, so I drove to Saskatoon in my pickup truck, located the CPR Freight Central Control and I just put up such a stink that they finally had an official open the car, take my money and let me have my shipment – rules or no rules – just to get rid of this stinker. But – I had stuff! I didn't care what they thought of me and I let them know it. Harold was as happy as I was when I got home with the order. However, McDonald's were not able to furnish the spar wood to repair the broken wingspan – broken 5½ feet from the end.

This posed a serious problem, because a wingspan is not made out of barn or outhouse lumber, but Sitka spruce, and Harold was a perfectionist. I filled their Aeronca with gas and Bill Tocker flew to Prince Albert for a piece of spar wood of proper quality. He was not received favourably, (Floyd was away) and was getting nowhere. So, he re-parked the Aeronca and stooged around. This took time, and at home we expected him long before he arrived. Harold assured us by saying, "If anybody can get it, Bill will!" What Bill did was to rummage around amongst a bunch of wreckage that had been

dumped behind a repair hangar, latched on to a piece of spar wood
from a Stinson of the right kind of wood, stole it, tied it to a strut on
the Aeronca and took off for Kerrobert. He arrived at dark and
nobody was more welcome at that time.

The boys had to plane down this piece of spar wood to
dimensions to fit EVO, slant-splice the remaining part of EVO's
remaining spar, clamp it, with special glue, for so long a period (to
comply with repair regulations), and a major part of the repair job
was accomplished.

Meanwhile, we had the fuselage upside-down in our shop, and
Harold was welding and repairing the main frame. A lot of fabric had
had to be stripped off, so when EVO was finally being assembled,
half of her was a skeleton, not a visual prospect for flight. I bought
a pair of pinking shears in Saskatoon, Mother sewed the approved
fabric according to Harold's direction, and the fabric cover was put
on. Boy, when one puts on the original fabric, it looks pretty sick –
wrinkles all over the place. But Harold, with my Binks Body Shop
paint gun, put on six or eight coats of protective spray, which made
EVO look like an airplane again.

Then there was the question of the engine, which had not been
run for two years or so. I had gone to North Battleford and secured
the right propeller from Hugh McPhail (second hand), and paid
$65.00 for it. EVO was finally READY.

We parked the plane out in the yard, blocked the wheels, cranked
'er up, with someone standing by all the time, and we ran the engine
at about half speed for several hours. This was on a Saturday – the
boys were leaving for home on Sunday, the next day, so time was
running out. All seemed well and we decided that if I could get the
plane from our shop uptown, down to the airport in the early
morning, Harold would test-fly it, make out the many-detailed papers
for a major repair report for the D.O.T. in Winnipeg, and the boys
could start back for Prince Rupert.

I was up at dawn and taxied EVO down Railway Avenue. The
street was a cinch but when I had to turn off to go around a
mercantile establishment and cross the railway tracks right where
there was a section house,[18] I had to stop the engine and do a lot of
hand-waggling to get by obstructions which would not
accommodate the 36-feet-two-inches (11 m) of wingspan. Once

[18] *Section house – A house for railroad maintenance staff.*

across the railway track, I was home-free and taxied the rest of the way to the airport. We had all worked night and day but Harold and Bill were soon there, ready to make the test flight. This whole thing was town gossip and soon there were cars arriving, bearing the curious. By the time Harold and Bill arrived, we had quite an audience – biggest thing since Fair Day.

Harold got into EVO, I flipped the prop and Harold made his takeoff. Everything seemed OK. But after takeoff, at full throttle, EVO took off like a new plane but started to miss and run raggedly and we knew we had engine trouble. Bill, who had been talking to someone, started running out onto the field, concerned for Harold.

Harold nursed the off-and-on power of EVO in a circle (we were all horrified) until he could land on the field, and landed. It must have taken a lot of raw nerve. The engine would idle OK and hold perhaps half throttle for all day but would not sustain full-throttle power. Taxiing over in front of the hangar, Harold shut off the engine, jumped out cheerfully and said, "Huh, we must have some gas trouble."

A small wrench soon took the gas line off the brass elbow which screwed into the carburetor. There it was – the pod that some dumb lady spider had laid her eggs in, acting as a partial stoppage of fuel flow. Removing that egg pod and putting the gas line back on took only a couple of minutes and Harold was able to complete testing EVO. This was a thrill for all, enough for the whole day or week, but to Harold, it was just 'one of those things' – he being used to it as part of his work.

Following the test, we hurried to the shop office to complete the papers and I was ready to pay the boys for the day-and-night work they'd done. They were in a hurry to get on their way, so we worked fast. Papers completed and signed, I had my cheque book out, ready to pay them. Harold said, "Oh, no, we don't want a thing. We like you and the way you live and what you have been doing for US." I objected, but couldn't break their deal. They asked that I pay telephone, power bills, send them the receipts as well as the bill for rent of the house, and they'd send me the money. Well, I cleaned up the bills but sent nothing to them for bills or rent. This was a wonderful gift and experience in my life.

Harold and I had an arrangement that you, Dave, and I would fly out to see the Kelloughs the following summer in the school holiday season. Instead of the risky landing on the seaplane dock at Prince Rupert, Harold wanted us to land at Terrace, B.C., where the Kelloughs had a cottage. He'd pick us up there and take us the 85 miles to Prince Rupert. No way did he want me to wreck EVO at Prince Rupert. He said, "I think you can do it, Walt, but I don't want anything risky when it comes to you and David – we'll play it real safe." Terrace would be a breeze, being a level landing field on wheels. So that's the way we parted, and never saw each other again – but that's another story...

Ready For Flight Again

After the repair of EVO, there was a lot of trouble about both the plane and I, from the D.O.T. before I could fly again. From Harold's standpoint, he had the added difficulty of being a B.C. engineer making major repairs to a Saskatchewan aircraft in an unapproved implement dealer's repair shop. They gave him so much static that it, on top of many other aggravations, influenced him changing his occupation, I'm sure.

From my standpoint, I went in for a Private Pilot's Examination and ran into a great many unexpected re-examinations due to my involvement of 'head' injuries, THEY said, but actually the injuries were facial. This ran into more than $65.00 in fees, besides the many trips to Saskatoon to affect them. Each time I'd get a telegram, informing me that I was grounded for another 30 days – letter following. The letter would explain that in the wisdom of the department… I was always skeptical about their sincerity of purpose because I was convinced that they were the all-powerful. However, I was forced to heed all their demands or perhaps be grounded for life.

They (the D.O.T., now M.O.T.) made a great thing out of the fact that I was barely inside the Winnipeg District, and even when I had a routine annual C of A done at Edmonton (another District), they gave me a lot of static. Since they were giving Harold such a rough time, they thought they might as well give me a rough time, too, medically. This went on all winter and they sent a nice Mr. Walker from Winnipeg to inspect the plane. Walker arrived in the evening, and we had dinner at a restaurant, and a coffee later and inspected the plane the next morning. That winter Larry Doerr's Piper Cub was in the hangar, too, and the two planes, dovetailed, really filled the hangar. However, Walker took his flashlight, in broad daylight, and made a perfunctory examination. It was silly, really,but I didn't let my feelings show. He cost the government plenty and had a report to make – and made it. Walker learned more from me the night before, than he learned from looking the plane over in broad daylight.

Meanwhile, unknown to me until I started flying around the country again, they were quizzing all the airport people about this Williams fellow. I guess my friends stood by me, from reports I received after I resumed flying.

Everything was held up through the winter, and I'd keep receiving those telegrams, pending a report from another doctor or test. I'll admit to mounting tension. Harold was getting the same treatment and I guess I helped the government boys fill in their time AND draw pay!

About April, I got one of the shocks of my life – a big bundle of papers in the mail. (They must have found someone else to pick on.) In it was my re-instatement as a Private Pilot, complete clearance of Certificate of Airworthiness for the plane – tantamount to an invitation to resume flying!

Harold was off the hook – I was off the hook – but Harold had had enough of their treatment and quit his job. We both feel they had been really mean to both of us.

In a last long letter from Harold, he wrote that he had taken on a job as pilot for a mining company, 'way up in the rough mountains north of Prince Rupert. They had an old Fairchild freighter and a 125 Piper. The place where he had to land at the mine was really a glacier, with a 15-degree tilt. It was a piece of cake for the little Piper, but when he flew in supplies, including blasting powder, in the Fairchild and flew out ore, he had only one routine to follow. This was to land with the incoming load, uphill. They'd load the plane again and he'd taxi down the slope as hard as he could and he said that when he reached the end he sometimes had to dive into the valley below to get flying speed. His description of the job was 'hairy,' but the pay was good and he had good insurance for his family. He also said, "Come on out, Walt, and bring your boy – we'll see that you have a good time."

At Kerrobert, we were making preparations like getting a survival kit for two from Leavens Bros. Winnipeg – I bought a Browning .22 in case we were forced down. It was a break-down model (I still have it), taking 100 shells, so we could shoot something to eat if we were not injured too seriously. We had minimum weight in mind and the rifle weighed only four pounds.

School was nearing summer examination time and about a week before examinations we received a telegram from Bill Tocker – "Harold killed in a mountain storm." Harold was the fifth casualty that summer in sudden storms that developed in the Rocky Mountains. Harold is still flying, because he slammed into a vertical face of granite, with a load of blasting powder aboard. It was sudden and a pretty good way to go. Mountain climbers wiped him up with a rag and they buried the rag.

So, the trip was off and we never did see Harold again. We sent flowers to his wife and a letter, but what was that compared to the feelings we had for Harold! Several years later, you, Dave, met one of Harold's sons in the Army. Later still, he stopped at our shop with his family in a converted school bus on a holiday trip. We repaired his generator for free and I asked him if he would consider reading my last letter from his Dad. He decided that he would. I left him alone while he read it, and when he returned it to me, he said it cleared up some things for him and thanked me very seriously.

So, I lost one of the best friends I ever had, and am still in the dark regarding a number of details.

Large Truck Transmission

It was summertime and we had a large truck in the shop. We had sent the whole transmission to IHC Motor Trucks in Saskatoon for an overhaul and I received word a couple of days later that the transmission would be ready about noon that day. I was pressed for time that day and both the truck owner and ourselves wanted to get the truck out of the shop. I told the IH boys that if they could bring the transmission out to the field, I'd take it home in the plane. They agreed and away I went.

Those days, there was a sizeable patch of prairie at the west side of Montgomery Place (near Saskatoon) still not developed, and I asked that I be met there. Timing was pretty good and along came Arnold Cosgrove (from the parts department) with the transmission in a pickup truck. It was pretty heavy so we both took one end each, lugged it out to the plane and shoehorned it into the passenger side of the cabin – one end resting on the floor and the rest of it leaning against the seat.

The trip home was humdrum and ho-hum until I circled the shop at home and did a steep side-slip for a quick landing on the field. Well, that transmission didn't have any brains, y'see, and for a minute I thought I didn't have any either. I had not tied or secured it, so with the tilt of the plane, it just rolled over, against and on my right leg – and it really was heavy.

I let off the left rudder, straightened up the wings a bit and managed to roll the transmission back, enough to free my right leg. This fooling around extended my landing a bit, but I was able to complete it OK.

Like it has always been said – one can learn something every day.

Mail – Groceries – Medicine

Some winters were worse than others with regard to heavy snows and many storms. Even the highways in those days depended on the weather of that winter. I remember one winter when our shortest road to Saskatoon was closed for four months. With all roads closed – even railways – a little airplane was the only answer. Farmers could not get to town to get their mail or even groceries, and I would get calls to deliver mail, groceries, and even medicine, all of which was arranged by telephone. For mail and groceries I had to land to deliver but for the light things as medicine, I would tie a big dark rag or a homemade parachute, and drop it into the yard – no charge. When I had to land, I'd make a small charge, but the medicines were usually dropped on the way to a paying trip.

I can recall a trip to the Earl Rolson farm with mail and groceries. The landing was pretty rough on snowdrifts, but I shall never forget the smiles on the faces of Earl and his wife.

'Drops' from flight were regulated as much as possible regarding wind direction and strength – the ultimate objective being, of course, to land the message or medicine as close or convenient as possible.

There was a time when my father was in hospital on his deathbed – Len Wansbaough, who ran a large farming operation, including grain and cattle (Len did everything in a big way) phoned saying that some of his men had been out searching for a whole carload of yearlings, something like 22 head. They had his brand on one hip for identification, and had not been found.

You and I, Dave, made a quick trip that afternoon, with no success. Early next morning, broadening the circle of search, we finally found Len's herd. On the way to fly over Len's farm, I found an envelope in my pocket, scribbled instructions on the back and saw Len standing in the middle of the yard with men and outfits hooking up for the day's work in the fields. Banking in a tight '180' over Len, I tossed out the envelope. Len made only two steps to catch the fluttering envelope, which told him where to find his cattle. We had circled to make sure he caught it, and then headed for home after Len gave us a big hearty wave. That's the closest drop I ever made from EVO. Len paid for that trip next time he came to town.

Finding cattle and horses by air took from five to twelve minutes on average. Bob Finlay had worn out himself and his horse for three days, looking for a horse. Then I took him up in the plane and we found his horse in less than 10 minutes. He is still amazed at how easy it was by contrast. I made a lot of other such flights.

Mrs. May – Vanscoy

The office phone rang one nice afternoon. It was Mrs. J.D. May, mother of Dorothy, my Uncle Dave Lockerbie's wife, to see if I could fly her to Vanscoy, Sask., that afternoon. Dave was a school principal at Vanscoy and Dorothy was not feeling well. Mrs. May wanted to go there and look after Dorothy and the home.

Mrs. May was the dearest and sweetest friend to us all and I immediately said yes – get ready, I'll be right along to pick you up. This was Mrs. May's first contact with a plane, but took everything in stride. I chattered a lot about planes and flying and she was a most encouraging listener. As we neared Vanscoy, I told her I thought I could land in a certain field and taxi to within a hundred yards or so of the Lockerbie house. This we did and, after a short walk in, entered the house by the back door. Dave and Dorothy looked around and there we were, and Mrs. May was having a good day.

This particular day, the Queen was visiting Canada[19] by air, and we were just in time to see on TV the rolling out of the red carpet for the Queen to tramp upon after she'd deplaned. Dave had managed to get Dorothy from the bed to the front room chesterfield, was getting her all propped up with cushions when Mrs. May and I came in. So, as well as a nice trip and visit, and as she touched Canadian soil, the earth shook a little as a result of the momentous occasion.

Anyway, I fondly recall that little flight, and Mrs. May's pleasure in it.

---

[19] *Queen Elizabeth II visited Canada as a queen in October 1957, her first visit after becoming Queen, and again in 1959. (http://www.canadianheritage.gc.ca/progs) Her first visit is likely the one mentioned here.*

Doc James – No Winter Roads

Doctor Clifford James, our family doctor, in whom we had infinite confidence, trusted me as a pilot and often used my service in aviation. He was one of the fellows who obtained his Private Pilot's Licence through our satellite flying school. Cliff asked me numerous times to bring in patients, whenever it was advisable in the best interest of the patient. He knew of advanced cases of pregnancy, snowbound in the country, that may not be able to make it to the hospital when that time came. He would suggest that I bring them into Kerrobert so they could be handy to the hospital at the right time.

I recall a time after the 1955 January 12th three-day storm, a very severe one which closed all roads, railways, caused two deaths and many injuries, when he suggested I bring in a Mrs. Bouchard. The Bouchard brothers had been opening the road to the highway (which was blocked, too) daily, and had to plow their way back home again. Mrs. Bouchard's maiden name was English, and sister Doris and her mother had the skin worn off their hands worrying about Mrs. Bouchard. The Bouchards had no phone. At Doc James' advice, when the storm abated, I flew out to the Bouchard farm to bring in Mrs. Bouchard so she could stay at her mother's place to be near the hospital when her time came.

When the great storm abated, I flew out to the Bouchard farm, landed in a clear field on skis and was greeted by the husband, standing on a big snowdrift that almost covered a grove of trees south of the house. He was all smiles and asked what brought me to his place (knowing all the while). I explained my mission (as I had to do on so many other occasions). He and his brother had done so much frustrating work, trying to prepare for 'the time.' He suggested we go in and have a talk with the lady.

Entering the house, we found her ironing clothes for the family, including former children. My persuasion, and some serious consideration on her part, made her finally ask, "Well, what should

I wear?" I suggested something comfortable and warm, and that the flight would be short. She was ready in a very short time, I flew her to Kerrobert and took her to her mother's home. It was a great relief to all that she was in a much more favourable position than on the farm. This was a time, many times repeated, when foresight and action really paid off.

Doc James was very sincerely concerned for his patients, but there was one time when I got real hell from a similar case, when the lady had to stay at the hotel. A week or two after I'd brought her in from the Cactus Lake country (roads impossible), I met her on the street and really got a dressing down for having brought her in too early. She hadn't had her baby yet and I was being blamed for causing her extra expense and a lot more that was not complimentary to my enthusiasm to help others. Well, you can't win them all.

I recall another time when I flew Cliff to the CPR station at North Biggar. He wanted to go to a meeting of some kind down East, and the only way he could make it, after caring for his patients and performing an operation, was that I fly him to catch a CPR train north of Biggar. En route, he asked me what would happen if we didn't catch the train. I soon put him at ease when I told him we'd just fly down the railway line, pass the train, and he could catch the train at any station down the line. Well, we saw the old steam train approaching North Biggar, I landed in deep snow and Doc James caught his train, after wading through waist-high snow.

There was another flight with Cliff to a farm near Major. An elderly man on a farm had a serious heart condition. The wife had previously passed away and only the father and son were at the farm. The son, through the night, told James that his dad was in real trouble. It was late enough in the spring that while there was frost through the night which froze the ground, the fields would be muddy later in the day, so I suggested a really early flight to avoid as much as possible the prospect of taking off on a muddy field on wheels. This was OK for James. So, we took off really early the next morning, landed on wheels on frozen summerfallow across the farm.

The old gentleman was in an easy chair in the front room. He had fallen out of it and the son had had a hard time getting him back into it. Well, James did everything he could but the old fellow passed away while we were there.

This extended time put it late enough that there was a coating of mud on the field where the plane landed. I said, "Well Doc, let's take our chances," and Doc was game. So, when we took off, there were mud balls flying, hitting the prop and putting mud blobs on the bottom of the wings. But we made it into the air and flew home. It was a struggle because every mud ball slowed the plane – but we made it!

Doc James got the greatest kick out of any risky situation and I'd keep him filled in on all aspects. He sure was a great guy – I think he would have jumped out to land in a snow bank if he thought it was deep and soft enough.

Wrecked Ryan

At one time, there was great activity in oil exploration in areas adjacent to the Kerrobert district. This began during the Second World War and the Discovery Well was right behind Alf Cole's farm, a couple miles south of the hamlet of Coleville. Exploration continued after the war, into my flying days, and there were times when I was called upon to do certain air services for this type of effort.

One such area which did not turn out to be as productive as the Coleville/Smiley country was in the hills near and around Fusilier. (Please understand that most of these little points on the railway have since dried up so that nothing remains, hardly, but the name of the location.) This is a particularly hilly part of the country and a test hole was being drilled at a certain place. A large number of these drill outfits were Calgary-based. I did a lot of welding and machine work for many of these crews during the years of their activities.

Whoever handled Ryan Aircraft in Calgary at the time thought they had the real super-answer plane for executives and men to fly from one well site to another, due to what they claimed was short-field capabilities, and offered a certain company a free demonstration flight to a drilling rig about 35 miles (56 km) straight west from Kerrobert. The pilot was their best and four well-fed executives were piled in for the ride.

The area around this particular well was about the worst this pilot could have chosen, hilly like a pan of buns, with many fences, which made any landing area either too hilly or too small – sometimes both. The overzealous pilot chose a relatively level but fenced-in field, too small for even little old EVO. Also, there were many stones and holes. Don't know what the pilot was thinking about – he must have gone to sleep. The Ryan was rated to be a good performer, alright, but when this one was dumped into this field, it was inevitable that something undesirable would happen.

It finally came to rest in an aborted three-point attitude[20] – (1) right main wheel, (2) nose on the ground with the bent metal prop dug into the earth and (3) right wing tip.

Word of this accident spread around among the other men in the same line of work and, that evening, a foreman from another company asked me if I would fly him the next morning to see this unfortunate incident. I was curious, too, so told him that it would have to be real early in the morning because I had a lot of other things to look after. We took off and found the location, and my first visual survey made me wish I hadn't come. However, I did some pretty hard figuring and chose another spot fairly near to the wreck and we landed, intact.

Nobody else was around and we had a good look at the wrecked Ryan. Fuel was still dribbling from the tanks since the day before, so this pilot-boy must have filled all tanks, too. It all looked a bit ridiculous and we went back to EVO to take off for home. We had landed at stalling speed on a field trail, uphill, but taking off on the descending steps of this lonely trail was another matter. We went over a hill without enough speed for takeoff, but the plane wanted to stay in the air. I had to slam 'er down to the trail again, to keep contact with the ground and to prevent stalling and crashing on the next hill. Full throttle all the way, we jumped off the next hill, and were in the air, intact. It took precise timing to pull it off. My passenger was apparently a drinking man, including the previous evening, and when I handed him a quart sickness container, he nearly filled it.

We landed at home OK and I put the container in a trash barrel I had at the hangar. We both went uptown to our respective work – wiser for what we had witnessed that day. I got a kick out of a remark from my passenger, when he said, "You can land and take off anywhere with this little thing of yours," – meaning EVO.

---

[20] *Three-point attitude - All three wheels touch at the same time. Under normal conditions, small-engine pilots land planes on the two large wheels and gradually let the tail come down and tail wheel touch. Wheel-first landings are made in cross-wind conditions.*

Sask Tel And Sask Power Flights

Dozens of times I had calls from Sask Tel and Sask Power Corporation repairmen for flights to remote and sometimes relatively inaccessible places. They were made both winter and summer, but mostly in winter. These men, most times, carried repair equipment and repair materials, which made us wish to land as closely as we could to the point of trouble. Lots of times we could taxi right up near the pole they had to climb. Other flights were to road-blocked farms, where the kickout switch had released and those people would be in a bad way until the repairman got there. Time was important.

In this case, the power serviceman would have to climb halfway up the pole and reach up with a 'hot-stick' which would let him reset the switch without getting too close to the hot wires and get himself killed. For the first two or three years, the sticks would be one solid piece, 10 or 12 feet long, and about as big or a little bit bigger than a rake handle. At the top end was a prong with a ball end sticking out at right angles, to engage a loop on the fallen switch lever. Later, a stick was produced which would splice at the centre, but many were the times we had to take along the full length pole. Often, we tied the long pole along or across the wing struts. Tools and such were taken in the cabin. Sometimes we had 'er pretty full!

Some of these flights were for inspection of several hundred miles of line, sometimes less, and my passenger would be making notes on special maps he carried or on a notepad. On flights like these, I would fly to the left side of the line, putting the line on his side. The line was just outside his window, so close that lots of times he could see the threads on the cross-arm bolts. Occasionally, when the observer was not sure, he would request another look. I'd do a tight 360-degree circle and zero in again on the spot in question.

One summer morning about five, Jack Drew and I took off for Eston to inspect the power line from Eston to Kerrobert. It was a fine sunny morning but the night before there had been a vicious storm, thunder and lightning and power service had been cut off somewhere along the line. I kept the line just outside his window so he could read the name on the insulators. We found several places where lightning had struck the line, breaking an insulator or shattering a pole, and Jack carefully logged all these places.

We returned to Kerrobert in good time and Jack was able to pinpoint all the trouble spots so each repair crew could go right to the right place and make speedy repair. Jack felt pretty good about that, but I just managed a couple of yawns and went to the shop for my day's work.

Near Primate, and in the Cactus Lake/Fusilier country, it was sometimes touch and go to fly down every hill and make the climb up the other side without hitting the hill (many times covered with bush), but we always did make it. I recall several times after such a hard climb, the line was higher than the aircraft. Service calls in those areas were something other than sensible according to flying regulations. A lot of times, the passenger serviceman would be quite scared, but I always managed to jump a fence or pull off some other trick and didn't hurt any power or telephone men. They liked it, though, and the beverage room stories often related flights with Walt Williams.

One day on skis on a power failure call in the Primate area, where terrain and bush made our mission risky, we spotted the trouble and then landed near Primate and walked into the hamlet. The storekeeper was the fellow in charge of the switch which could cut the power on the section that was in trouble. A rule by the Power Corporation stated that a man in his position was not to turn on the power again until he had definite word or indication from the repairman that he was through his work and clear of the line. So, to save time and another landing at Primate, it was agreed that the man responsible for the switch would turn on the power again when the line was repaired and clear (it was a broken insulator this time) and the repairman and I would buzz his store.

After the buzzing, we circled around, got a wave from this man and we headed for home. That time the power was off only an hour and five minutes and EVO surely had to wiggle to get in and out of the place where that pole was located. The Power boys were pretty well pleased with that particular incident.

Police Flights

EVO flew many policemen with various missions. These included delivery of court summonses, discovering winter tracks to homebrew stills, investigating fires and deaths, and bringing in a prisoner (police waiting at my hangar).

One clear morning 1,000 pounds of meat and bones walking on eight legs came to the shop, asking to be flown to Tramping Lake – now-like. These four big guys had been 'doing the town' the night before in Kerrobert and now, party over, it was time to get home for recovery from their present condition. Ample evidence was obvious regarding nature of stimulant. So, I pushed out the plane and started out to make four trips – Tramping Lake took an average of around 40 minutes for two takeoffs, a trip each way, and two landings.

It turned out I made six trips because by the time I had moved these fellows out of Kerrobert, our big Mountie wanted to be flown to Tramping Lake, too. Something had turned up which involved the men I'd just flown out of town. With all roads blocked, EVO was the only means of transportation, so I flew the Mountie out to Tramping Lake.

He walked into town while I made another short flight and was waiting to be flown back to Kerrobert when I returned. Apparently one of the four original passengers that day was needed to keep a jail cell warm and occupied in Kerrobert. First, I was to fly the Mountie back to Kerrobert, then fly in the culprit, who had agreed to return. All turned out well and it was quite a day, for me at least.

Another time, a sunny summer afternoon, two Mitchell kids and another kid were driving all over the Kerrobert streets at high speed in a car. Soon a police car gave chase, and they tore around town for awhile, then headed for the country. Hector Gouliquer was at the shop, just going to start working for us, and he and I jumped into the pickup to see what was going on. When the chase started east on

Highway #51, I drove back to the hangar and got the plane out quickly. Hec, when asked if he'd like to go along, elected to do so. We took off without a warm-up (the only time in my life), and headed east. We picked up the cars a few miles out. They had been going one way and then another, and when we came over, the cars were headed south. The police car was just staying clear of the dust, waiting for the fugitives to make a mistake or run out of gas or road or whatever.

Well, the kids came to a place bordering the PFRA pasture, and were approaching a corner where they would have to turn left. Perry Thun's farm was at that corner. The kids zigzagged with indecision and finally, more or less out of control, left the road and hit a power pole that suddenly jumped up in front of them. They stopped! Along came the police car in the dust, and they saw two of the kids running towards some bush in the pasture, about a third of a mile away. They were soon caught and returned to the car, in custody. However the big question then was, "Where's Gary Mitchell?"

Hec and I had been circling and had seen Gary go a short distance into a field of standing wheat, flattened down on to the ground, and he was hidden by the wheat crop. There wasn't much of a place nearby to land EVO, so I dived at Gary in the field, pulling up from the point where he was lying. I did this several times and came so close a couple of times that afterwards the police told me I cut off some of the wheat. Must have been quite an experience for Gary, and I'm truly thankful he didn't panic enough to jump up or we'd have been in a lot of trouble. Anyway, the police got the point, went into the field and apprehended Gary.

This small wheat field was close to Perry Thun's farmyard, just west of his shelter belt of trees. Perry had been in the army and had gone into the house and brought out his old Army rifle. Good thing Gary didn't meet HIM! And poor old Hector – who survived the dives, pullouts and stall returns for another dive – admitted later that he'd had all he could take.

One winter day, with practically all roads closed, the Chief Mountie asked me if I could fly him to a number of places scattered all over our general locality. I said sure and away we went. It turned out that he had a fist full of summonses to serve for court appearances as witnesses to the upcoming court assizes.[21] We landed at one farm after another and at times he didn't even have to unfasten his belt or get out. I got a couple of dirty looks that day. For his part, he said he'd never had it so good!

One stormy winter, an elderly couple was living on the home farm in the very hilly country near Cactus Lake. Mr. Olsvick was 65, a paraplegic. His wife was a reputed 85, strong, vigorous and lively for her age. The family had all grown up and moved away. The only means this couple had for getting anything to or from the farm was for the old lady to strike out afoot. The family seemed to exhibit no interest in or obligation to them. The rural municipality was concerned and arranged that Dr. Cliff James make a welfare inspection of the Olsvick circumstances. Cliff called me and away we went.

This farmstead consisted of a large two-storey square house, a few old rundown granaries and sheds. Three ravines converged near the yard. Landing space was scarce so I chose a bare small field which had been summerfallowed, and the stones really tore at the skis. Just as we were coming to a stop, we fell into a ravine, where the snow had drifted in many feet deep. Cliff asked if he could help get the plane out, but I said I thought he'd better make his call first and I'd do what I could to get EVO back to level ground. Cliff took his bag and scrambled and waded his way out of the ravine and headed for the house.

I broke a couple of layers of snow crust ahead of the skis in the hope that this would make it possible to advance and climb the other side of the ravine. This, I had to do with my feet. In winter, a ravine fills in a little more every time there's a snow or ground drifting. Then every hard frost, thaw or mild spell will produce a hard crust. In time, the ravine has many such layers. EVO had penetrated one, maybe two.

When I thought things were ready, I slammed the throttle wide open while remaining outside the plane that I may jiggle, lift, pry – anything to help the engine move the skis ahead, be it ever so

---

[21] *Assize - A trial held before a travelling judge.*

little. It was a matter of half an inch or an inch at a time. Several times in my exertions I broke through more crust layers and, at one time, the bottom of the doorway was above my head. However, I eventually made enough progress and EVO went up over the other side so fast that I nearly lost 'er. Big flight boots and heavy clothing didn't help me to be nimble – but I did make it OK.

By the time Doc James came from the house, I'd made two or three takeoffs and landings, and determined the way we'd leave the place. We got home OK.

One windy Saturday night, less than a month after Doc James' visit to the Olsvick farm, that house burned down. It was situated on top of a small hill, so the wind really burned it down so that nothing remained but the square cement footing for the building and a chimney standing up from the centre of a round hole which served as a semi-basement for the house. All else was reduced to fine ash and remnants of metal parts of furniture, stove, etc.

The next morning was quite windy, too. Our regular Mountie, Bert Fisk, had left for Prince Albert, where he would be for about a week and the Kindersley detachment was to cover his area while he was away. So I received a phone call from the Mountie in charge at Kindersley, asking if I could fly him out to the Olsvick farm. I said sure and met him at a field behind the Kindersley Hospital. Recalling the ravine incident with Cliff, I let this fellow off at a nearby farm, where he wanted to begin his investigation. Then I was to bring out a coroner from Kerrobert.

The law says that a coroner (doctor) cannot act as such if he has attended the victim(s) within the prior 30 days, so Doc James could not act. His colleague, Dr. Munkley, was IT this time. Munkley had an operation to perform that morning and I knew I might have to wait until he was finished before I could fly him out to the Olsvick farm. On returning home, I glided quietly over our hospital on the hill and, looking down through the skylight window of the operating room, I got a glimpse of surgery still in progress. So I thought I could rush home and get a bite to eat this time. It was just about noon. Hurrying home, I was on my third mouthful when Doc Munkley came to the back door. So that was the end of the lunch for me, and Doc didn't eat at all. Away we went, and the wind was still blowing pretty strongly.

Arrived at the farm, we made a short landing in the strong wind. I put the cover over the engine and we went to the place where the house had burned down. The Mountie was waiting, so they went right to work. In one corner, just inside the concrete foundation square, was what was left of a human being. Both arms and legs were burned right off and the skull, still balancing in line with the spinal column, face down, was what remained of the old man's appendages. All that remained was the torso, very badly burned, too, and as soon as the torso was touched, the skull collapsed. The only thing we could find to wrap up the remains was an old binder canvas in a shed, with the slats on, so that's what we used.

No sign of the old lady. It must have been a very hot fire, fanned by the high wind, and what had not been blown away and scattered was in the cellar dugout. Munkley and the Mountie, by reason of their responsibilities, were bound to sift through the ashes, closely examining for any trace of the lady – a bone or piece of one – anything. Finally, with the short winter daylight and the big job only started, it was decided that the Mountie would remain and continue the sifting and stay at a neighbouring farm. Munkley and I would fly back home before it became too dark.

A day and a half later, I received a phone call from the Mountie, asking if I could fly him and the Olsvick torso to Rosetown. I said sure and set out to make the pickup. Since I'd seen him last at the farm, there had been stormy weather, closing most roads and highways. It was a lovely day and the Mountie, with the torso stuffed into the small space behind the seat, made quite a load, although the torso wasn't very heavy.

Subsequently, EVO was used in many searches all over the surrounding area for traces of the lady. As well, RCMP tracking dogs were used, to no avail. Bert Fisk and I made free trips out to scan snowdrifts in the remainder of the winter, and on into the next spring and summer, scanning weed rows along the fields, low spots full of grass and weeds, etc. and on one occasion we landed where a man was summerfallowing and Bert had a talk with him. No trace of the old lady was ever found.

Bert made many flights in EVO – some easy and some not so easy – landing in snow with EVO's belly lying right in the snow and the propeller fanning snow all over us – missing surprise rock piles – strumming the top wire of a fence to get 'off' – we had quite a variety of 'fun' together. Also, Bert seemed to know, continually, what EVO was doing and there were some times when I was glad he drove down to the hangar just as I was coming in from a difficult flight. He was there, too, when I'd come in illegally after dark, and I was ever thankful that the dear old Department of Transport didn't do anything about THAT.

I trusted Bert and told him a pretty straight story of all that was going on. Part of his apparent tolerance was due to the fact that I laid my entire future of the line many times when I thought it was in my power to help someone else. One flight we made together, he asked me to circle a certain farm that he just may see a track out in the snow to a still. This man was selling moonshine and it was Bert's job to try to find out where the moonshine was coming from. We saw no tracks on that occasion.

Train Wreck East Of Biggar

One year, when John Garstang was our head Mountie, he came to me one early summer afternoon and told me there had been a serious freight train pileup 12 miles east of Biggar. He wondered if he and I could fly out there, see it and take pictures. I said, "Boy, that's real rough country but sure, we'll fly out and see what we can do." John had two cameras and I had a new 36-roll in my colour slide camera.

John had flown bomber-type planes during the war, so felt like a bird in the air with no wings in EVO. However, he was game and we took off soon afterwards. The weather was good enough, though dull, and we thought it might rain later (which it did, but not very much).

Finding the wreck was easy enough and it was an unholy mess. An 86-car CNR freight train had piled up 47 cars in a cut through a large hill. Through this one cut, both CN and CP ran their respective tracks as close to each other as regulations would allow.

This was one heck of a wreck – tank cars of oil had split open, squirting oil right up over the high bank of the cut – carloads of wheat burst and thousands of bushels of wheat were in the mess, and someone was hitching a ride in a gondola car[22] and perished. (His body was found later, soaked in oil, and identification papers were soaked in oil, too, so it took quite awhile to find out who he was.) Steel rails were twisted into pretzels – a carload of wheel-and-axle assemblies was scattered around like tin cans at a wedding. Mixed freight in boxcars was being salvaged by B & B crew, one showing a size-10 footprint on his posterior. I think they were Italians because "No-speaka-da-English" was prevalent among them.

Mounties were there from Biggar, in their jurisdiction, and John Garstang was off base but suffered no censure for that – he was just another man and was never reported. He was in uniform, but Mounties are pretty good to each other, generally, and John rated well with his peers in the Force. We took our time and were satisfied

---

[22] *Gondola car - A low-sided metal car for carrying coal or mineral ore.*

we had covered the whole thing by the time we left for home. By then, there was light rain.

Now – initially approaching the scene, in the hilliest country you can imagine, we flew at low altitude, first one way and then the other, so we could get close pictures from the air. Meanwhile, I had a keenly speculative eye on where we could land not too far away from the wreck. We could land on a stubble-covered hill 1½ miles away and walk back to the wreck – or land in 'low and close' on soft summerfallow, real close – between hills and a real plane-trap.

I decided to land on the close field, but had no idea how soft the summerfallow was. We had a heck of a time, at full throttle, to get off it onto prairie. John cursed me for all kinds of a fool and was quite upset. I said, "Just quiet down, Johnnie, and we'll figure our way out, after we've completed our observation of the wreck – one thing at a time. We've landed and we'll get away in whatever way we can calculate, after the main mission is accomplished. We're here now, and we're going to make the best of it." I jokingly asked him if he trusted me and he said a definite, "No!"

There were cars from all over the surrounding area, as well as cars of investigative people, and there must have been a couple of hundred people there. They had railway 'wreckers' there, hauling out one car after another, and dumping them out on either side of the hill beside the track. Bulldozers were there to drain oil from the ruptured tanks into a nearby field downhill. When we climbed the hill, a woman said, "I wonder why that plane landed in such a God-awful place." John said, "Y' see, everybody else thinks you boobed, landing there." I told him he worried too much and we'd get home OK.

Few people can describe the havoc in such situations, but I have a series of colour slides which are more eloquent than words – they are facts, photographically recorded. The day was Thursday and on the following Sunday, flying to Saskatoon, I took pictures of the first train through that cut, creeping through on the new road bed that had been reconstructed. They had wreckage and oil-soaked dirt bulldozed off the right-of-way, both sides of the hill. Then they bulldozed dirt from both sides of the cut to fill in a new level for the tracks – laid the tracks and they were in business again.

Now, back to John and I getting home again...

A light shower had begun and I suggested that he let me, alone, get out of that soft hollow and that he walk to whatever field I might find for our takeoff for Kerrobert. He said, "You'll never get out of there!" but I made light of the situation and asked him to have a little faith and wait and see how I made out. So, alone on the plane, I took all 65 horses out of the barn and went downhill in the soft summerfallow, knowing that I was heading for a trap in the surrounding hills. Finally, EVO began to lift, but I was getting pretty close to the hills when she finally cleared the earth. I had to do some dodging at stalling speed, but MADE IT!

Finding a hill a mile or more away, I landed, and John came walking along and got in – still cursing me. I just made light of the whole thing, saying that he lacked experience and we flew home in fine shape. He just didn't know how slow a small plane could fly, that's all, but he found out that day. I'm sure that he thought the Good Lord had 'spared' him that day, but it was just another adventure for me.

Dr. Eyde – Macklin

Late one summer morning, when I didn't know how I was going to keep all my shop-work promises, I was called to the phone. It was Dr. Eyde, long-time doctor in the town of Macklin. He had a son who had been in a Saskatoon hospital for a long time and the doc had received a call that he should get to Saskatoon as soon as possible. Would I fly him in? Well, I told him I was over my head in work but out of respect for his worthiness, I would come right away. We agreed to meet in a field north of Macklin, where I had landed before.

As soon as I could gas up and get EVO out of the hangar, I was on my way, still bothered about the time I'd be losing at the shop. Arrived at the field and there was Dr. Eyde, waiting. He got in and away we went. Talk between us was meagre for we really didn't know each other very well and he would be preoccupied with knowledge and thoughts about his son. As we taxied toward the hangar in Saskatoon, he reached for his pocket, asking, "How much?" I pointed to a waiting taxi with a nun-nurse in the back seat and said the pay could wait, he'd better get going. He said, "Of course," and that taxi rounded the corner on two wheels on the way to the hospital.

While I was gassing up, the boys told me that the nun had given them a rough time, which was common of people who expect to arrive by the time they'd hung up the phone just because they'd called an aircraft. I gassed and paid and left for home. On the way, I did some pretty serious thinking. Here I was, leaving work undone until I returned from this or that flight, always for someone else. I loved flying too much to get rid of EVO and had a reputation for helping whenever I could, and the public expected it.

Several days later, I received a letter which helped me make the decision to continue flying. The letter was from Dr. Eyde, with cheque enclosed. He said it was the amount other flyers had charged and if I wanted more, he would gladly send it. He expressed appreciation for helping him out, and here's the payoff sentence – "Your help allowed my son to die in my arms."

That one sentence really melted me down, to continue being of service to those in need. You see, Dave, I had a son of my own...

Mrs. Russel Bielby – To Biggar

One fairly windy winter morning, Russel Bielby, near Kelfield, phoned asking if I could fly his wife to Biggar. I said, "Sure," and was soon on my way. There was enough snow in the air that I followed the highway and road to Russel's farm. They were waiting, so there was no delay. Russel asked if I could get him a good pump jack as his old one had petered out, and I assured him that I could get a good one from Davies Electric in Saskatoon. Told him I'd pick one up for him and Mrs. Bielby, and I took off for Biggar.

I was never curious about the reasons for a flight, so didn't know why Mrs. Bielby was going to Biggar. That was none of my business. All I was concerned about was transferring the passenger from Point-A to Point-B safely.

We stuck pretty close to roads and highways, and finally came out into better conditions before Biggar. We made a nice wide turn to land upwind at a field I'd used many times before. I think it was Russel's brother Harold who picked her up in his car. Then I flew back home.

The roads opened and I made a trip to Saskatoon by truck and picked up the pump jack for Russel. Soon after, and because Russel's road from the highway would not be open, I muscled the pump jack into the plane and flew it out to him. Landing near the buildings, I met Russel and we wrestled the pump jack out of the plane, then went to the house where Russel settled up for the jack and the trip to Biggar. Russel's young daughter made us a coffee.

I can still remember the twinkle in Russel's eyes when he told me that he'd got a bargain, since I thought I was flying one person to Biggar instead of two.

His wife had gone to Biggar Hospital to have a baby! Everybody was happy – even me.

Winter In The Air

Prairie winters in the 1950s were much harsher than they are today, with days and sometimes weeks of impassable roads and school closures.

Walter's niece Faye Climenhaga remembers when she was a child that sometimes the tops of the snowdrifts were level with the roof of the town's dance hall, a prominent social gathering place. Farmers tied long ropes to the doors of their houses to help them make their way to their barns and back in blizzards, she said, and a hospital bus picked up pregnant women who were expecting to deliver, if it could get through on the roads before a storm hit.

Faye's sister Brenda Lawrence recalls one particularly hard-hitting storm in 1958 that began during school hours and caused problems for school buses. Brenda and her girlfriend were lucky that their bus got stuck in front of the Williams home, where they happily stayed for the next two to three days. "The snow totally blocked the back door to Grandma's house, so you had to go out a bedroom window upstairs to access the roof of the shed and then go to shovel out the door!" said Brenda. "Another bus got stuck at the church, so the church basement was full of kids who had nothing to eat or drink, and nowhere to go to the bathroom. Men from the town had to go there and walk the kids to houses down the block to see how many children they could take in."

These were the conditions in which Walter Williams was called on to fly his airplane. Even getting to the plane was sometimes a huge challenge, never mind getting EVO ready for takeoff and then trying not to freeze to death in a plane that had no heater and was in constant danger of icing up and falling out of the sky.

First Winter – Drunk Passenger

The first winter I had EVO – got her in September, so really had only three months experience with her – I received a call from a distraught wife whose husband had been missing for about two weeks. He had finally turned up at Biggar, and had been on an extended alcoholic bender.

I said OK, I'd go for him. I wanted to have his friends bring him out along the highway leading to Kerrobert and I'd land as near the road as I could in whatever field I thought was suitable.

It was fairly cold, so I dressed up heavy in big flight boots, the whole bit. It wasn't too early, so I'd have to make things click to get home before dark.

On arrival, I saw the car and landed in a typical Biggar field, lots of hills and bluffs of trees, and pulled up right beside the fence – facing a bluff of trees. We managed to get the man through the barbed wire fence OK and harnessed him into the plane. He was in very high spirits. Then I had to go around to the front of the plane and crank the propeller.

The throttle was set at idle engine speed but by the time I'd reached the prop, my passenger had gleefully slammed the throttle shaft right to the dash, in wide open position – full throttle. At the first flip of the prop the engine roared – wide open, the plane started ahead, and in my inexperience and surprise, I nearly had my future eliminated right there and then.

I managed to throw myself sideways so the prop missed me and I grabbed a wing strap as it passed over me and swung up inside the cockpit. I pulled back the throttle just before the plane got into the trees.

To put it mildly, I was quite upset by this unexpected development, but this man was so far gone there was nothing I could do but pretend it was a great joke. I had to take the chance of going back to the tail assembly and twist the plane to an angle where I could avoid the trees – on his promise that he would not touch that throttle again. Finally, I zigzagged out of the field and we were headed for home with just enough light to see the land.

This man was a particularly good friend of mine for as far back as I could remember in my years in Kerrobert, and he sure babbled a lot on our way home, revealing things I shall never reveal to anyone. One of our shop and truck driver men was waiting at the hangar when we approached the field.

It was a foolish oversight, but on that trip I had not taken out the right wheel column controlling the ailerons.[23] I was all lined up for setting down and was about 200 feet in the air when my passenger got risky and began yanking and twisting on the wheel control at his side of the plane, laughing and thinking it was a good joke. I slammed the throttle full on and counter-wrestled his movements, gave him a bang across the front and told him to let go and quit fooling around.

He became quite trite when I unsnapped his belt, unlatched his door and gave him a shove, telling him, "You're getting out RIGHT NOW." This caused a semblance of sensibility to my friend, and he behaved long enough for me to circle around and make a quick landing, sliding right up in front of the hangar.

Fred Lalear from our shop was there waiting with our pickup truck. My passenger landed with his safety belt off and the door on his side unlatched. He joked with Fred for one half to one minute and then he just keeled over. Fred, a big fellow, caught him and carried him over one arm to the truck. The guy was in real trouble, so we took him right to the hospital.

He spent some time in hospital and they barely pulled him through. He had been there before for the same reason through the years. One day when he was feeling much better, he jokingly said to his doc that the advice would be 'no more drinking.'

The doc said, "No, we're not going to say that but while we used all the tricks in the bag to save you this time, we can't do it again – ever. You've had your last chance and it's entirely up to you whether you go on drinking or not."

My friend never took another drink – turning down AA's offer of assistance, and did it all by himself. If you visited at his home, he would serve all who wanted liquor but would never take any for himself. THAT takes a REAL man, after so long a drinking habit.

---

[23] *Aileron - The control panel on the back of the wing that enables the plane to turn.*

Sharing The Big Day

Sharing in a BIG DAY for a family was always a very satisfying reward, regardless of difficulties or ease of accomplishment, effort, time, or inconvenience to me. An average instance would go something like this:

There would be a farm family – Mom, Dad and say, three to a half dozen children. It would be winter, with roads drifted full and, even if opened, could be closed in again by even a short storm. Mom would have to go to the hospital for awhile, and sometimes I flew her in and sometimes she'd arrive by other means.

In due course, she would recover to the point where I'd get a call to fly her home, sometimes with a new baby and a suitcase containing a good supply of a milk formula for the wee one. (Sometimes I thought that suitcase weighed as much as the mother.) I would make the pickup at the hospital and transport to the hangar, where I'd shovelled out a path to get the plane out and had warmed up the engine.

In her absence from the farm home, Dad would have been doing his regular chores plus looking after the house and family, and today "Mom was coming home," which made it a BIG DAY in the family history of all concerned.

Mom, baby and suitcase loaded, we'd take off and head for the farm. Mom would be very wide awake as we'd talk of this or that, and in a few minutes I could point out her farm home, which would give her a visual target. On skis in winter, the relatively open prairie country lent itself admirably in providing landing fields almost anywhere, although sometimes there were circumstances of fences, hills, sloughs and tree bluffs but EVO had a slow landing speed and I could usually land near or onto a sleigh or stoneboat[24] trail leading out to a feed stack or manure pile, which was a good path for the family to walk into the yard.

---

[24] *Stoneboat- A flat-bottomed sled on two skis used especially in removing stones from fields.*

As we taxied up, there would be Dad with the kids all bundled and lined up to welcome Mom home. The thrilled mother would usually remark that Mary didn't have her scarf on or John his warmest coat, but this was soon forgotten in the excitement of the meeting. Stopping across the trail, so that her door was above the path, I'd open the door, unfasten her safety belt, and reach behind the seat for the suitcase. She would give Dad a short kiss and a hug, and then she was on her knees in the snow, hugging the kids. Dad would say, "How much?" and settle up, take the suitcase and close the door. I would give the prop a flip, or sometimes I'd leave the engine idling if there was no dog around, and away I'd go for home, or to another farm or village.

Thus, I had 'shared' in that family's BIG DAY. Now, many years later, Romona, in her work of chaplaincy at the hospitals, sometimes hears of one of these trips, so I guess everybody doesn't forget after all.

Alsask – Injured Boy

One winter day, I was phoned by a mother at Alsask to fly her and her eight-year-old boy to Kindersley Hospital. She said that it was urgent. The weather was fine, so I assured her that I would be there as soon as I could warm up the engine and get going. She and the boy should be ready to be picked up at a certain field on high ground, a short distance south of Alsask.

Alsask was not easy country, even on skis, due to hills, fences and what-not. I had used this field before, not too large and fenced, but the best available in that area.

When I arrived, I was pleased that the mother was a smallish person and she had her son with her, with his face and head all wrapped up. Apparently the boy had been frolicking with their dog. A storm window had been left leaning against the house and while playing with the dog, the boy had fallen into the window, face-first. The result was a very seriously cut-up face, but the mother thought the eyes had escaped injury.

Takeoff successful, we streaked for Kindersley. That winter there had been a lot of snow and storms, and while at that time there was a fairly large field to land in, there was a giant snowbank right outside the rear door of the hospital. Not wishing myself to carry the boy a long way under existing conditions, and realizing that this little woman could have a difficult time, too, I managed to taxi EVO right to the top of this big rounded snowbank and shut 'er off right there, before falling in against the hospital. We were then at the level of the second floor of Kindersley Hospital. I took the boy and told the lady to dig her heels in real good, and we descended to ground level, just a few feet from the Emergency entrance.

Delivery accomplished, all I had to do was climb the bank, turn EVO around a bit to face away from the building, and give the prop a flip. I let EVO slide down to field-level fairly quietly, out of respect for patients in the institution, and then roar off for home.

A couple of weeks later, I received another call from this family asking me to pick up the boy and fly him back to Alsask. His face had been cut up pretty badly alright, and though he'll be a grown man before this, his lot will be a very badly scarred face.

The only unusual fun for me on that trip was seeing patients of the second floor looking at us from only a few feet away. Perhaps it 'made' their day, too.

First Forced Landing

One fine day, on skis, John Herron and I took off, and not knowing too much about dew-point, I turned off the carburetor heat too soon after takeoff. Very soon after becoming airborne, the engine started to miss out and act erratically. It was not an important flight, just a Sunday jaunt. Apparently the dew-point was such that ice was forming in the intake manifold, which starved the engine of the amount of air to sustain maximum power. Very soon, the engine began to 'miss,' diminishing power seriously. We were not far from the home field so I turned back, hoping to land back at the hangar, which would be home ground.

So, flying downwind with an erratic engine performance, loss of power and only about 200-feet altitude, we had our fingers crossed. Finally, though, the engine just quit – DEAD. This was a serious situation, what with such low altitude and going the wrong way for an up-wind landing. Fortunately, though, to my left was a little five-acre field, fenced all around, with horses and deposits, and trees all over it. When the engine quit, there was only the sound of several boiling tea kettles, due to airflow over wings and struts. There wasn't even a hundredth of a second to think. Making a severe 180-degree turn, I banked in and landed on a small path, to make about the slickest landing I ever made in all my flying. But we were down and safe and didn't bust a thing.

We fired 'er up again and had taxiing revs, so taxied through gates and ditches back to the hangar, a distance of a couple of miles. I recall that at one point of effort, I split the bottom out of my trousers, right from zipper to the belt at the back. It was a cold winter day, so the first thing I did when we got the plane back to the hangar was to go to the house and put on a whole pair of pants.

This was my first experience with an icing carburetor intake. It was part of learning the hard way.

Mother With Sick Child – Major

I had made a trip of my own to Saskatoon and stayed overnight. In the morning, I went to the airport, had gassed and warmed up EVO, was in the office paying my bill, when the phone rang and I was told it was a long-distance call for me. From Major, someone asked me if I could fly a lady with her child (who had pneumonia) to Kerrobert Hospital. I said I was just ready to leave and would fly straight to Major. Then this party asked if I could fly 'in this weather,' and explained that the weather wasn't very good at Major. I said the weather was 'fine' in Saskatoon, but I'd sure try anyway.

The weather was from the east, so I made record time, encountering worsening weather conditions from about Biggar westward. Passing over Kerrobert, I could still see well enough to have made a landing and put EVO to bed, but not wishing to be a quitter and having promised, I didn't pause but continued along to Major. When I arrived at Major, the wind and snow were so bad I had to skim the houses to see them as I passed over the village. I was blown downwind half a mile, just making the turn-around for landing into the wind.

As with car driving, one will suddenly realize a very serious situation but one hopes to come through without any damage to body or equipment. Then, when the serious facts face one squarely, one's goal diminishes through "Let the equipment go but save my skin," to the ultimate concern of saving one's own life. Well, this was a case like that, and finally I would have settled for saving my life, injured or not, before I touched the snow-covered stubble field.

Visual reference was just about nil and the plane was kicked around like a football. However, I managed to touch the skis onto the field, and the wind was so strong it took nearly full throttle to taxi against it. When I had nearly hit the fence at the end of the field, I had to maintain half throttle, stick forward, just to keep the plane in level flight attitude. Otherwise, if I had let the tail down, the increased angle of incidence of the wings would have let the wind blow the plane right over backwards, whether I was in it or not.

I had used this field before, and as soon as people heard the plane pass over, quite a number of fellows came out to the field and I certainly needed them. Motioning that they should grab the struts to hold the plane steady on the ground, they did so, and I shut 'er off. We manoeuvred EVO into a nearby gateway where we tied down the tail and the wings to the two gate posts. Someone had the mother and child in a car but we soon decided that it would be suicidal to try to fly to Kerrobert. Everybody went into the village where the baby was taken care of by an elderly nurse, Mrs. Edmonds, on advice from Doc James by phone, and the child came through alright. I was put up in a room in a vacant hotel, wrapped up in blankets that some of the boys had rounded up.

The storm continued the next day and a snowplow cleared the railway, and I bought a ride on the CPR mixed[25] which made three trips a week between Kerrobert and Coronation, Alberta. The following morning after that, the weather had cleared, so I came back out to Major on the 'Coronation.' Then it was time to dig out EVO and try to get 'er fired up.

Well sir, I cranked on that thing until I was nearly played out and other fellows helped, too, but she wouldn't start. So I went into town and phoned Bob Graham, an engineer and friend at Saskatoon airport – Mitchinson's in fact. I was advised that the carburetor intake was probably 'iced up,' perhaps even full of ice. Best way was to use heat from a blowtorch, which I did.

Remember, EVO was out in the field, and it was COLD. Bob cautioned against fire and sure enough, she caught fire, but I was ready with a fire extinguisher and put out the fire. A lot of water ran out, and I finally got the engine going. But it was getting late in the winter afternoon by then and a lot of frost had covered the windscreen and windows. This meant that I took off up a slight hill facing the brighter western sky without being able to see straight forward. The takeoff was sluggish, but over the hill the plane picked up speed. Just as I was leaving the ground, I passed a big stone pile on my left. Sure was glad I hadn't hit THAT one!

So, respectively, the baby made it and so did I. It was a very nice

---

[25] *Mixed trains – Freight and passenger trains.*

gesture on the part of the fellows of Major who had helped me, when I received a short note of appreciation for trying and $17 the boys had chipped in.

Not connected with his incident, but funny, was that before this flight I had bought a raffle ticket, the draw (at Major) to be for a gas-powered washing machine. Not long after the mother-and-child affair, my usual draw luck went all screwy and I won the washing machine. Went out and picked it up, traded somebody (Cliff Pedersen, I think) the gas engine for an electric drive, made the conversion and shipped it out to my sister Grace, who was living in Vancouver at that time. She had no washer and it pleased me to send her a new one.

Dad Rising Early For Me

About the last year of his life, my dad, if he wakened, would come downstairs and make coffee and some breakfast for me. Mostly, I would quietly rise, eat a bite and be gone, sometimes all day, and not stop for lunch at noon, making the last landing after winter darkness had set in. I would have to rise really early, get all my flying duds on and walk the mile or more to the hangar, and by flashlight get the plane ready for the day's flying, which often began before dawn. I'd leave on the first trip while it was still dark sometimes, in order to be at a distant first call by daylight.

There had been a long period of 40-below Fahrenheit (-40 C) weather, which took more and more preparation for the day's flying, and with no cabin heat arrangement, I wore clothing that was about three inches thick and heavy flight boots, since I'd be sitting in that cold plane all day. It wasn't too bad on each passenger, because their particular flight would be comparatively short. The short times I'd be out of the plane to get unstuck or carry luggage or a patient to or from the plane through the snow served to warm me up once in awhile. However, other times I'd have to fly with the windows open, to get the frost from people's breath off the inside of the windshield, so I could see ahead.

The first thing I did when I came downstairs would be to check the temperature, wind, fog, etc. One morning, Dad was really amused when I reported that it was only 10-below (-23 C), and I should have a relatively easy day. He said, "Only 10-below," and had a good laugh.

I am extremely thankful that my dad and mother never exhibited apprehension over the hairy trips with which I was involved. Of course, I sometimes forgot to tell them ALL of the details, and I had a habit of calling home if there was an unforeseen delay, to report the reason and that all was in hand. Perhaps this helped them…

Blood Poisoning – Greene Elevator

One late winter afternoon, after flying all day and having put the plane away, on going to the office, my partsman Harold Patterson gave me a message that a man would be waiting for me on a snowbank so far this-way and that-way from the grain elevator at Greene, near Alsask, just inside the Saskatchewan border. This man had blood poisoning in a hand, which was travelling upward in the arm as far as the elbow, so it was becoming urgent that he get to a hospital.

Well, it was late in the afternoon of a short winter day, but I went back to the hangar and took off to find a man on a snowbank in the dark (by the time I got there), 60 miles (96 km) away. When, in the gathering darkness, I could pick out the Greene elevator, I gauged Harold's directions generally and, sure enough, there was a man-sized dark spot in the snow. Landing, it turned out to be a man walking towards me. Yes, he had blood poisoning alright and decided to give up home remedies and seek 'expert' assistance. He was a sore boy and I was inclined to think he was a tough old bachelor who found 'giving up' a very hard thing to do, but that's what he was doing.

He had chosen a field, for which I was thankful, and takeoff was therefore made simple. He said, "Kindersley Hospital," so I headed about due east and we were flying in the dark. I attained enough altitude to see Kindersley lights clearly and we were on our way. He asked if I flew in the dark very often and I assured him that I felt I had to 'lotsa times.'

"Well," he said, "you've got to be either crazy or a damn fool, but I hope you get me there OK." I assured him that I was both crazy and a damn fool, that he would be delivered safely and whole, and that helping others was costing me the taking of many risks.

When we arrived and landed in what then was an open field behind the hospital at Kindersley, he paid me and started walking to the hospital. I had never seen him before, didn't take his name and haven't seen him since, but I'm sure he came out well.

From there it was the same old story all over again – fly home in the dark and put the plane away.

Howard Carter – Out of Propane

It was a Sunday morning in winter and Mr. Carter, farming south of Kelfield, phoned to say that he had run out of propane gas, which was a very serious circumstance in his home. I said I'd do what I could and contacted Skinny Dunfield, who handled propane tanks in Kerrobert.

Got a large propane tank from Dunfield and went down to the hangar. Had to take out the seat cushions to get the large tank in. Warmed up, and away I went to the Carter farm. The weather was good and when I circled the Carter farm, he was out and ready to receive the tank. I landed in a near field and when I dumped the tank out, with his assistance, he wondered how I got it into the plane in the first place, alone.

Anyway, he had his propane and would get it to the house some way. He paid me and I took off for home. He really appreciated the service.

Warm Winter Days – Sticky Snow

A very disappointing thing about winter flying, which would compare with muddy roads in summer time, is sticky snow on a warm winter day. This was caused by water content or dampness in the low temperature top layer of snow, which would let the plane taxi but not attain enough speed for takeoff, as there was too much suction and drag. A similar circumstance occurs for floatplanes on glassy water. (This can be alleviated by having a boat criss-cross the takeoff patch of water, which provides air between the ripples to lessen the drag, enough for the floats to become unstuck.)

There was talk of plastic bottoms and I saw some which could be fastened on with rivets and they'd handle the warm snow problem. My skis were made of Duralumin[26] and were pretty tough for stones, etc. The plastic was easily torn and the few I saw were usually a sorry mess. Also, they were expensive.

Well, I'd have to buy the plastics and they wouldn't last very long on my kind of flying. So, I reasoned that my head hadn't cost me very much (being given to me by my parents), and it would last as long as the rest of me. After a lot of figuring how to beat this problem, I decided to think of a lubricant – KEROSENE. That should do it.

I got a cork to fit a Coke bottle and a rag and carried that behind the seat, waiting for the next warm-snow situation to come along. This little kit didn't take up much room and weighed very little.

At the next occasion of this nature, I found that the kit was the easiest part and the application a strenuous job. I had to lift each ski, one end at a time, hold it by one hand with my wrist over my knee. Then I'd ball up the rag in the other hand and take the uncorked Coke bottle out of the snow where I'd stuck it, tip the bottle so some of the kerosene would soak the rag, set down the bottle and proceed to wipe the kerosene on as much of the bottom of the ski as I could reach, which was about half way. Then it was all repeated for the other end

---

[26] *Duralumin – Trade name of one of the earliest types of age-hardenable aluminum alloys, containing copper, manganese and magnesium. (http:wikipedia.org)*

of the same ski. Then it was time to go around to the other side and do the same thing to the other ski. By that time, I'd had enough exercise to do me for some time. Put away the rag and bottle, climb in and presto – the skis slid over that wet snow and I was airborne in jig-time. IT WORKED!

However, each application would do for only one takeoff and, many times, I'd have to repeat the whole process several times in a day. I felt pretty good about that idea, and passed it along to other flyers who couldn't, or wouldn't, do it alone. It was amusing when I'd demonstrate and they couldn't duplicate the lone effort. It was HARD WORK!!

The only alternative was to hang around long enough for the snow to become more crisp, but this would be lost time. We could LAND on the sticky snow. The takeoff was the problem.

R.M. Mariposa – Books To Audit

The R.M. of Mariposa #350, where my grandfather Lockerbie was secretary for several years at a previous time, wanted their books flown to Kerrobert for auditing in the mid-winter. For some reason, the auditors preferred Kerrobert, perhaps because of hotel accommodations, etc. Could I fly in their books? I had a vision of books, large and small, and said sure, because I thought they could be piled into the plane – I'd just have enough daylight to make it that day – so get the books out to the field – I'll be there shortly.

It seemed like a nice winter day but by the time I reached Broadacres, I ran into a kind of white-out haze near the ground. Flying over and looking down through it, one could see a fifty-cent piece lying there but when one levelled off near the ground, it was like flying in a fog and the ground level was hard to find. This layer was relatively shallow.

I tried twice to land but didn't feel safe, so gunned out for some altitude again. I had used this field consistently right beside the United Church, for Broadacres people, I suppose nearly a hundred times that winter so far.

Then I got what I thought was a bright idea – there was a fence all along the south side, the wind was from the east, so all I had to do was keep the fence to my right and that would tell me the ground level. As things developed, it could have been the end of both my flying and my future.

Lining up with this fence, I went past the corner furthest from Broadacres – a part of the field I had never used before, or didn't remember. Descending, I missed the cross-fence at the end of the field, lined up with the east-west fence to my right. Keeping the plane in a nearly three-point attitude, I relaxed a bit, thinking I had it made.

Everything seemed to be going fine, but another glance at the fence revealed that the fence was quite a bit above me. This could mean only one thing – I was dropping into a pothole! There wasn't a split second to think, but I put on full throttle, pulled back on the control wheel, just in time to tilt the plane sharply upwards to start sliding the skis up the fairly sharp bank at the east side of the pothole. (Had I not acted instinctively, I would have slammed right into that bank with disastrous results.) Once I had ski contact with the snow, I let back the throttle and was on the field at last. The main thing was that the plane was intact, and so was I.

From the moment of arrival, I had seen a big wooden box at the corner of the field near the church, containing all the books involved in the audit. I think everybody trusted me, but I reflected that it wouldn't be proper to just hand a guy, even me, a bunch of loose books that were so important. At the same time, it absolved me from any tampering or loss, but I sure had one heck of a time to get that big heavy box into EVO without any help, and with all the fooling around landing, it was beginning to get dark.

I had to take off the right door, remove the cushions and heave and pry to get that darned box into the plane, and then put the right door back on. However, I fooled everybody and made it. The box was so large I had to fly back home with the door on my side partly open, and in the dark at that. Arrived at the field, I labouriously removed the box, put it in my pickup truck (it was about all I could lift), put the plane together again and into the hangar. When I arrived at the hotel, I asked for the auditors. They came on the scene and were just going to take the books without identifying themselves.

I said I nearly lost my life and had to take my plane apart to get this big box into it, so how about showing me that you are the proper people to receive the box. More to ease my own frustration, I made them produce their credentials, and then I let THEM handle that big heavy box. I had had to handle it alone but those two pink-fingered guys could hardly handle it together, and I just stood by and let them sweat.

I didn't make any more flights like that without asking more questions. After all, EVO was not a freighter.

Trips For Two Sick Women

One winter evening, I had a call that there was a very sick old lady in a farm shack with her husband. It was imperative that she be transported to hospital that night or she would likely not be saved. Could I bring her in? I said a little moonlight would help, but even though it was pitch dark, I'd try.

Theirs was a lonely little shack with not much else around it, and the fields were pretty level with no phone line to run into. So off I went into the dark to see if I could find the place. When I finally saw a little red square of light, perhaps from a kerosene lamp, I decided to try a blind landing and take the chances. The skis finally touched, I throttled back, and the plane came to rest. I thought the shack was 'over there, somewhere.' It was a wonder I even saw the dim light of the window from the air – just luck, I guess. This was before the days of farm electrification and yardlights.

By this time, my eyes were fully adjusted to night vision level but even so, I knew I could get lost in the field trying to find the plane after leaving it, so I left the engine idling so I could then be guided back to it by sound. Then I waded off in the snow and found the shack fairly soon. Snow had drifted into a high bank all around it. I found the door and knocked. An old man, not very strong, greeted me, and I explained my purpose. He was desperate enough to agree that I should take his wife, although he knew me only by name and had only my word for that.

We bundled her up, and although she was not able to walk, I was thankful she was not a large lady. So, the old man opened the door, I picked up the lady and waded off into the dark and snow. It was easy finding EVO by sound and I talked lightly and encouragingly to the lady, despite my own misgivings. I put her in the seat and fastened her safety belt, went around and took my own seat, and gave 'er gas. Straight ahead, seeing nothing, a few little bumps later, and we were in the air. We didn't hit a thing – no rock, fence, power or telephone line. Our good fortune was extreme, and so was my foolhardiness.

The landing at home was the usual feel-and-hope system, but successful. Taxiing near the hangar, I carried the lady to my pickup truck and took her to the hospital. There, I carried her in, and the staff had a hard time to believe I had found the farm and flown her in on such a dark night. I could hardly believe it myself. Don't remember ever being paid for that trip, but I've always felt good that I pulled it off OK. I broke nearly every rule in the book that night.

Soon after dark on another dark winter night, I had a call about a lady with pneumonia who should be brought to hospital that night if possible. Roads were all closed, air was about the only means of transport for her. This was a few years after the former occasion and there were fences, telephone lines and power lines to watch out for. However, I knew the area pretty well and these folks were friends and customers, so I decided to give it a try. I didn't have much trouble finding the farm and thought I could make a landing and takeoff across the road from the farm site. Touching down accomplished, the plane had slowed right down when the left ski ran on to a patch of bare ground. Nothing short of a brick wall can stop a ski quicker than bare ground, and there I was – STUCK.

EVO weighed 920 pounds empty, which means no gas, no oil or tools, etc. It took all my strength and ideas to get that ski back onto the snow.

I finally made it, picked up the lady, who was a young strong German. I had a hard time believing that her case was that critical, but we made it back to the home field – mission accomplished.

Sebastian Schell – On A Suitcase

Sebastian Schell was a farmer in the general area of Broadacres and a member of the municipal council of the R.M. of Mariposa, #350. Their office was at Broadacres. This one real tough winter, there was the annual meeting in Regina of all the reps from Saskatchewan R.M.s. We still had trains those days and Sebastian phoned to say that if I could fly him to Kerrobert that afternoon, he could stay at the hotel overnight and catch the train for Regina the next morning.

The weather was not violent, but very dull and muggy and snowing part of the time. I had made other flights that day, never getting more than 300 feet from the ground at any time, following roads, railways and fences – just feeling my way from place to place. Flight time was increased, generally, for I had to fly mostly 'on the square' instead of straight across country.

However, I told Sebastian I would pick him up later in the afternoon near his farm. I had to make a circuitous route to get to his farm, which made me a bit later than I originally estimated. Arriving at his farm, I observed him out in an open field nearby, sitting on his suitcase, which was standing on end. Sebastian had one short fat leg crossed over the opposite knee, and he was holding it from slipping off. His grin covered his whole face, almost.

It was a routine pickup and it was not long before we'd backtracked and landed at Kerrobert, just at dark. Sebastian was very pleased and afterwards his story was that, "I vass sidding on de suitcase in de fieldt, yet, unt here comes Valder!"

When he returned from Regina, the weather was fine and I flipped him out home in jig-time. To Sebastian, the whole thing was a big deal.

Ralph Wright – To Saskatoon

Ralph Wright asked me if I could get him to Saskatoon on a very stormy winter day. He had married a girl in Scotland when he was overseas in service, and they had two daughters. Finally there was a separation and Ralph was to get one of the girls. She would be put on a certain flight from Scotland and would arrive in Montreal or Toronto on such-and-such a flight.

Ralph, desperate, wondered if I could get him to Saskatoon so that he could catch a flight to meet his daughter. I said I'd try and I remember having the plane out (it was really storming). Ralph and I were in the plane, which was idling, and I told him that the moment we saw the phone line at the old highway half a mile away, we'd gun her and follow the roads and highways and get to Saskatoon some way.

We finally got a glimpse of the phone line and I gunned EVO, for better or worse. Made the highway (there was no point of return) and, flying low, followed known ways to Saskatoon. Weather was far below D.O.T. limits, so I explained to Ralph that I didn't want to land at the airport and be grounded for flying 'below limits.' I suggested that I land him in the area west of Montgomery Place and he could walk downwind to the highway and bum a ride into town. He said that was OK. I didn't try to turn the plane around in such a high wind. He got out and started wading to the highway and I gunned EVO off for home.

Flying back home with a more-or-less tail wind didn't take so long, and when I circled the shop to let them know I was home again, Fred Lalear took a WD-9 IH tractor out of the shop to meet me. There were big drifts by this time and he thought the tractor could make it, rather than a truck. I hung in the air, facing the wind, throttled back a bit so that I stayed in one place over the ground, stationary. Saw Fred come out of the shop with the tractor and head down to the hangar. When he got to within about 300 yards of the hangar, he got into a big drift and got stuck. He came the rest of the way on foot and

I landed as close to the hangar as possible and was sure glad or his help in getting the plane into the hangar. Then we walked back to the tractor, dug it out and returned to the shop.

Ralph managed to catch a ride into Saskatoon. He took a taxi to the airport, to find that his flight has been delayed because of the storm, but he was eventually able to get away in time to pick up his daughter down East.

Flew Baby To Lloydminster

One winter I was asked, on a Sunday, to fly a 1½-year-old baby from Coleville to Lloydminster. I stated that I would prefer that someone went along with the baby. Art Brampton, who had a sister at Lloyd, said he would go along to look after the baby and visit his sister, too.

I picked up Art and the baby at Coleville, and we had a really nice flight. We delivered the baby to the proper people, Art had a visit with his sister, and we flew home again. This was not really exciting, but I had never landed at Lloydminster before, so in a sense, it was a 'first' – the only time I ever landed at Lloyd.

It was a nice day and we took our time, and it was one of the easiest flights I ever made. Art got quite a kick out of the flight and visit, and it was a pleasant Sunday for me.

Mechanic's Wife And Baby

In the cold weather of late fall one year, no snow but sloughs frozen, the plane was still on wheels. I had a mechanic (name forgotten), whose wife and baby had gone to visit her folks somewhere in the Paynton area, and it would be a lot easier to get her back to Kerrobert if I flew the plane and picked her up. So away I went, to find a farm about so-far this-way and that-way from a given reference. I wore enough clothes to keep me reasonably warm for existing conditions and did locate the farm.

But, this certainly was not airplane country – helicopter, yes, but airplane, no. The ground was far from level and between the bushy areas, there were potholes full of ice – some larger than others. I thought that as long as I was this far out on a limb, I may as well make the best try available.

After some observation, I found a place where two potholes were separated by a small ridge with a gap in the bush, so tried and made it. I nearly ran EVO into the bush to get stopped. This was near the right place, alright, and soon the family brought out the well-fed mother and her child. I said it wasn't warm enough weather for the light clothing she was wearing, but she insisted that she would be OK, so I took them aboard. I had over a hundred miles (161 km) to get home, and thought she could get pretty cold in a flight of over an hour.

We managed a kind of hairy takeoff but made it after dodging some bush, turned for Kerrobert and settled back for the flight home. Sure enough, we hadn't gone far before I noticed the woman getting cold. Quarters were cramped (she was kinda plump), but I wasn't going to have her suffer the cold the rest of the way, so I unfastened my coat and we had quite a time of getting it onto her in flight, but we made it. Then it was my turn to get cold, and I sure did. When I landed I was really shivering, but she and the kid were OK.

Mrs. Murray Lowe – To Dodsland

The calls began coming in the morning (it had been storming all night) of a stormy day during a winter when storms were fierce and frequent. Murray Lowe asked if I could fly his wife to the hospital 'right now.' I explained that the storm was still too bad for me to come right then but that I thought it would abate later in the day. When I could see to travel, I would be glad to make the trip.

He would not hear of any delay and during the prolonged call I asked him to look outside and tell me how far he could see. There was a short pause and then I was informed that he could see the henhouse. I told him that that was practically zero visibility, the same as at Kerrobert, and I had no intention of committing suicide or killing his wife. Nope, he would have to wait. I promised that I'd have the plane ready for the first signs of the storm letting up, at which time I'd start out for his place.

From then until mid-afternoon, his repeated calls averaged less than an hour apart. By the middle of the short winter afternoon, the storm showed signs of abating and I phoned Murray to tell him that I had shovelled the snow from in front of the hangar, the engine was warmed up and I'd be starting out to find his place. He'd better have a team of horses and a sleigh-box ready to bring the wife out to the field, because the wind was still too strong and drifts too high to risk turning the plane around.

So off I went, hardly able to see my way, but by keeping track of known landmarks and farms, I kept pretty well on course. Gradually, as I flew along, the air cleared considerably and by the time I arrived at the Lowe farm, visibility was quite sufficient for our purposes. I landed, rocking and bumping on large drifts against a strong wind. Murray soon had his wife near the plane and I helped the lady to her seat and fastened her belt. I didn't lose any time because the plane was rocking quite a bit from the wind. The safest place for EVO right then was 'in the air.'

We took off and I asked, "Where to?" She said, "Dodsland Hospital." She seemed very assertive and strong-minded, but we didn't say much to each other along the way. But after we'd gone about two-thirds of the way to Dodsland, this dominant woman asked me how many people EVO would hold. I replied, "Two – you and I."

She then said, "Well, you'd better hurry or there'll be three here." We were a snug fit in the cabin, both bundled up for the weather, but I managed to squirm sideways enough to face her and said, "Is that so? Well, Lady, you've waited nine months by now and if you hang on for another nine minutes – and I don't care how you do it, tie knots in your legs or whatever – you'll make it to the hospital." After that, further conversation was unnecessary.

I approached Dodsland from the west with a tail wind and there was Charlie Dowd with a team of horses and a flat sled with two men and a large stuffed chair on the sled. They were on a side hill. I made a tight '180' to face the wind and slapped EVO down on the slope of the side hill. Charlie's horses nearly bolted, but he held them. I unsnapped the belt, pushed her door open and the men took Mrs. Lowe and suitcase. When I last saw them, the team was plunging through the snow, headed for the hospital.

Wow – another close one, I thought. Soon I was home, just at dark, and I put EVO to bed for the night. Tomorrow she'd be making a dozen flights to and from all directions and for many reasons.

John Vaber

It was a fine, though dull, winter day when I received a call from the doctor telling me that John Vaber should be brought to the hospital. Could I handle it? I said I'd give it a try, right away. John was a very longstanding friend of mine, pretty old by now, a Russian who had moved to the Argentine for 25 years and later had moved to Canada and farmed about six crow-miles northwest of Kerrobert. I'd known him since I was a young fella. We dealt with him and I'd repaired his machinery. He was a very heavy man, not over average height – the solid fat with tight skin – and it would be hard to get hold of him or lift him.

John had suffered a stroke and the only one home with him was his son Joe, with the same physical characteristics as his Dad. I told Bert Fisk about it as I was leaving the shop and Bert remarked that this one might be a 'toughy.' I agreed but decided to go through with it if I could. A skip and a jump later, I landed EVO in an overnight horse run behind the barn – big enough for horses but not for airplanes. However, I wanted to land as near the house as possible. There were fences and gates everywhere and several gates later, I was at the back door. There was Joe, who hadn't even heard me land, and John was in bed, with Joe trying to put covers back on as fast as John, in a kind of coma, threw them off.

Well, Joe and I had a real time getting John dressed, for it was pretty cold outside. When we'd managed to get him all bundled up including overcoat, muffler, fur-helmet hat and mitts, he was so big we couldn't handle him. Getting him out through the door and several gates was a combination of science and brute strength. John stirred and fussed quite a bit, which wasn't much help to us.

EVO was parked at the back corner of the barn and then we began the chore of transferring John to the passenger seat. Boy, what a job! At best, he would not bend enough to sit back in the seat – the safety belt would not reach around him. His feet were much too close to the rudder pedals for my peace of mind. He could tramp one of the pedals and wreck us. EVO must have thought we'd loaded a horse – not a man.

With all the waiting while we got John ready and out, EVO's engine had really cooled off and stiffened up. However, with plenty of luck and teasing of primer and choke, she finally started. After a brief warm-up, I headed for the far fence corner with all the 65 horses out of the barn. We got barely enough speed to lift at stalling speed over the corner post and out-fly the rising ground ahead.

It was only about six miles to the home field, but with my neck out so far with broken rules and John's condition, the short flight seemed to take an hour. John was fairly quiet while we were flying because it was smooth, but the landing was sure to arouse him. In order to minimize upsetting John when the skis began to rattle on the icy landing surface, I made a power-stalled approach and greased 'er on as slowly as possible. Sure enough, John stirred violently, straightened out, and pushed the left rudder to the floor, and EVO did a violent left ground loop. The right wingtip almost touched the icy surface and unbelted heavy John nearly crashed out the right door. I countered with pressure on the right rudder pedal but couldn't make it – John had stretched right out straight. Anyway, the plane lost speed, tipped up on the right ski and I was glad when the plane came to rest right side up with no damage.

At that time, Bert Fisk was driving a two-door Plymouth and there he was, waiting at the hangar. His concern and foresight made me appreciate the wide Plymouth door, and this made the less difficult transfer from the plane to car. When I taxied in and shut 'er off, Bert asked, "What was THAT all about?" meaning the ground loop. When I told him, he just shook his head and said I was going to 'get it' sometime.

We managed to get John to the hospital and helped get him on to a high stretcher. John's case was too serious, and he didn't live very many more days.

Forced Landing – Jack Allen

Every winter, International Harvester Co. held schools for dealership servicemen or mechanics, and this certain winter, Jack Allen and I were going to attend. We were both inclined to fly in to Saskatoon and back – go Monday and return Friday afternoon.

Everything seemed fine when we left Kerrobert, but we encountered fog about 20 miles from Biggar and decided to fly 'under it,' following the highway. However, by the time we got to Biggar, the fog was so thick, EVO was becoming slow and sluggish because of ice forming on all leading edges[27] and the propeller. This meant we'd have to land – pronto! Imperative necessity required that we ditch on a little triangular piece of ground, very uneven and uncertain, at the northeast corner of Biggar alongside the old highway. I managed enough turn to approach this spot and at full throttle, 'landed.' What a landing! I thought we were coming 'down,' but I guess the ground was coming 'up,' too, and we really slammed 'er down hard. I took it more in stride, but it was obvious that Jack was extremely appreciative of the fact that both we and the plane were all intact. Boy, did we have ice!

It was near enough to noon that we walked into town and had something to eat at a café. The meal over, we went to the Cornish garage where I was known, especially by Arnold Cornish. After a short visit, we noticed that the fog seemed to be diminishing from the west. Arnold drove us out to the plane and we took off all the leading-edge ice we could by hand. I 'milked' the ice off the prop with a blowtorch. It was a relatively mild day and on the way over from Kerrobert, we had encountered a layer of warm air above the fog level. The air seemed to be clearing, so we fired up EVO and I took off, alone, to have a look around upstairs, and flew in the warm layer which took off the remaining ice from the plane. It ran off the trailing edges like rain. Then I landed again, downhill on the slanted field, and taxied back to the boys.

---

[27] *Leading edges - The front edges of the wings. A plane's lift is created by the wind blowing over top the wing, so ice on the edges would negatively affect the plane's flight.*

Jack and I decided to take off again and fly over the fog, which levelled off at about 2,000 feet above the ground towards Saskatoon, on compass, for the estimated time it would take to reach Saskatoon and look for a 'hole' where we might get down to ground level. Well, we made some extensive circles at our estimated destination and saw nothing but a solid layer of cloud all the way. So we turned back, on compass, to return to Biggar. We were delighted that when we came to the edge of the fog layer, which was just at the east edge of Biggar, we were only about a mile from the town.

Circling over Biggar at 800 to 1,000 feet, we saw Arnold run out the front door of the garage to meet us in his pickup. I slid back my door window, idled the engine and called down 'Arnold!' He stopped, looked up, and I said, "Bring out five gallons of gas." He waved and went back into the garage, and we proceeded to land in the same small field. Arnold soon came along with the five gallons of car gas.

One interesting thing was that when I landed after my de-icing flip, I had just missed a large rock, sitting there in the snow – only by inches. If I had not been landing downhill, I might have seen it.

We gassed and went back to the garage with Arnold, where I phoned the tower at the Saskatoon airport. A 700-feet ceiling was reported. So Jack and I decided to fly over again, not directly over Saskatoon, but perhaps northwest, and break a rule by descending through the cloud layer, hoping to see the ground before hitting it. I had done this before, but I think it was the first time for Jack. I explained to him that everything would be a dark-wool colour until just a moment before we broke through the bottom of the fog, whether we were at ground level or not. At that moment, everything would turn brown. Well, we waited, getting lower and lower, until everything turned brown, and we broke out about 500 to 600 feet above the ground. We were northwest of Saskatoon alright, in country we didn't know. But we soon found Saskatoon, jumped the airport fence and were ON.

Harold Mitchinson had been out in the Rosetown country the same day. He got to Saskatoon the hard way, too, by flying in the gully of the Eagle Creek, so he had a pretty twisty trip. We both had a laugh about bustin' rules all over the place and making it.

The trip home for Jack and I, after school was over, was monotonously favourable – just sit there and let the time and country pass by...

Dr. Dicola – Veterinarian

A few times I flew Dr. Dicola, a government veterinarian, and would sometimes get him to fly in wintertime when flying was the only way he could get to the point of service. This time, he had a call from someone in the Handel area – a cow in trouble, giving birth to her calf. It was pretty cold weather – say 25 below Fahrenheit (-31C).

We arrived and it was pretty difficult terrain, and the nearest we could get to the farm was the darndest kind of field – rolling ground and fenced in tight. However, we landed, taxied near the farmstead and walked in. I always helped in these cases, but by the time we had pulled the calf out of the cow, a lot of time had passed which under the circumstances passes more quickly than under ordinary times. By the time we went out to EVO to take off for home, the engine was really cold. I had a hard time to coax EVO into life, but barely and finally succeeded. Warming up took quite awhile and I knew I had to have a hot engine to get out of that field – it was a real dandy.

The field had many ups and downs and heading for the far corner of the fence, uphill, we barely made it. I was glad that Dicola took it 'right in stride.'

We got home OK – Lady Luck, again!

Percy Klaen

There was a real ground storm on a winter afternoon, when I got a call from the Byrnes farm, six or eight miles (11 km) out on the south highway. It was Percy Klaen of Saskatoon and his car had gone as far as it could through the drifts. He was, or had been, a military man and was doing D.V.A. (Department of Veterans Affairs) work. He asked if I could fly him to a town with train service (we still had passenger trains those days), and I said sure, I'd pick him up in the field directly across from the Byrnes farm, but he would have to walk a short way out to the plane since the wind was so strong I didn't want to risk turning around for fear of having EVO blow over.

In a short time, I was there and so was Percy and we were in the air, flying sideways because of the strength of the east wind. Percy explained that his next business was at Luseland so I just bypassed Kerrobert and let him out at Luseland, where he would have a relatively short walk downwind to the hotel. That was on a Friday.

Sunday morning, a much better day, Percy phoned to ask if I could fly him home to Saskatoon, so I fired up EVO and flew him home. Years later, we met and had a good laugh about a remark I'd made on the first flight. I had said it amazed me the number of people who, not even having heard of me before, would so willingly jump into the plane, storm or no storm. He asked what was so amazing about THAT? I replied that for all he knew about me, I could be a damn fool!

Some years later, Percy Klaen went on to be one of Saskatoon's mayors. On October 4, 1977, Percy came into L & S Equipment and asked for Walter Williams. I had seen him approach and thought it couldn't be – he's dead. But when one of the other boys pointed to me, I put out my hand and said, "Percy Klaen – how are you?"

We had a long visit, including a session in the upstairs coffee room. I had thought he was dead, but there he was, an old man, retired to an apartment where he didn't have to do gardening, etc. He said he was mayor of Saskatoon about 1964 – the most thankless job in the world. He'd get calls at 2 or 3 in the morning because someone's toilet wouldn't flush due to a broken water main, etc. He is a good friend of Dick Pittaway because his wife and Jean Pittaway ski together, and my name happened to come up and he remembered. I was greatly thrilled.

Cutter Near Tramping Lake

I got a call from a farm northeast of Tramping Lake one morning from a man whose son was quite ill, and would I be able to fly him in. It was early enough for me to remind him that it was train day, if he should choose that alternative. However, I would come if he wanted me to. He said, "Yes, you come." I said OK and left for the hangar.

On my way, I passed Broadacres, then Tramping Lake and began to pick out the farm ahead where I was to call. There it was, the farm, but I was distracted by some movement out of the corner of my left eye. Turning that way, I observed a man standing beside a cutter sleigh and team of horses, waving his overcoat above his head. Banking left, I landed in the field and was soon at his side.

This was the man who had called me, and soon after the phone call, had changed his mind, and elected to take the wife and son to the train after all. But it was too late for the boys to stop me, for I'd already gone. So there he was, with a broken sleigh in the middle of a field and he thought I wasn't coming. He was really desperate.

We put his wife and boy in the plane and they were in hospital before the train left Broadacres. If I ever wonder if I was welcome anywhere or any time, all I have to do is remember that incident. My, he was glad to see me.

Corpse – Consort To Castor

One winter, there had been so many severe storms and so much snow that every means of travel except by air was cancelled right out. Even walking up and down the drifts soon exhausted a person who was trying to make a short trip on foot. Drifts were big and hard and I was forever trying for a short space I could use for landing or taking off, with the least pounding and hammering of the plane any more than was necessary. Mostly, it was a game of touch and go – lots of 'touch,' and wondering how long one could 'go.' Most years, after a hard winter of flying, I'd have to take the plane for serious repair work. Storm after storm would build up a long list of necessary flights and one time it was in the evening when I received a call from an undertaker at Castor, Alberta.

His plight was that a lady died in the hospital at Consort, Alta, and with all means of transport wiped out, he could not reach the corpse, nor could the corpse reach him. Consort and Castor were about 50 miles (80 km) apart. Could I fly the corpse to Castor? I explained that I was a couple of dozen flights behind and asked if he could get a plane nearer his district. He told me they were all too busy and anyway, they didn't want to fly a corpse. I told him I couldn't give him a firm booking, but would list him, in case I had a flight west of Kerrobert that would minimize the time necessary to help him.

Well, it turned out that I had a flight for a man, his five-year-old little girl and a case of beer for 'Dad,' to Bodo, Alberta. This would take me near enough to Consort, so I phoned the undertaker and told him I was able to take on his trip. Boy, was he relieved!

Bodo is in a kind of hollow with hills and fences all over the place, so our so-called 'landing' was more like a smash-on, but we made it. They wanted to return to Kerrobert later in the day, so I told him I'd likely be back to pick him up by four or five in the afternoon, and please be ready. I'd be making a couple more flights in the meantime. Didn't tell him any details. Then I took off, jumped a ridge of hills and landed at Consort in a field at the east side of town, which was the smoothest I could find in that area that day with the wind in the right direction.

A bit after landing, a team and dray[28] came out, saying I should land on the other side of town near the hospital. I told them that I had previously used that field but under the present circumstances it was very unsuitable and unsafe, being too small, fence-bound and with trees around it, and the wind was from the wrong direction. I said, "No, you'll have to bring the body out here."

Well, there was quite a delay and I was beginning to fume and thought of taking off, aborting the mission. However, they finally came along with the corpse, dead two days, wrapped up completely, a flat box containing clothes, and there was a large envelope of papers. This was my first corpse in EVO and I didn't know if it would be five or seven feet tall, and was afraid of rigor mortis, which could have posed a real difficulty. However, this lady's body was of average size and as limp as a rag.

Placing her in the passenger seat was no trouble, but her head kept falling over backwards into the baggage space behind the seat. So, standing the clothing box on end, it just fit the nape of her neck and the corpse sat there, straight as could be. Checking with Doc James later, I learned that rigor mortis relaxes after 12 to 24 hours, which explained the limpness.

Takeoff was no trouble and I headed west for 50 miles to Castor. At that time, there was a relatively open field south of the CPR station and that's where the undertaker was waiting, with a hand toboggan and a young lad to help him. By the time EVO had slowed down, I was into a place where there had been tall weeds. The plane broke through the crust and there I was, stuck, and my passenger was no help. Managed to wriggle out of there, and the undertaker handed me a blank cheque to fill in the amount.

It's odd how many corners can be cut and red tape forgotten in desperate times. Here was a situation where a plane dropped out of the sky anonymous. No questions asked. A corpse, clothing and documents were taken aboard, and the plane took off and disappeared. A short time later, the plane landed to meet two more

---

[28] *Dray – A cart without sides used for hauling items.*

people, still anonymous, passed over the corpse, clothing and documents, received a blank cheque made out to 'cash,' and disappeared. Boy, talk about shortcuts!!

When I received the body at Consort, I was told that their Dr. Day would appreciate being flown to Coronation, Alta., on my way back. I said I'd be glad to comply but time would not permit delay, so please could the doctor be ready when I called back? Sure enough, as I was gliding low over Consort to land in the same field, here came the doctor, walking down the street with his little bag. By the time I taxied back to takeoff point, he was there and got in. Chit-chat during the short flight revealed that we were distantly related. At Coronation, there were not very many nice places to land, so I let him out in a field across the tracks, where he would have the least walking to do. We parted and I wondered who would be pleased that he arrived!

From Coronation, I took off and headed for Bodo to pick up the people there. Being a difficult place for an airplane, I decided to use a sleigh trail up over a hill so I could keep one ski or the other on something solid, praying that a team and sleigh was not coming to meet me in the other direction. The load consisted of the man, his little daughter, and he'd picked up a suitcase and a dog, too. Put the suitcase in the back and made the dog lie down on that, and he panted like mad all the way to Kerrobert. This added moisture soon fogged up all the windows, so the only place I could see out was to slide back the little slide in the side window. That wasn't much help, but we met no team and got into the air anyway.

This man was very happy by this time and after my tough day, I thought I'd like to diminish his exuberance. With all the extra flying and getting stuck, my gas supply was getting short. I let my over-happy passenger know this, which gave him something to think about. I asked him to check the gauge on the rear reserve tank and he reported that it was empty. I said, well, the front one's nearly empty, too. His happiness fell off to some extent.

We made Kerrobert OK and put the plane away, loaded everybody and everything into the truck and then the man became over-happy again. So, I told him about flying the corpse, which caused him some alarm. He said that if he'd known I was going to fly a dead woman, he would never have gone near the plane. "Flying a dead lady, weren't you scared?"

I replied, "The dead ones don't bother me – it's the live ones I'm afraid of."

So, that was most of another day in the life of EVO and I.

P.S. Later, I heard that this undertaker did other things, too, like buying horsehair – you name it and he was doin' it. Also, it was said that he had a couple of gunny sacks full of false teeth and he'd give you a pretty good deal if you took a pail of water for rinsing and found a good enough fit!

Prince Albert – Radio

EVO was not blessed with any extras when I got 'er, just the basic instruments. After the Second World War, many farmers bought war planes for a song – to make winter cutters[29] out of – and mostly because it became the 'in' thing for farmers at that time. Adolph Henning had one with all the instruments in it, let me remove one or another item from the one he bought. First was a Venturi,[30] along with a sensitive altimeter. Later, I went back and got the turn-and-bank[31] and a directional indicator. These changes all added weight to EVO, further taxing the little 65-HP engine. Finally, it was like adding half a tank of gas. Oh yes, I also mounted a clock which Bud Henson had removed from a shot-down Hawker Hurricane overseas (Bud had spent a '48' with the pilot[32] who was lost with the plane). I took out the clock when I sold EVO and gave it to Alan Cameron for his first plane – a Champion.

But I had no radio, so bought what they called an Airboy Jr. – battery operated – about the absolute minimum in aircraft radio. Removed the glove box door, made a mounting, then phoned Prince Albert, where the Kerrobert boy, Floyd Glass, was manager. He now operates Athabasca Airways out of Prince Albert and Lac La Ronge. He said they would install the radio for me, etc. Also, I had to get a radio rating on my licence.

This was in winter and cold enough to freeze the hardware off a monkey – something like 42 below F. I got there, they did the work the next morning, I paid something like $60 and lifted off for home. I had enough daylight to make it but Nature makes one seem to have three or four kidneys under such conditions of cold. Around Cando, I knew I wasn't going to make it, so landed in a large field. As I landed, I noticed a team of horses was hitched to a sleigh-box at a nearby farm. I was in a hurry and side-slipped in and slapped EVO

---

[29] *Cutter – A horse-drawn sleigh.*
[30] *Venturi – An instrument mounted on the front side of the airplane which assists to indicate altitude.*
[31] *Turn-and-bank - An instrument which assists a pilot in making proper turns.*
[32] *A '48' – A 48-hour leave.*

down real quick and left the engine idling. Guess the guys thought I'd crashed.

I was so cold and wearing so many clothes, it took me a bit longer to accomplish the necessary. Before I was ready for company, here came the team and a couple of fellows – horses plunging through the snow. I wasn't in a visiting mood, so jumped into the plane, gunned 'er off just as the horses arrived and tried to fasten my clothes up the rest of the way to Kerrobert. I sure got cold that day!

But, I finally had a radio. This was one I could take out of the dash, take in to the house or to a hotel room, clip it to a bedspring and I was in business. That way, I could tune in on the airport weather reports 24 times a day. It wasn't much, but a lot more than I'd had before. This meant I could follow radio beams, etc. Those days, practically nobody in my class needed a radio. Now, things have changed so that it really isn't a plane if it hasn't got a radio, and most airports make the use of one mandatory. Guess I lived in the lucky days.

Meadow Lake – Lake Landing

It was a Friday, near Easter, I think. I made a trip to Meadow Lake to pick up Dave so we could have a little holiday visit at Kerrobert. When I arrived at Meadow Lake, there was a strong wind from the north and I decided to land on the lake and taxi into the creek or river which ran close to the town. Drifts on the lake were hard and the landing a bit rough, but everything went OK.

When I arrived at the school, I was asked if Clayton Mills, Dave's teacher, could squeeze in as Kerrobert would be near his home on a farm north of Kindersley. Otherwise, he would not be able to make suitable arrangements to get home and back in time for school. He said he could make other arrangements to get back if he could get home that day. Well, I thought that with the stiff wind, EVO could get into the air more quickly despite the overload, so said OK. We had to go out to Little Chicago[33] to his shack for his bag. Dave's bag was ready.

Back at the lake, we loaded up using every inch of space, packed almost to the bulging point. Taxiing out on to the lake clear area, past a peninsula, we met a Stinson piloted by Vic Pearsol of Cochin trying to taxi crosswind into the bay we had just left. The oversize dorsal fin and udder section of the Stinson made the thing keep weather-cocking, or facing into the wind and towards the trees along the shore.

We recognized each other, waved, and then he opened his door and beckoned to me to come over to him. I left you boys and ran over to Vic's plane. He wanted me to hold back on his left, or downwind, strut long enough for him to get into the lee of the trees where he could have much better control of the Stinson. This I did, and he was soon able to continue on his own.

About Vic: Vic Pearsol was a noted overloader of aircraft. When he should trim out or level flight, his plane was always high-nose, low-tail, flying uphill all the way. On this trip, he had 600 to 700

---

[33] *Little Chicago – A tougher section of Meadow Lake in those days.*

pounds of fish, heaven knows what else, and an Indian woman and child aboard. Of course, this was years after he'd started flying but when his family lived at Luseland, Vic became the youngest boy to get his flying licence at that time in Canada. He took the darndest chances and always seemed to come through. Finally, though, he did manage to wreck a plane on a far northern lake. He lived through it, but got it right in the face – like I did in my worst wreck.

After helping Vic, I ran way back to EVO, still idling, shoehorned myself back into the seat and gunned 'er for takeoff. The brisk wind made our ground takeoff speed slower, but even so, we finally hit a hard drift which bounced us into the air. We didn't touch again, gained speed and altitude and headed south with a good tail wind. EVO was overloaded that day, with two grown men, a husky Dave, and double luggage. I smiled when I reflected that this was the way Vic Pearsol flew all the time – nose up and tail down!

We had a normal flight to Kerrobert, making good time, where I let Dave and his bag off. I think we started the truck and turned on the heater, so he could wait until I had delivered Mills to his home near Kindersley. Later, Mills told us that he walked in on his folks just as they were cleaning away the supper dishes. The flip back to Kerrobert was no sweat. We put the plane up for the night and drove up to the house where Mother had a really good meal ready for us.

Thus, another of the Kerrobert-Meadow Lake trips has been accomplished, though this one was just a little bit different.

Doc Jones – Upset CPR Snowplow

One winter day, afternoon, Doc Jones phoned to say that there was an upset snowplow in a big cut[34] on CPR track between Kerrobert and Broadacres. In other flights, I'd seen this plow slamming away at this cut through a large hill for days. It was a winter of much snow and many storms, and nobody could get anywhere until a road had been plowed. Perhaps that night or the next day, another storm would close up the road that had been cleared.

The day Cliff phoned, I'd noticed from previous flights that the Froelich brothers from Tramping Lake were opening a road from Tramping Lake through Broadacres, southwards to Highway #51, which was 'open' in a questionable sort of way. The road the boys were clearing crossed the Black Slough,[35] north side, and the upset snowplow was only several miles from this crossing.

Doc said that one of the crew had sustained a broken leg and the rest of the crew had moved him to the caboose. Could Doc come out? Doc said yes, if he could get Walter to fly him out there, and he would call back. It was quite awhile before he could pass back the news because news-hungry farmers all over the country had every telephone party line busy continually. Finally, though, we took off, hopped a dozen fence lines and were at the scene, where we landed in a little triangular patch, all fenced in, beside the wreck. (Soon after starting off, Doc had turned to me and said how different and how much 'fun' this call would be for him. To me, it was just another 'trick in the bag.')

We climbed a fence and a mountain of snow and slid down beside the caboose. Inside were the crew with the broken-legger (from Wilkie) down on a bunk. This guy seemed kinda crabby, and I discovered on later occasions that this was his true nature anyway. We found a crude piece of wood and Doc splinted him from foot to

---

[34] *Cut – A valley that railroad companies cut through for their track rather than going up over the hills.*
[35] *Black Slough – A slough near Broadacres, Sask.*

armpit and told the crew that if they backed up to that Black Slough crossing, Walter would drive out with his Travelall[36] and stretcher and convey the patient to Kerrobert Hospital. Doc gave him a pretty stiff shot of morphine and then he and I got in EVO and got out of that small patch – ticking the top fence wire with our skis. Doc was really havin' fun!

Back at the hangar, we hurried uptown in the Travelall. I dropped Doc off at his office and went to the shop to get the stretcher. You were there, Dave, and you and another man whose name escapes me, went along. It was a pretty rough trip, what with meeting the farm-tractor blower outfit and fellows digging out stuck cars and trucks, but we made it out to the backed-up engine and caboose. Now we had a fellow with a busted leg aboard and couldn't go smashing along like we did on the trip out. Sometime before our slower return to Kerrobert, the morphine wore off and our passenger was becoming a noisy individual. Several days later, he snarled his way out of Kerrobert Hospital and it was my doubtful pleasure to ambulance him to the Government Ambulance Plane for transfer to Wilkie or Saskatoon – anywhere but Kerrobert suited me just fine.

Y' know Dave, when the skis touch the fence wire, one has to kick the tail up to keep the tail wheel or ski from hooking the wire, and I think Doc and I finished our takeoff in the next field. It was failure to do this that pulled me down on my second wreck at Altario, when one ski came right up through the belly of the plane when we thumped down. (That time, Joe Kreiser's brother was with me.) We welded it all up again and I flew the rest of the winter with that big hole in the belly fabric. This makes for a draughty plane. Got 'er fixed in the spring.

---

[36] *Travelall – A pickup truck-sized station wagon built by International Harvester, similar to today's Chevy Suburban.(www.wikipedia.org)*

Jim Charteris – Damage – Repair

One winter morning I flew out to the farm of Jim Charteris to bring him in for a school board meeting in town that day. It was early, a perfect day. Jim had never flown before but I had previously flown in other members of the board from Denzil, Luseland, etc. and Jim said, "Now they'll have nothing on ME!"

That morning I didn't land on the runway but just barged in over the neighbouring prairie area. Hit a big rock that was just barely covered with snow with the right ski, heard a big 'crack' and knew I had broken the fuselage frame in the general area that had been repaired when John Herron backed the truck into the plane.

Let Jim out, drove him uptown and later discovered that my guess was right – she was busted alright. I made a makeshift repair several times during the rest of that winter, not wishing to be away from home long enough for repair. (For the job they have to strip the fabric off the whole area, make the repair, then put on new fabric over the stripped area.)

There was a long ski period that year and I made many, many flights up to springtime. I learned to favour the right side of the plane, putting the initial stress on the left ski as much as possible. I'd hear it creaking away while taxiing over some rough drifts or areas, and many were the landings made with fingers crossed.

The final flight in early spring was a scary deal. I had flown to Biggar, to pick up a man and fly him back to his home in the Kelfield Coulee. I had flown him to Biggar the week before. It was late enough in the winter, or early enough in the spring, that snow conditions were capricious – from dirt-mix to high drifts, and we can't always control what is our lot in so many different situations. This time, on a calm day which required longer takeoff distance, I tried a couple of times to get this man off the ground. There was dirt in the snow. The last attempt ended in a stall on or beside a farm machine, and the frame of the plane was really creaking by this time. I taxied back to the Biggar corner of the field, looked over the frame condition and asked my passenger to find another way home or risk crash of some kind. I knew then that I would be lucky to even get the plane back home.

A mechanic friend of mine in Biggar at Cornish's garage came out and we wired up the busted frame, but all we had was soft wire. This, at best, was only temporary and inadequate, but I took the chance to try to get the plane back on the home field. When we were finished wiring it up, I went into Biggar, phoned George Cunnings, and told him he was the only contact I'd make but I wanted him to be on hand at the field, win or lose. I told him I'd be leaving in so-many minutes, and should arrive at such-and-such time, which was in the noon hour, and I didn't want any more witnesses to whatever was going to happen.

Taking off from a different field at Biggar after the makeshift repair (it was a perfect sunny day). Leaving Biggar, I made a circle or two to see by shadow on the snow the angle of that right ski. It was hanging down at an alarming angle and I was in the air! I thought I'd rather crash at Kerrobert than at Biggar, so proceeded to meet George as scheduled. Being a calm day didn't help very much because it meant a higher landing speed, and knowing I had a ski hanging down, I came in real slow and dropped that ski on the down-slope of a big drift, lost speed, and slowly and thankfully taxied to the hangar – the last trip of the season. My flying was over for that winter!

Subsequently, when the grass was green and I had changed over to wheels, one Sunday morning I planned to fly to Swift Current where I had arranged with Al Smith to repair my plane. Had quite a time to un-stick a stuck valve, and finally got 'er to run on four cylinders. Had to taxi to the far end of the field – then the tail wheel fell off! I had to walk half a mile to the hangar, leaving the engine idling, to get two bolts for attaching the tail wheel. This chore being accomplished, I climbed in and took off.

Halfway to Swift Current, one cylinder cut out (and I knew which one it was), so I finished the trip on three cylinders. Arriving, I knew my right landing gear was a real hazard, but I crunched onto the field and very slowly taxied to Smith's hangar. Nobody was there – but I was in one piece – which was important to me.

Later, Smith came on the scene and we put the plane into his repair shop so he could see what repair was needed. He had a hoist for lifting the whole plane, and when he did, the right wheel and axle fell off. That, and the fact that the engine was running on three cylinders, really upset Al. Some of his other boys were there, so he took me over to a corner of the shop to tell me off. Before he was finished, he was yelling at me, pounding the bench, and you could have heard him in Swift Current, 3½ miles away. He yelled, "The Lord doesn't owe you NOTHIN' – He doesn't owe you a thing!"

Al did all the regular work and finally informed me that my plane was airworthy again. I liked him (and in spite of the fact that he knew I was crazy – he liked me, too). Anyway, I got somebody to drive me down to Swift Current. Paid my bill and flew home with a good plane again. The bill was several hundred dollars but look at all the fun I had flyin' a busted plane most of the winter! And, I didn't hurt any person, or myself.

Wilkie – Flying Santa Claus

One winter, the town of Wilkie asked me to fly Santa Claus up and down the main street of Wilkie, so he could wave at the populous at an advertised time. We agreed to pick up Santa at the Scott Corner, about six miles west of Wilkie, along the highway. You went along, Dave, and rode to the Wilkie airstrip in the car that brought Santa out. After the main street caper, we were to land old whiskers at the airstrip, where some sort of conveyance would whisk him into town, in full view of the kids.

So, we were pinned down to a certain minute, or a few – we had a schedule to keep. However, it was a real muggy day, with visibility quite limited. There was even a bit of snow in the air. This was nothing new for a couple of experience-hardened characters like you and I, but it must have detracted from the main object in mind. For instance, when I buzzed low up and down Main Street with Santa wavin' away, I'll bet a lot of the people couldn't tell whether it was Santa or a girl with a red hat.

Anyway, we did our part, the Wilkie Board of Trade paid their part (fifteen dollars, if I remember correctly) and, to keep the records straight – mission accomplished.

'Lady' To North Battleford

One winter morning during a thick snowstorm, I received a phone call from a friend in Ruthilda asking if I could fly a lady to North Battleford, now-like. I told him about the storm at Kerrobert and he said it was the same at Ruthilda, but the lady seemed to be in urgent need of getting to North Battleford. I said OK, I'd try, but when I landed on the high ground west of Ruthilda, she'd better be ready and there. I didn't like fooling around in storms.

I flew low and close to the highways all the way and landed where I had designated. She was there and ready and got into the plane. She was big and strong and healthy-looking, so I thought it must be family trouble of some kind. I didn't ask, nor did she say. The man who called me was a good friend of mine and I was there because it was he who called rather than a desire to fly under those conditions. I was to fly this woman to North Battleford, stay overnight, and fly her home the next morning, which would be Sunday.

I had to keep running my hand along the highways to keep from getting lost, and she took the sudden turns of the road between Biggar and North Battleford right in stride, and nothing registered on her handsome sphinx-like mien – she was a real deadpan.

Landed at North Battleford Airport, we called a taxi and she wanted to be taken to a farm a few miles north of the city on the west side of the highway, and I then recognized the farm of a bachelor. She was a married lady, or woman. Well, I politely agreed to pick her up by taxi the next morning, and I spent the night in a hotel downtown.

Sunday morning, the storm was over and I secured a taxi and we picked her up at the bachelor's farm. The trip back to Ruthilda was made cross-country without the perils of storm and the necessity of following roads to keep from getting lost. Landed at Ruthilda, I was paid for the trip plus expenses and I was willing to, up to that point, believe that the bachelor could have been a brother, father, or some other relative, but my naiveté was upset later by snide remarks and raised eyebrows about this particular trip. Only once before had I been accessory to such a purpose but it was by truck, not by air – innocently, both times. However, my conscience was clear since I simply did not know…

The thing I privately resented was the risky trip in the snowstorm to facilitate an unworthy purpose.

Lady From Chicago – Father Dying

One winter Sunday morning, Len Ashdown phoned me from the Windsor Hotel in Saskatoon (where he clerked) to say that a lady and her son had come in on the Saturday night train from Moose Jaw and wanted desperately to get to the hospital at Consort, Alberta, where the lady's father was dying. The next train out that way would be the Coronation – Tuesday. Could I fly them out – now-like? It was a nice enough day and I said, "Sure, I'll pick them up right away."

Called at the Windsor, picked up mother and son, cranked up EVO, and we were on our way. She told me something of her life, holding her son between her knees, and she had been born and raised on 'that farm,' just before we got to Consort. Well, the wind that day was such that I could land in a very small fence-and-tree-bound field just across the fence from the hospital. I took off again, just missing the fence, since I was alone for the takeoff.

Two large men greeted their sister from Chicago. One paid me as the other helped sister and the boy through the fence, and away I went for home. They were all very thankful that I had made the trip.

Later, I learned that she saw her father for one hour before he expired. He recognized her, and that was a lot better than waiting until the following Tuesday.

One thing – the setting of the town of Consort is unique, in that you approach that certain little field next to the hospital by passing just over the grain elevators in the valley, count the shingles if you like, and you're right on approach to land beside the hospital.

I felt good about that little trip, since that nice little lady did get to see her dad.

Taxi Services

Some winters, the stormy deep-snowed ones, required so many flights that many were the days when EVO was in the air all day from before daylight until after dark. On a lot of flights, I would bring someone in, make a quick change of passengers, and fly one out of town. This required a great deal of taxi work (and saved an awful lot of my time) – advice as to what to wear, timing for my next arrival or departure, waiting at the airport until that little pair of wings showed up, etc.

Passengers came from hotels, homes, the hospital, or just off the street, so the 'taxi driver' advised, and was always waiting to receive or deliver one, perhaps both.

There had to be close liaison between myself and the man who made it unnecessary to wait at the field for the next passenger. It had to be 'Drop one – take one – and get goin'.' This vastly increased the use of the short winter days. Some flyers would have thought themselves to be a hero with one flight while, with the help I had, I made dozens – no heroics about it – we were just 'helping someone.'

The odd time it would have been one of the men from our shop, but I remember two winters when two really good friends, unselfish almost to a fault, furnished taxi work, just for the fun of helping someone in need and filling in their time.

I pay tribute to two men who could have stayed in bed all day through the winter or just listened to the radio or whatever. They were both farmers, of the older school of ethics, and again I use the word 'unselfish.' They were Emery Rolston, one winter, and George Cunnings, another winter. These men, both in their turn, were of inestimable assistance in the non-stop service we were giving, whether it was a guy I had to bring back to town to go to jail or somebody who had to reach or leave a hospital as quickly as possible, they were on deck and very efficient.

When I came in with a patient for the hospital, lots of times they were there, waiting with someone who was returning home from the hospital. My everlasting thanks and admiration go out to these men, who wouldn't take a thing for their efforts. They were both farmers with ethics which included 'Help your neighbour,' even if you never heard of him (or her) before.

Emery would joke about all the nice ladies he met and George just loved to help someone. For both of them, it helped to pass the winter in town and again, I praise their efforts and unselfishness.

I kept the road to the airport open for wheel traffic with our shop 'Chore Boy' Farmall "H" tractor, sometimes having to work nearly all night to keep the road open. I didn't get paid for my extra efforts in this regard and Em and George wouldn't take anything for their efforts. We all just liked to 'help someone – anyone.'

Kelfield Agent's Wife

One winter day, I got a call from the station agent at Kelfield, whose wife had been visiting her folks at Traynor, Sask. I didn't know where Traynor was but found it on the map, northeast of Landis. The weather was fine and I told the man I'd be glad to fly his wife home to Kelfield. I'd land nearby, to eliminate his waiting and get his wife back to the station where they lived.

Traynor was just a name on a railway map. I flew there and found the place. On skis, I was worried about the number of stones that showed through the snow, but managed to land without damage.

The lady was brought out to the plane and I strapped her into the passenger seat. It was apparent immediately that she was an unusually nice person – a thing which is often revealed in the afflicted. She was a paraplegic.

Ready to take off, we gunned EVO, missing as many rocks as we could, and we were soon in the air. This was a comparatively short flight but I was very much impressed by the worthiness of this lady. I'm a sucker for the afflicted anyway, but this was a distinct pleasure to fly this fine lady back to her husband.

At Kelfield, I landed in a difficult little field next to the station. It was a tall-grass and weedy field but I landed there (never again) in the deeper snow that I usually used. Her husband was soon out to the plane and carried his wife, piggyback style, to the CPR station – home.

I was happy to think that I had helped in an unusual case. The lady said she enjoyed the flight and it would stand out in her life as a special experience. I was glad to have had a part in it.

Lady To Wilkie Hospital

One winter, all roads closed, about suppertime – dark, anyway – I received a call from a grain elevator operator at Handel, Sask. His wife was having her 'time,' and this would occasionally be a very bad time for her, and he was afraid for her this time because she was so very ill. Could I fly her to Wilkie Hospital – now? We were in the middle of a very cold spell, it was dark, no lights at any field, and I also reminded him that their weekly train from Wilkie and back had made its trip that day – I'd seen it from the air.

His story was that she hadn't been sick enough when the train came through, but she was much worse now. I would land in 'that field just east of the hotel,' and he would have her brought out to the plane. I said no chance, there isn't even a moon, I was not acquainted with that field, Handel is in very stony country anyway with the odd bluff of trees here and there and it's not very level terrain. No, I didn't want to kill his wife or myself either for that matter. I would come in the morning and be there at first light but not tonight – it was the best I could do.

He pleaded, said the field was clear and level, he'd light gasoline on the snow, went through a lot of crazy promises, but I knew the facts, and he was desperate. He finally agreed that if she made it until morning, I should come then.

Next morning, at 43 below F, I waded down to the hangar in the dark – took awhile to wake EVO up that morning, and finally made it into the air when it was still dark enough one could hardly see anything. Headed for Handel, light gradually improved until by the time I reached Handel, I could see well enough to look things over. For one thing, this 'clear and level' field was rolling land, had several tree bluffs in it, and the odd stone pile stuck up into view through the deep snow. The land had not been cropped, perhaps ever, so the tall weed and grass growth would make the snow deep with hard layers of winter storms in it. What a gyp that guy tried to talk me into the night before!

There was a sleigh trail across it, where farmers came to town, so

I lined up a little space where I could squash EVO down and stopped the plane across the trail. So there I was, stopped across the trail and there was no evidence of a team and sleigh anywhere in the hamlet, but I saw a few dogs running around barking. Waiting a few minutes, I finally saw a man starting to walk towards the plane. He explained that he could not arrange to bring his wife out to the plane but could I bring the plane into 'town' and pick her up at the house. I was dumbfounded!

I told him this was against all the laws of aviation, but told him that if he went ahead and told everybody to keep their dogs away from the plane, I'd try it. By now, other people were out. Following the trail, I passed the hotel and went up the street a couple of blocks, turned right on to the highway street, went another block and was finally in front of his house. By now, the street was half full of people.

Stopping the engine, I turned the plane around by the tail and asked, "Well, where is she?" He said she's still in bed, but they'd get her ready. Boy, I was getting cheesed off! Ladies helped, and I advised how they should bundle her up. I had told the husband to inform the ambulance at Wilkie. He wanted to have some kid make the call but I wouldn't go for that. Finally, I made the call myself and the Wilkie people were to call back when there was a car at their airport, waiting for our arrival. I said it was a lot better for 'them' to wait a few minutes than for me to sit out there in such severe weather with a deathly ill lady aboard – hoping someone might come along.

I got the call back – they were ready at Wilkie. We carried the lady, completely helpless, out and placed her in the plane. Then, it was 'get out of town and away from all the people and dogs.' I made it to the field and after a difficult takeoff, we were in the air, headed for Wilkie, and it was really COLD!

Arriving at Wilkie, I was stuck briefly and taxied back to a waiting car with two mad-lookin' guys in it. They started to beef but I soon shut them up and told them to 'get busy.' She was transferred to the car, and I lost no time heading for home.

Corp. Bert Fisk knew of the trip and as soon as I saw him, told him everything. He just shook his head and told me I didn't know how far out I was getting my neck, or how much red tape could result in case of failure.

Well, the lady lived…

Merle Kirk – Swan River

Merle Kirk – son of Mr. and Mrs. Albert Kirk of Kerrobert – had a position as teacher at a country school near Swan River, Manitoba. He spent the Christmas–New Year's holiday with his folks. Apparently he would have a hard time to get back to his school due to blocked roads and inadequate travel schedules, so I got a call.

It was 40-below F weather and the time of year for shortest days, and I knew I couldn't make the return trip in one day. I think I quoted $80 and had to make the flight. We set it up for pre-dawn the next morning and I told Merle he should wear all the clothes he owned or could borrow. I may stop in Saskatoon for gas, maybe not, depending on our luck.

It must have been a different experience for Merle next morning when we carried his things a mile over railway tracks, fences, deep snow in the open, to the hangar, then warmed up the engine, pushed out the plane, and hustled off in the dark. Visibility was pretty reasonable that day, and we finally arrived at the farm where he lived in the fairly early afternoon. As we circled the bush country to decide which field to flop into, we saw two nice deer, not very far into the trees behind the barn.

Landing in a field nearest the farm, I helped Merle in with his things (more to get out and warm up with a little exercise than anything. After all, we'd been sitting in that thing, cramped up with all the clothes we had to wear, with no heater.) Then it was back into EVO and head for home, only this time it would take longer, since the light wind of the day had helped us make better time heading east. It must have been the winter of 1951-52, because I recall following fence lines, etc. while I, at the top of my voice, practised my memory work for going through the degrees of joining the Masonic Lodge.

By the time I had reached Humboldt, 70 miles east of Saskatoon, it was getting towards dusk, and I knew I couldn't make Saskatoon in legal daylight. I didn't have night endorsement on my licence, and no lights on the plane. I found their so-called airport, something like Kerrobert's, taxied over near a clump of trees and let EVO freeze down for the night. Put the prop crosswise, and walked into town, about two miles.

I asked for the hotel's warmest room, undressed to normal clothing (but still feeling the chill of a whole day of flying in such cold weather), went to a restaurant for a warming meal, back to the hotel, and sleep which was just warm death. I'd asked for a wake-up call and in the morning, early, it was up and at it again.

Walked the two miles out to the plane in the dusk, realizing that I was one of the 'strange ones.' Got out the blowtorch and rain pipe, and stooged around for 40 minutes making sure there was no frost on the wings, etc. When the 40 minutes was up, I took away the canvas cover, rainpipe and blowtorch, and fired 'er up. Funny, in 40-plus weather one can chin himself on the prop and it won't move until the engine's warmed up. That morning it was 42-below but it turned out to be a nice day otherwise.

The engine started up easily enough, but I had no oil pressure at the gauge (1/16-inch copper line frozen up – finally got oil pressure reading after about 50 miles), the Pitot tube was frozen[37] so there was no air-speed indication, and there was frost on windshield and windows, so no see. However, I had a pretty good pair of pants (fly by the seat of your pants), EVO got into the air, and I headed west for Saskatoon.

The air was reasonably clear, but when I neared Saskatoon (only 2/3 the size it is now) the fog and smog from the city stretched halfway across the airport. So, I felt my way onto the field inside the north fence with no forward visibility and taxied a mile or so to Mitch's place, and the gas pumps. Gassed 'er up, borrowed a bunch of coats and blankets, covered the cabin part of EVO, lit the blowtorch and sat inside while the cabin got pretty warm (couldn't leave the blowtorch unattended). Then I shut off the torch, left the door open a bit, and waited for awhile inside the building. After awhile, I went outside, took off all the coverings and all windows were clear of frost.

Took off for Kerrobert, 110 miles (177 km), arrived safely, put EVO away in her berth, phoned the Kirks to report all was OK, and got back to work in the shop.

---

[37] *Pitot tube – A tube that comes out under the wing to sense the air speed. Air passes through the tube to the air speed indicator which is on the instrument panel.*

Trip Home From Swift Current

It was late in the fall and I still had wheels on EVO. I had to take her to Swift Current for some work to be done at Al Smith's – Smith Airways. I forget the nature of the repair or maintenance work now, but Al had given me a rough estimate as to how long the work would take, so I told him I could arrange to be there. I was there when I said I would be but Al, as usual, did not even come near his estimation of completion, and didn't have the work done until a couple of days after his guestimation. This surely played heck with my plans at home, and I became very annoyed. I think I tied my skis onto the outside struts on that trip and Al was to install those, too.

I kept listening to weather reports, which were worsening as time went on. I kept in touch with my mother each day (Dad had passed away before then), so that she would know that I was not in trouble somewhere.

Came the day (late), finally, when the work was finished, and by then I was so angry with the delay I felt desperate. I asked them to take EVO outside and fill both tanks. A real blizzard was in force there at that time, and I didn't want to hang around there any longer. They thought, "Well, what the heck, it's storming too badly and he can't go anywhere anyway," so they humoured me and gassed 'er up. Reports from further north, closer to home, were not very severe. I hurried inside while EVO was still outside and paid my bill.

Then I went out, bundled up, gave the prop a flip, and took off. It was quite a storm and the fellows all tried to keep me from leaving. It would soon be dark and they were really worried – (so was I). Nobody laid a hand on me for fear of getting hurt – they knew I was thoroughly disgusted.

It was a dim takeoff and I established a general compass heading as I crossed #1 Highway right alongside and fluttered off into the storm. I was soon alarmed at the seriousness of what I had done, but was still too mad and stubborn to turn back. One thing – I was alone and mine was the only neck there. The worst place was when I had to cross the South Saskatchewan River and not crash on the north

Above: Marion Lockerbie and Blake Williams on their wedding day, November 17, 1910.

Above and below: The farm home built by Blake Williams near Revenue, Sask., where the family lived until Walter was eight years old.

Above left: Walter Williams as a Boy Scout, with his sister Grace, June 1923.

Below: On the steps of the Williams home in Kerrobert, about 1933 (left to right): Unidentified, Marion Williams Jr., Unidentified, Jane and David Lockerbie (Marion Williams Sr.'s mother and father), Unidentified, Marion Williams Sr., Walter Williams, Katherine Williams, Unidentified, Unidentified, Grace Williams, Blake Williams.

Below right: Walter Williams, about 1938.

Above left: (left to right) Walter Williams, Oscar Neubaeur and Blake Williams at the first IHC shop.
Above centre: Front row (left to right): Katherine's children Janet and Alan Cameron.
                    Second row: Katherine (Williams) Cameron, Grace Williams, Marion Williams Sr.
                    Back row: Walter Williams, Blake Williams, Marion Williams Jr.
Above right: Walter Williams (centre front), playing cornet in the Turtleford band, 1936-1938.

Above left and centre: Walter Williams and Frances Jean Allcock on their wedding day, February 15, 1939.
Above right: Walter Williams with infant son David (Dave), 1940.

Below left: Blake Williams (far left) and Walter Williams (far right) with friends.
Below right: The company truck surrounded by snow, Winter 1942-1943.

Left: Blake and Marion Williams, Easter 1943.

Right: Walter Williams on Old Smokey, his Harley, 1945-1947.

Below: Construction of the B. Williams & Son IHC shop, October 22, 1945.

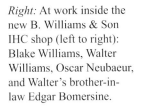

Above: Walter Williams on Old Smokey, with his sister Katherine (Katie/Kay).

Right: At work inside the new B. Williams & Son IHC shop (left to right): Blake Williams, Walter Williams, Oscar Neubaeur, and Walter's brother-in-law Edgar Bomersine.

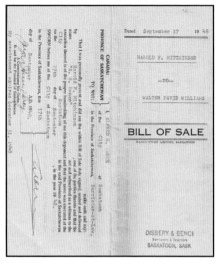

Above: Oscar Neubaeur and Edgar Bomersine at work in the new IHC shop.
Right: The bill of sale for CF-EVO to Walter Williams.

Four photos: CF-EVO struck a fence near Altario, Sask., on a failed takeoff with Joe Kreiser as Walter's passenger, Fall 1948.

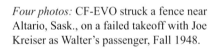

Right: A view of CF-EVO and the Saskatchewan prairie from the cockpit of CF-DRY, a Piper Cub owned by Norm Easton of Eston, Sask.

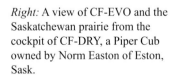

Above: Marion and Blake Williams.

Above: A highway snowplow in for repair at B. Williams & Son. Walter Williams is standing on the far left.

Above: Marion Williams Sr. (left) on the front step of the Williams home in Kerrobert.

Right: A snowplow travels over a cleared road near Kerrobert.

Below left and right: Walter and Dave Williams outside and in the cockpit of CF-EVO, about 1950.

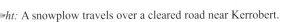
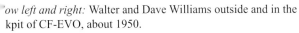

Left: The view from 10,000 feet above Kerrobert in the summer of 1957. "The little squiggle in the highway is six miles away," noted Walter about this photo he took from EVO.

Left: Kerrobert airport and town, facing south, 1957.

Right: Dave Williams (left) and his cousin Donald Cameron with CF-EVO, about 1957.

Left: Walter Williams took this photo of the No. 4 highway on his way north to Meadow Lake, Sask., March 1957.

Left: International Harvester crests were purchased by Walter Williams as promotional items for his business.

Right: Walter Williams, October 1969.

Above: Walter Williams and Rev. Romona Underwood Williams on their wedding day, March 3, 1973.

Above: Miriam and Dave Williams, December 1975.

Above: Gathering in Walter and Romona's Saskatoon apartment on their wedding day. Back (left to right): Merle Cameron, Gerald Bomersine, Faye Bomersine. Front: Walter Williams, Dave Williams, David Lockerbie.

Above: Walter and Romona, about 1975.

Left: A hillside sign welcomes visitors to Kerrobert, Sask., 2008.

Right: A view of the town of Kerrobert, beyond today's airstrip, May 2008.

Above: View of Kerrobert from the airstrip, 2008.
Below: A wind sock helps today's pilots land at the Kerrobert airstrip.

Above: Kerrobert airstrip and hangar, 2008.
Below: Today's landing strip is across the tracks east of Kerrobert and north of Highway 51.

Left: The 'immigration hall' that became home to the Williams family in Kerrobert in 1920 is home to the Hansen family in 2008. The original fieldstone front entry and steps are intact as well as the second floor built by Blake Williams.

Right: The large shop built on Railway Avenue by Blake and Walter Williams in Kerrobert is still serving the agricultural industry in 2008.

bank. But, luck was with me and, with both eyes wide as teacups, I finally saw the north bank hills in time to miss them. From there onward for 70 or 80 miles (128 km), it was a case of crawling along pretty close to the ground. Then the air seemed to become clearer and I could see lights, like the town of Eston, and it had been dark for some time.

By this time in Saskatchewan development, there were many power lines across fields where there were none before, and I didn't want to chance having a wreck by landing blind. Therefore, I followed roads, railways, etc. having a hard time to see them sometimes, and by the time I flew over Kindersley, visibility had vastly improved. Only 30 miles to go, and by then I knew I had it made – just follow the highway north to Kerrobert. Halfway, I could even dimly make out Coleville, four miles from the highway.

When I arrived at Kerrobert, I didn't buzz the town, but did circle to view the field and get my bearings for approach. This all had to be done by feel, since I had no light to read instruments or find ground level. I would use the hangar for ground reference.

It was just suppertime and I was amazed when eight or nine cars and trucks streamed down to the airport to help me land in the dark OK with their lights. My friends knew I had been wanting to get home – I had not called to say that I was on my way – but they all assumed that it just had to be me as soon as they heard the plane overhead. This concern was moving and very much appreciated by me. Everybody flocked around, we put EVO to bed and I caught a ride uptown, finally back on home base.

Now for Al Smith:

Next morning, I was working my way through a pile of mail that had accumulated in my absence. The phone rang and I answered. I was asked if this was Walter Williams' office. I recognized Al's voice and knew that he thought it would turn out to be a case of search and rescue. I paused a little, then assured him that he had the right number and said he was talking with Walter Williams. There was a long pause and then Al, who possessed a vast vocabulary of profanity, said, "*xyz+#! You must have turn-and-banks for eyeballs!" A turn and bank is an instrument. He had been really scared after I left his field and just knew that nobody could make it in that Swift Current storm.

Sure, it was foolhardy on my part, but I did make it and had the satisfaction of scaring heck out of Mr. Al Smith. I didn't forget to again bawl him out for making everybody fly home after dark or stay overnight in Swift Current.

Al thought I was crazy for making that flight, but he wasn't the only one – because I thought so, too. I wouldn't admit that to him, but told him he didn't know me very well – that's all!

Snowbanks – Bare Ground

One year, the spring breakup took an odd turn. Our airport was on the line separating two opposite conditions – west of Kerrobert was all snow and winter drifts while east from Kerrobert had lost all or nearly all of the winter snow. The landing strips of the Kerrobert airport were ice, due to the ski traffic all winter. This meant that I could use the field either on skis or wheels. But I had to change from one to the other whenever I had a flight from the east area to the west area or the other way 'round.

Many times, I'd land with a passenger and he or she would have to wait for me to change from wheels to skis, or from skis to wheels. This was an odd situation and I made a set of jigs which allowed me finally to affect the change either way, in 20 minutes alone.

This only happened one year, which was enough to suit me. The only thing that worried me was the fact that I had to leave the plane out on the field, as the hangar doors were frozen solid and I couldn't use that. Fortunately, weather stayed good long enough that I could later get the plane into the hangar before any dangerous weather developed.

Schoolteacher – A Load Of Books

One mild winter day, I received a phone call from the Cactus Lake country. A schoolteacher had managed to get home for the weekend visit. His teaching job was in the area of Handel, Sask. I forget his name but I can recall some of the names I invented for him on that occasion.

I said, "Sure, I'll come and getcha." He told me just about where I could find him. I said, "Well, just to be sure, you be out in a field waiting so you don't waste a lot of my time lookin' for you."

I must explain that many times, snow conditions could be good at Kerrobert but warmer and less favourable for ski operation at points west like Compeer, Cactus Lake, etc. Well, it was one of those days, and when I landed in the Cactus Lake hills, the temperature was lower and I had sticky snow to deal with. Also, almost all the fields had dirt blown into the snow, which made for greater difficulty.

So, he was waiting – poor trusting soul. I was hoping more than trusting, more than he was. When he got in, he had a suitcase full of books, which must have weighed as much as he did. When I lifted it, the handle nearly broke off. Well, so be it, I thought, and decided to give it a try. I'll admit that at that moment I wasn't bubbling over with enthusiasm and happiness, and the only thing he got from me was, "Get in." I put his belt on real tight and not a word was spoken.

We taxied up a hill, full throttle, and I hoped to get 'off,' going down the other side. So, still at full throttle, we taxied up another hill and another, but we still didn't get airborne. By the fence lines, I knew we were running out of hills, so taxied up the last one and the far side was pretty steep, so I thought this was it – we'll get off. The only fly in the ointment was that between this hill and the next was a farm in the bottom, with corrals full of cattle – straight ahead.

EVO's engine was getting pretty hot and I couldn't stop anyway, so I pulled back on the wheel for liftoff. EVO left the snow, just before a pen of cattle. The ravine lowered to the left, so I eased her that way. We didn't hit the next hill, the cattle pen or the buildings and were finally out in the clear, where I could get flying speed with an overheated engine.

My passenger didn't say a word – nor did I. I hope he was scared, because I sure was. Forty or so minutes later, we landed on a field on the east side of the Kelfield coulee, near the farm where he boarded. Parting, I was barely cordial – the 150 pounds of books was mainly what bugged me – and the close shave we'd had.

Reflecting, I wonder if such fundamental facts registered on his intelligence. Well, he didn't learn anything from me because I told him nothing – just took his money and was glad to still be alive. We should have died in that cattle pen.

Snow Or No Snow

Spring breakup was in full force, and we were still on skis and there was diminishing amount of snow at Kerrobert. I thought the snow might last another day so, on Sunday morning, I asked John Herron if he would like to fly to Saskatoon to visit our friends there. The answer was immediate and affirmative.

It was a fairly warm morning and snow on the airport was spotty, so I asked if he would walk more than a mile to a pasture field south of the Wallace Pangman farm, where there was more snow. He said OK, and started walking. I managed to get off the airport, alone, and landed on the larger field of snow I'd indicated. John got in and away we went.

Reaching Saskatoon Airport, we found the snow quite intact on the areas where the big rollers had been packing it all winter. Landed, we stooged around and visited until late afternoon. We enjoyed ourselves so much, we forgot about the shortage of snow at home. It had been a nice balmy day, and when we thought it was time to leave, soon discovered that a not-too-serious headwind had developed – just enough to delay our arrival at Kerrobert to just about dark.

Arriving home, we found that the temperature at Kerrobert had been warmer than Saskatoon and most of the snow was gone – just patches here and there. The bare ground would be sloppy mud.

Well, here we were, arriving home and it was practically dark and we were wearing skis. We could see the contrast between the snow patches and the bare areas, didn't have enough gas to get back to Saskatoon in the dark, illegally, so it was time to figure out a way, here and now. The wheels for the plane were right over there on the hangar and this, after all, was the HOME field. The wheels wouldn't have worked in the mud anyway.

We schemed and thought that if we bounced from one snow patch to another a couple of times, we'd lose enough speed to get stuck in the mud without flopping the plane on to its back and wrecking it. John was game and so was I, and that's exactly what we did. It surely was a sudden stop when we slid off the last snow patch and got stuck in the mud, but no damage was done, thanks to a little good timing and a lot of good luck.

Walking up to the shop (really slithering in the mud), we got out the old DS-30 truck, chains on, and brought a long rope. Finding the plane in the dark, we tied each end of the rope to a ski and the middle of it to the drawbar on the back of the truck. Then we dragged poor li'l ol' EVO to the hangar door – safe and sound – still no damage done. We owed a lot to Lady Luck, and it was the last trip on skis for that winter!

Fun And Foolishness

Walter Williams loved flying his little plane around the countryside, whether it was to help people or simply to go for a ride, by himself or with others.

Terry Allen grew up across the back alley from the Williams family and said the relationship between his father, Squee Allen, his Uncle George Allen and Walter Williams was memorable. "As a youngster in Kerrobert, I clearly recall having Dad take me down to the airport to look at Walter's airplane on many occasions and I vividly remember Walter doing loops and chandelles over Kerrobert for us kids. This was the start of a lifetime fascination with flying for me."

Lyle Busch, a childhood friend of Dave Williams, fondly recalls stories of his father Art Busch's days as a coyote hunter on the prairies. Lyle recalls Walter occasionally assisted with these adventures and created a few of his own, taking the passenger door off EVO so his friend Art could find his target from the air. Walter would then land EVO on skis beside Art's two horses and cutter, dropping Art off before being on his way again.

Sharon Fluney has fond memories of Walter flying out to the home of her parents, Ralph and Gladys Fluney, just to visit. "One time he flew out and took Dad up in his plane. It was quite a thrill for us to see this small plane land across the road from Mom and Dad's farm home about five miles west of the village of Tramping Lake. Walter liked to play cribbage and would bring his own board to play with Dad," added Sharon. "He must have thought I needed to learn the game, too, as he gave me a cribbage board for my own. Whenever I see a cribbage board, I think of Walter and the way he took an interest in all of us."

Walter Williams enjoyed being behind the controls of his little airplane and having fun with his neighbours, but there were many times as well when his recklessness got him into trouble.

First Flight To Pick Up Dave

Early in my flying experience, the first winter, I didn't have many hours in my pilot's log book. I propositioned Harold Mitchinson about renting the J-3 EGF to fly to Meadow Lake and fly you, Dave, back to Saskatoon. Mitch knew the general situation of the separation, thought a bit, said I was used to driving up there, and li'l ol' EGF was pretty slow – just a pasture plane, but if I wanted the experience badly enough and paid the freight (per hour), then OK, go ahead. It was a lot for me to ask and just as much for Mitch to give, but as I have already pointed out, Mitch accommodated me at the same time as he refused others.

Leaving our DS-30 truck at the airport, I was off in the early morning with a lump in my throat. This was a first for me. Seventy-two air miles per hour indicated, I stopped at North Battleford, with a light head wind en route and gassed up. This was my first of many stops at North Battleford Airport throughout the ensuing years. Took off again, straight north, flying at some altitude over more bush country than I had ever seen from the air. Finally arriving at Meadow Lake, I put the wooden skis onto a small field at the southwest corner of the town, not too far from a mink ranch. Boy, that snow was deep! EGF didn't go very far in it.

Now, it was stated in the rule books that this J-3 should be flown single from the rear seat but everybody flew it from the front seat because it made for better visibility, etc. However, this changed the centre of gravity so much that it tended to make the little Cub nose-heavy. I learned about this the hard way when I wanted to taxi to the edge of the field for, almost at once, the tail went up and the prop was threshing the loose snow. After that, I sure held the tail down – stick back.

I picked you up, Dave, and we cleared the field and headed back. Halfway to Glaslyn, we encountered snow in the air, which meant that we had to descend and follow the highway. By dusk, we passed low over North Battleford and landed at the airport. Conditions included heavy snowfall and a 26-mile-per-hour (42 km/h) wind. I sure felt green, and your presence didn't ease my misgivings. We managed, in the failing light, to park the plane near a hangar for shelter (which burned down a short time later, burning also the planes it contained).

Walking over to the airport buildings, we registered and I phoned Mitch to tell him we were OK and would go on to Saskatoon in the morning. Mitch played it down but must have been relieved to hear that all was well up to that point. We took a taxi downtown to a hotel. One thing comes to mind about that night, which still amuses me. We both took a bath, and that was when I taught you how to bathe like a man, without a wash rag (like the ladies always nag us boys to use). You learned that night that one becomes clean using only his hands.

In the morning, we were back at the airport. It was a nice clear day and the flight to Saskatoon was safe and easy. I remember feeling pretty proud that we'd pulled off the flight OK and I think you were pleased, too. You were eight years old then.

Local Barnstorming – Gift Rides

Before acquiring EVO, I had been getting my 'kicks' out of an old 1936 side-valve Harley Davidson 47 motorcycle for three and a half years, which I completely overhauled every year. When EVO came into my life, Old Smokey (the motorcycle) seemed tame. A truck driver wanted the old bike pretty badly and kept badgering me, so a month after EVO moved in, Old Smokey went to the truck driver.

Originally, friends helped me to buy EVO, and I paid them off when and as I could. One way to add to my earnings was to do 'barnstorming' – a 10-minute circling of Kerrobert at two dollars a ride. John Herron would do the booking and collecting, so there was little lost time. He had 'em lined up and ready.

As soon as I stopped, he would unbelt the passenger, get the seat empty and have another passenger in and belted in jig-time. He was a real little hustler and a great help. When gas ran low, I'd warn him and he would have the chamois funnel and a jerry can of gas ready for the next stop.

We didn't do much other barnstorming than at home. One time, there was a big family gathering in the Tramping Lake/Revenue area, and somebody there thought it would be something different if I took the plane out and gave them all a ride. This gets pretty monotonous – just 'get in,' circle around, and then 'get out.' One fellow, thinking he was braver than the rest, wanted 'stunts,' so I gave him a few stiff stalls and a loop, all in quick succession, made a quick landing before he dirtied up the plane, poured him out on to the ground minus his gizzard. I dropped that off on the next trip.

Nobody else wanted stunts and maybe I spoiled his day, but I think the whole thing made for a good party. For one thing, the weather could not have been better.

Other times, I would be invited out to a farm, where a whole family or two would all want rides. The old man would pay the shot and these were nice experiences and a big day for those involved.

Doug Bick, our druggist's son, was handicapped to the inclusion of a cloven palate, a right arm which was hardly useful and a dragging right leg. You, Dave, and I seemed to associate with him more than other people and we saw a lot of him. He would make frequent trips to the country in my pickup truck and many times I gathered him up to make flights with me. I'd take along a thick cushion and set him on it so he could see out, and strap him in. Once on course, I'd let him take the wheel to keep the plane level. His feet couldn't reach the rudder pedals, so my feet did that part. Gosh, Doug was in the clouds in more ways than one!

Sometimes, I'd touch one rudder or the other, which automatically banked the plane slightly, just to give him something to do. I'd praise him and he seemed to be in heaven.

Mrs. Evelyn Connor (Clayton's wife) was another ride I recall giving. She's only a little thing but with a game courage, which led me to suggest that I shut off the engine while in flight at about 3,000 to 4,000 feet altitude. We'd glide for a short period without power. Then I would have to dive the plane straight down and attain an airspeed of 120 miles per hour (193 km/h) in order to windmill the prop over compression and into action, and we could continue powered flight. Well, she was game and we did it. She enjoyed it. At that time, we were operating a satellite flying school at Kerrobert, and there were several other planes in the air then.

Ricky Chen, Japanese, and widow of Steve Chen, Chinaman, who used to run the old Canada restaurant (long since torn down), was another friend whom I invited to go for a ride. I had previously taken her two sons, together, and the mid-day rough summer turbulence of that day made them both get air sickness. I always carried a couple of quart sickness containers behind the seat and those two boys sure tried to fill them.

The satellite training school was still on when Ricky accepted my invitation to go for a ride. Instead of the usual ride at one or two thousand feet, we went up to 10,000 feet. It was pretty smooth air that day, but Ricky said she was tired afterwards. Maybe something else was bothering her.

The Wolf Cub Pack was having a contest of some kind and hadn't decided on an award when I suggested that I would give the two top boys a real good ride in EVO. This was acceptable and the contest was sparked. The boys got their ride and 15 years later at St. Martin's Church in Saskatoon, I met Lyle Wright, one of those Cubs, and he reminded me of the event. Before the ride, and to give myself a few minutes to finish some work, I gave them the key to the hangar and asked them if they would 'count the wings,' and if the count was two, we'd go. They walked the mile and back, gave a favourable report and by then I was ready.

The Dave Turk family lived east of Kerrobert, north of Dodsland, and I knew them pretty well. One of the girls was the teacher at Roslyn School, staying at the farm of Adolph and Mary Henning, midway between Kerrobert and Broadacres. Well, it was a stormy winter and naturally, the girl got home for the weekend whenever she could make it. The distances were short, and three times that winter I was called to fly her back to work on the Monday morning. I charged her five dollars for each of the first two trips, but the third time I said, "Put away your purse – this one's on me." They were fine people.

Many other times, teachers were stormed in at home, 'off base,' and I recall getting a call from Oscar Peters, south of Superb. Could I fly his sister to Dodsland or Druid, or somewhere in that area? It was on the stormy side and I said I'd have some shovelling to do at the hangar, warm up the engine, and I would get out as soon as I could. He said he would start out with team and sleigh-box, and I said I could easily see and recognize them, land beside the rig and pick up his sister.

My chores didn't take long that day, with the result that I spotted Oscar and his outfit only a couple of miles from home. I crossed over him and landed in the snow pretty close by. His horses reared a lot, but Oscar held them down. The sister unwrapped from her blankets, jumped into the plane and was soon at her destination 'on base.'

The Draves family, near Ermine, between Kerrobert and Dodsland, called me one winter day, telling me that they were all assembled to celebrate Grandpa Draves' 83rd birthday. Was it a nice enough winter day for me to fly out and give Grandpa a ride, his first?

I said, "Sure," and went out, taxiing right up to the farm gate. This fine old gentleman got in, I fastened his safety belt and away we went. I flew him around for 15 to 20 minutes, and when I was coming in for the landing, I asked him how he liked it and he replied, "Just like in a car!"

Jean Porter was a public health nurse in Kerrobert when my sister Marion started in at that work. Marion and Jean became great friends and Jean would frequently be a guest at our table. Our mother was with us then. Jean was a very pleasant and gentle person who was raised on a farm near Stranraer, Sask.

Those years, with our Dad having passed on, I missed a lot of home mealtimes. Many times, I would be out in the country or delivering machines and lots of times I missed meals altogether. I had told Jean that I would give her a nice ride in the plane – "sometime." I suppose quite a time had passed and she still had not been given her ride. So, one time at our dinner table she smiled at me and asked, "Walter, when is 'sometime?'" I said I could take her up right after the meal was over, and that's when she got her first ride. Driving our own respective vehicles to the hangar, we got EVO out and took off.

That first ride, I was careful in the smooth air to make it a straight-and-level flight that would not alarm her in any way, because we all liked and respected her very highly. I explained this or that as we went along. After about 20 minutes, we made a very smooth landing and pulled over to the hangar. By this time, Marion had helped Mother with the dishes and driven down to the hangar to meet us.

We sat in the plane for a minute and Jean made no move to open her door or unfasten her safety belt. I asked her if she had enjoyed the ride or was she in shock? She gave me a nice smile and said, "Walter, that's not the way you fly!"

I asked her if she'd like to horse around a little and tear up the air and she said yes, she'd like to try it. So, I got out, waved to Marion, flipped the prop and we took off again.

This time I started with stalls, graduating from mild to quite severe. She liked it all. Then I went into stall turns and loops, and everything that wouldn't tear off the wings. When we landed, Jean said she'd enjoyed that ride very much. Marion was surprised and shocked that so gentle a person would ask for such a ride.

I gave Jean many rides after that, and every time I would have to promise to give her 'stunts' – otherwise she was not interested. Huh, y' never can tell, eh?

Dave And Alan – Banff Mountains

It must have been in 1949 and you'll remember, Dave, the trip we flew to the Calgary Stampede. With both tanks topped, we managed to get to Elnora, Alta., OK but the big question then was where to land in such hilly and bushy country. Grain fields were small and in crop. Summerfallow would be too soft. Finally, I decided to try a pasture west of Elnora, with a twisty ridge running more or less east and west, well decorated with debris and stones, and we'd have to do a lot of steering to stay on the ridge and miss trees and debris as best we could. But – we made it! Whew! Oh, one other thing that was not a blessing – the two to three-degree downhill tilt. We shook up EVO a bit, but everything was still OK.

Bob Cameron drove out to pick us up. Later, we went back to the pasture and cleared the ridge of junk and stones, preparing for our takeoff for Calgary Stampede the next morning. Tied the plane down, and the only worry was that horses might chew parts of the plane. There's something about the smell of doped fabric[38] that makes horses chew the fabric, and cattle will lick holes in it with their tongues.

Next morning, with Bob shaking his head a bit, you and your cousin Alan and I made a teetering, skiddy takeoff but we made it, dragging out like a sick calf. In those days, Calgary was no sweat without radio, so we finally got a green light and landed – my first time at Calgary. There, we looked after the plane and got a taxi to take us downtown.

In the central part of town – the Station, I think – we arranged for staying overnight at a private home, took down the name and address. Then we hit for the Stampede. I had attended the year before on Old Smokey, the motorcycle, so I got my kicks out of the kicks you kids got out of it.

I think you kids enjoyed the Stampede, the Indian section, etc., and when it was time, we took a taxi to the private home billet we had been assigned. Spent a restful night, paid up in the morning and took

---

[38] *Doped fabric - Aircraft dope is a protective coating, similar to varnish, for the plane's cotton fabric to strengthen it and make it smooth and long lasting.*

a taxi to the airport. I thought it would be nice to fly out to Banff, to enrich our adventure.

Arriving at Banff, elevation over a mile, and with a little 65-HP fly like ours, I didn't realize what was in store for us. There, they had a windsock at each end of the field and sometimes they pointed in different directions. At the base of Mount Cascade, it's OK for high-powered planes, but I got a real scare before that day was over. On our first approach, heading straight for the mountain, we had fun looking at the bears at the city dump. When I turned in for final approach, I was 600 feet too high, so circled around again. This time I forgot about the bears and powered down through an up-draft to make a landing.

So, there we were, on the ground. Took a taxi into town so we could say afterwards that we'd really been to Banff, had a lunch there, didn't fool around too much, got a taxi back to the airport. On takeoff, I went to the extreme south end of the runway, turned around and gave EVO full throttle. Well, she didn't want to lift, but being a stubborn fool, I kept on, hoping to lift in time to jump the trees at the other end of the runway. You kids were having a pretty good time with each other, so I didn't express my apprehension as to our welfare at that point. Two men were standing on our left off the runway, and when it became apparent that I was not going to abort the takeoff, started running for the trees. But it was too late then to stop, so I pulled EVO off the ground.

I still don't know how we got over those trees, and I'm sure we must have brushed the tops. It took me three miles to gain 300 feet of altitude, turning to the right over the railway. I didn't say anything to you kids, but I surely was scared that day. Alone, I wouldn't have worried so much, but responsibilities multiply with son and nephew aboard. But – we did stay in the air, turned around, headed for Calgary, and made it.

From Calgary, we headed for Three Hills, Alta. We had phoned the folks at Elnora, telling them that there was a landing field at Three Hills, and asked if they would pick us up there, about 25 miles from Elnora. Remember the big rocks sticking out of the prairie, along our way at one point? Remember me opening my door a bit, acting as though I were going to get out, and saying, "I'll be right back!" You guys sure laughed over that one.

So we landed at Three Hills and a fellow named Smith came out. He had a Stinson and had landed at Kerrobert once before that. He had a new hangar and sure wanted to see if there was room for my plane in there with his. I said I thought EVO would be OK, just tied down outside. But he was so insistently curious that I decided to humour him, and we worked like the dickens, nestled the two planes together and got the door shut.

EVO was under cover and it was one of the luckiest things that ever happened to her. Bob and family picked us up and drove us all to Elnora.

That night there was a fierce storm – lots of wind, rain and hail. At Elnora, a neighbour's big tree blew down and struck Bob's house. Power and telephone lines were blown down. It really was a terrible storm and if EVO had been out in the open, she would have been shredded by the hail storm. As it was, she was safe and intact, and you and I flew home the next day, landed safely, and we'd had quite an adventure together.

Coyote Hunting

About 1950, there were so many coyotes in the country that farmers were suffering serious losses of chickens, sheep, etc. They carried rifles and would shoot this pest at every opportunity, but this didn't make much of a difference in the numbers of this cunning predator. Several years later, the Saskatchewan government carried out a province-wide cyanide poisoning operation which cleaned out most of the coyotes and some farm dogs. After all that, all we had left was a super coyote whose progeny were more wary and wise but a lot fewer. Like germs that learned to endure penicillin – the survivors were tougher. Also, after the coyotes were nearly extinct, we had so many rabbits, which winter on bark and small branches of bush, and the damage was great in that respect. So it was another example of the upset of nature's balance, or cycle.

But, back to 1950. One old farmer, a very fine fellow, Mr. Goodhart, south of Major, had lost just about all his sheep. And by then someone thought up the idea of a 'coyote shooting bee,' and I was right with it, with the plane. EVO had been used for killing coyotes many times in southern Manitoba before I bought her, because she was small, could fly slow and was superbly manoeuvrable.

The first of these events started with everyone gathering at Mr. Goodhart's farm. There were several hundred fellows, all with shotguns – no rifles allowed, because the shotgun had a shorter range and was therefore safer for this kind of crazy activity. The idea was to disperse all these men and shotguns around an area four miles square (16 square miles). (Incidentally, the shotguns ranged in quality from expensive models down to what could be likened to a piece of pipe and a hammer.)

Milton McCracken of Kerrobert, one glass eye but good with a shotgun, rode out to the Goodhart farm with me but Art Busch, who farmed about halfway between Kerrobert and Goodhart's, was my shooter for the event. Art was an expert shooter and impervious to the violent flying required in the hunting, which was always low and risky.

We would spot a coyote, fly near him, then I'd side-slip to the right so Art could shoot the coyote with the shotgun sticking out through the open window on his side of the plane. Art didn't miss very often. After the shot, I'd put on full power and yank the plane upwards to gain enough altitude to turn around and see if the coyote was still alive or done for. Art used #2 shot, which is a pretty big pellet, and the shell had a lot more #2's than, say, buckshot – more pellets to a 'hill' (like potatoes), so to speak. If the coyote was done for, we'd make a quick landing, pick up the dead coyote and take off again.

We put the first dead coyote on the floor under Art's legs and flew over a truck full of men, deploying to their section of the 4 x 4 square, and pushed out the coyote, which the men picked up after it hit the ground. Well, that coyote must have had a million fleas. Art and I were scratching ourselves all the rest of the day. (I still get itchy just thinking about it.)

We found a long piece of cord and after that, we tied the dead coyotes to a strut with a bow knot, and when we wanted to drop the coyote, just pulled the cord and the coyote would drop just like a bomb.

At the outset, it was agreed that when Art and I saw that the 16 miles of perimeter was pretty well filled in, we would loop-the-loop in the centre of the square and everybody would start walking towards the centre. While we were waiting for all those guys to get into place, Art and I flew outside the hunt area and shot seven coyotes and delivered them via bombing method to the men below.

As the hunt progressed and men got closer together, coyotes were cornered into an increasingly smaller area. When one would make a dash to get out of the circle of men, several fellows would shoot at it, more or less towards each other, and it was a miracle that someone didn't get shot, but not one person did. Nobody ever knew how many coyotes died that day, but there would easily be a hundred.

This was rolling country, pretty rough (in fact, Mr. Goodhart's house was on top of a fairly high hill). One thing Art and I had agreed to do was that when the circle was fairly small, we'd shoot one coyote from the air so everybody could see how it was done. Finally, at that point, there were six or seven tired and wounded coyotes left, we dived at one, Art shot it and I full-throttled upwards again.

Then, I made the unforgivable error of turning downwind at near stalling speed. The plane shuddered and I just knew we'd had it this time, with all our bridges burned behind us. Men, cars, trucks all over the place; there was nowhere to even crash-land.

I left on full throttle and managed to point EVO straight for the ground. In our vertical power drive, I saw partsman Morley Nord, whom I loved as a brother, holding his shotgun and looking straight up at us and we were diving straight for him. I remember thinking that, whatever else, I wouldn't hit Morley, so I twitched the right rudder a bit and missed him, but it meant that when Art and I finally and desperately 'pulled out,' the right wing cut the grass. We didn't quite make contact with the ground, and a half a mile later had acquired safe flying speed. This all happened in just a few seconds. I think I was more 'shook up' over that one than Art was. All he said was, "That was close, wasn't it?"

We landed near the crowd. Everybody was excited by the whole experience of the day, and I felt particularly lucky re: our averted disaster. Art drove home, McCracken flew home with me. Morley, being a former Mountie, knew more than most the miracle of our escape, and wouldn't talk about it for a month.

There were other similar coyote hunts but I never turned wind at stalling speed again. I rather felt that God didn't want to call me just yet…

Baldy Bell – Barnstorming

One summer Sunday, when John Herron and I decided to do some barnstorming, we went upstairs and did a few stunts to let people know we were around, and sure enough, there were soon a few cars and people, curious, and customers. We flew a lot of people that day. At one time, just as I'd taken on a fairly good slug of gas, it was Baldy Bell's turn.

Now Baldy, nearing retirement as a CPR engineer on the Kerrobert/Coronation line, weighed 265 pounds (120 kg). I had noticed that on other flights, that low atmospheric pressure of the day made EVO lazy on the lift. When I added weight by fuelling up and taking on half a moose like Baldy Bell, I went the whole 1,200-feet (360 m) of the north-south runway and barely got off the ground. We missed the railway phone line a mile further on and Baldy, sensing the situation, cheerfully suggested that the plane was taxed to its limit. I agreed.

We did gain altitude, though, and he got as good a ride as the rest of the people, notwithstanding. When he got out, I felt relieved (and maybe he did, too). Anyway, on a poor-lift day, there's a lot of difference between a 65-pound kid and Baldy's 265 pounds, especially since one might be light on gas for the light passenger and heavy on gas for the heavy guy. That's one of the bugs of having only 65 horses in the barn, at the most.

Denzil Girl To Prelate

One early spring day, there was a call from Denzil, Sask. Phil Reiniger was another IHC dealer and his sister wanted to be flown to Prelate, Sask., where she worked in a Catholic institution. We had not lost our snow yet, so I was still on skis. It was a fairly cold day, and when the girl was getting into the plane, I asked her if she was dressed warmly enough. She cheerfully assured me that she was and showed me a warm-looking jacket, and she wore ski pants.

So, we took off and had not gone far when I noticed a couple of inches of bare skin on both her legs, between socks and ski pant bottom. I thought, "Well, I've asked her," and she was a strong-looking young German girl, so I let it go at that.

Our flight took us almost due south and across the South Saskatchewan River. We ran out of snow before we reached the river, and south of the river was bare ground. This sure bothered me because we were in the air, waving a pair of skis!

There was a road from the river to a town, southward, where people had been crossing all winter but the ice looked pretty rough for a landing, so I proceeded southward, following the road. By reflection of the sun, I saw a strip of ice in the stubble where the snow had drifted in from a summerfallow field more deeply and while snow had disappeared from the rest of the stubble field, there was this thin icy strip along the edge. I lined up with one of these strips leading towards the river road and made a good landing. I got to the road just in time to catch a ride for the young lady, in a car that just happened to come along.

I thought everything was turning out well – the car took off down the road and I took off, too. Gaining altitude, I happened to look towards the town and saw 'Leader' printed on the elevator! This was the wrong town I had taken the girl to, due to my concern about landing in a snowless country on skis!

I circled over Leader and saw that the car that had picked up the girl was heading out for Prelate, so I flew home. I decided that it would be better for me if I told this story as soon as I got home so that gossip could not catch up to me – meaning travellers who called at our business. The first was Spud Morphy of Davies Electric. He was the one who enjoyed this mistake the most. And every time I see him after all these years, he laughs mostly about the motorcycle trip I made to Saskatoon in wintertime and the time I dropped a passenger at the wrong town.

Well, he loves me and loves to kid me, but it was one of the things which enriched our association. He knew well that I did the things that nobody else did, and I'm one of his best friends.

Meadow Lake Trip – Bush Fire

One Sunday in summertime, my Dad and you, Dave, and I got into EVO with you half-sitting, half-standing between Dad's knees. We were bound for Meadow Lake to make a short visit there and return the same day. There was a bit of forest fire smoke in the air and this increased as we went northward, until finally the air was quite hazy.

We landed there and met people you went to school with, and the ones I'd met on my many trips to visit you, including the people who ran the Avenue Hotel. One of your friends was Charlie Graham. A small bush fire was burning across the tracks south of town and I took Charlie for a ride. We foolishly flew right over the bushfire and I was soon sorry because of the smoke, turbulence, and especially the fiery pieces of bark and junk rising from the heat of the fire. Our plane could easily have caught fire if some piece, glowing with fire, had caught in the right place on the plane. We could have come down in flames.

We three stooged around, had something to eat, and left for home. The air stayed quite hazy until about halfway home, we burst into clear sunny air. Guess the wind had changed and was chasing the smoke back up north. Landed at home OK, we had had a nice visit and something different, that day, just the three of us.

Reminded me of the time when we three had stayed overnight in the little old Windsor Hotel in Saskatoon (still there), when you were seven years old and drove with your cousin Brenda in the Traveller's Parade, in the baby car we'd made for you in our shop. That was another story.

Brenda – Biggar – Right Wheel

One nice summer morning, my youngest sister Grace asked me if I would take her daughter Brenda to Biggar to visit her grandmother, Mrs. Madden. Brenda would be with her grandmother for several days. I said sure, and decided to use the plane to make it more dramatic and memorable. Brenda was a very cute little girl and she and I got along well.

Takeoff was normal and we headed east. It didn't take long to reach Biggar and I decided to land really 'close-in,' so we landed on the same field where Jack Allen and I had had our iced-up forced landing on skis, at the northeast corner of town.

There's a lot of difference between wheels in summer and skis in winter on the same field. This was not really a good field. For instance, a badger hole covered with snow in winter is no problem on skis. But in summer, on wheels, one can come to grief if a wheel drops into the hole – it just fits the wheel and you-are-IT!

Well, we approached the field, made a smooth landing and were slowing down and were lucky that as we were just stopping, the right wing went down because the right wheel had dropped into a badger hole. Had we been going faster, we could have wrecked. No damage – and a few lifts later, I had the wheel out of the hole, and we were 'home free.'

I was used to carefully watching for rocks and holes, but with the tail down and the engine hood up in front of me (I was in the left seat and the hole was at the right side), I surely missed that one. 'All's well that ends well' was the order of the day that time.

Winnipeg Flood – Arnold Cornish

The year of the 'Winnipeg Flood,' I thought I'd like to view it on the weekend. Since Arnold Cornish (a Biggar fellow in the garage business with his father and brother), a good friend of mine, was interested, too, I agreed to pick him up at Biggar at four in the morning. It must have been about May 25, but I forget which year it was.[39]

This put me in the air by 3:20 or 3:30 in the morning and I landed at Biggar on a pretty rough field at 4:00 a.m. Arnold was there to meet me and in minutes we were on our way. I had a jerry can of gas behind the seat and both tanks full. At the Yorkton Government Airport, still early in the morning, we landed and put the extra gas into our tanks.

Then we continued our flight, passing the south end of Lake Manitoba, which was still mostly ice. We stopped at Neepawa, gassed again, and got advice about getting into the Winnipeg Airport. Approaching Winnipeg, we saw more water than land and by the time we got to Winnipeg there was water almost everywhere. Part of the city was flooded, but the airport was OK. However, the air was full of airplanes, and I recall crossing a couple of miles in front of a four-engine job, probably an airliner. But we finally got a green light and landed. A Grumman Goose[40] was right behind us, and I didn't stay in front of it very long but turned off the runway. Boy, things were crazy around there – aircraft all over the place.

We found a quiet place and walked in to register. We were just country boys and I came in for censure for not having gone to the end of the runway instead of turning off, but suffered no penalty. Registering was a matter of standing in line. We wanted something to eat, gas up, and leave. I phoned a cousin of my mother and they said they've wave a blanket from an upstairs balcony if I circled. (Another plane nearly got me when I circled.)

First, after registering, we wanted a bite to eat. There was such a lineup that I suggested an open window at the kitchen. So we went

---

[39] *The Winnipeg Flood named here occurred in 1950. (http://wikipedia.org)*
[40] *Grumman Goose – An amphibious flying boat. (http://wikipedia.org)*

around to the back and made a deal with the cook. Eventually, we were handed our lunch out the back window, paid, and ate.

The next difficulty was to fire up EVO and get into the lineup for the gas pumps. We made an inadequately mature individual pretty angry when we crashed the lineup, but when he realized that I was determined to not spend the rest of my life waiting for a fill of gas, he let me pass and I got EVO filled up – they were just getting rid of me, so it pays to have nerve sometimes. Then we idled the engine for 15 to 20 minutes, to get clearance for takeoff.

Finally, we were off and free in the air again, having to dodge the darndest bunch of aircraft I was ever among. We kept the rendezvous with the blanket-waving relative and headed south. It was like flying over an ocean. A few miles out of Winnipeg, I dropped down to low level so we could really see things, take pictures, and wave at people whose farms were completely inundated.

It was really awful. I was surprised that there was such a strong current – enough to sweep a large barn into a nearby hollow, against a bluff of trees, and the barn was a complete wreck. Another place, a railway had damned the waters so the flood just broke through the grade and turned a quartermile of the line upside down. There were ties on top of the rails and at each end of this situation, tracks and ties were vertical. Another place, where the highway went over a rise and was above flood level, there would be an ox or two with nothing to eat, but just not drowning. Some farms had gas barrels to hold planks for getting from one building to another and we got vigorous waves from those people when we circled low over them.

The whole thing was crazy, flying so low, because if we'd have had trouble and fell into that mess, we would have been casualties.

We flew over the town of Morris, Man., which was completely flooded. Piles of lumber at the lumber yard had floated and lumber was everywhere. Police boats were going up and down the streets to keep order or help as necessary. By then we had seen enough and at low altitude, we could not see land. So we flew higher and headed for Portage la Prairie Airport. I wanted to top the tanks and start heading for home.

Gassing at Portage, the fellow who gassed us recognized EVO

and said he knew 350 coyotes had been shot from her in that district, prior to my owning her. He sure had a good word for EVO.

We took off and headed for Neepawa. There, we gassed again and took off, but after being in the air for awhile, I decided we should not continue because we could not reach a decent place to spend the night, so we turned back and landed again at Neepawa. There, we gassed up again, we arranged for an early morning takeoff, got a room at a hotel, and went out for supper.

I don't remember much after that because I had a bad head cold, had flown 10½ hours that day and was just dead tired. When one flies with a head cold, altitude doesn't bother but coming back down, one gets a real bad-head feeling – it's very depressing and debilitating – plus, we had left Kerrobert/Biggar at 2,000 elevation and Winnipeg is in the minus-1,000-feet area.

I recall eating supper with Arnold but not much more until he wakened me early the next morning. I asked him how I got to bed and he said he undressed me and put me to bed. My head felt better but I was very tired.

We took off from Neepawa about five in the morning, stopped at Rivers, Man. (I think it was), got the people out of bed to give us gas, and kept on course for Saskatoon. I was so sleepy and 'beat' that at one time Arnold took over the plane for an hour (he was not a pilot), while I slept. He was to waken me if things got out of hand, but everything went well. Arnold was pleased to be the only one awake in the plane at that time.

We finally reached Saskatoon, gassed up again and I dropped Arnold off at Biggar, safe and sound. We had both taken dozens of pictures of the flood and thought we'd pulled off a DANDY.

Doug Herriott – Harris – Deer

Doug Herriott was our IH blockman for several years, and an avid bow-and-arrow man. He once took top honours in Saskatchewan, although he modestly allowed that perhaps better shooters than he had not been at the meet, but that he'd had 'a good day.'

In certain areas in Saskatchewan, archers can hunt a deer a month earlier than the gunpowder boys, and Doug always arranged a week of holiday in that period. He had several brothers and they were archers, too, and this was a good time for them to share a common interest together. Doug was a big strong fella, and even with the broad-cutting hunting arrows, he had to hold back a bit or his arrow would pass right through the deer and the deer would be hard to track, blood trail and all.

One year, he phoned me from the hunting area south of Harris, Sask. He had shot a deer, the deer took off, and Doug couldn't find it. Would I fly over and we could try to locate it from the air? I said sure, and was soon picking him up in an open field nearby. We criss-crossed that whole area but never did locate his deer. We did, however, see a dead deer and after landing, walked to it.

It's one thing to spot a deer from the air and quite another to find it while one is walking. Camouflage is so effective that I stumbled over or onto one (dead several days), went a few feet away, looked back and had a hard time to pick it out, so well was it camouflaged against the fall-coloured grass. Well, in Doug's case, the deer we saw from the air had been dead for several days, too.

While we were in flight and not very high, we saw other hunters hidden in bushes, etc. They must have had a pretty bad opinion of us, although we did spook the odd deer which the hunter may have missed if we had not made the deer move. We gave up the search for Doug's deer. It may have been dying or dead, in brush or thicket, invisible to us from the air. It was a disappointment for both of us but that's life sometimes. I left Doug with his brothers and friends, and flew home again to my work. It had been just another experience, or adventure.

Trip To Calgary – Dad – Los Angeles

One summer day, dull and rainy at home, Dad received a telegram to learn that his youngest brother Ewart had passed away in Los Angeles. We inquired about air schedules and found out that if he caught a certain flight in Calgary that evening at about nine o'clock or so, he could make it to Uncle Ewart's funeral. Since it was raining at home, I phoned the tower at Calgary, learning that they had perfect weather there, visibility 70 miles (112 km). In other words, 'Come on over – everything's fine here.' Dad cleaned up and changed, Mother packed his bag, I got EVO ready for the 220-mile (354 km) flight, and we left as soon as we could.

Since it was raining, Dad asked if it was wise to fly and I assured him that just light rain was no threat to our welfare, and we proceeded on course for Calgary. Sixty-five miles later, we burst out into bright sunshine and clear sky. I wasn't taking any chances with my own dad for a passenger, and when I saw a large rainy (real storm) area ahead in the Hanna area, I detoured southward to avoid the storm. I remember passing over Youngstown eventually. From there, it was almost straight west to Calgary.

Arriving at Calgary, we saw great pools of water all over the airport. They had had a rainstorm since my phone call, but the sky was clear again. With li'l ol' EVO, it was easy to circumvent the pools of water and we taxied to the gas pumps. Filling both tanks for my return home in the morning, we parked the plane in a hangar which was run by Charlie Adie's brother Jim. (Charlie was the Pool elevator man at Kerrobert and a friend of mine.) I arranged with Jim that I could take my plane out any time I wanted to (which happened to be before dawn the next morning), so long as I closed the big hangar door before leaving.

It was beginning to get dark by the time Dad and I walked across the airport to register, and for him to catch his flight. We walked near the fence at the south end of the runway, but they flashed the runway lights to let us know that we were not welcome there. I explained this to my Dad and he worried a bit, but I assured him that we'd just continue on our way and nothing would come of it. No plane landed or took off while we crossed. It was almost dark by that time.

At the terminal, Dad confirmed his flight, and I saw him off. It was arranged that he would advise us by telegram when he felt free to return to Calgary, and I would fly over again and pick him up. He appreciated the idea of flying all the way from Kerrobert right to Los Angeles. The only walking he did was walking across the Calgary field, with runway lights winking angrily at us, to the terminal where they have that old Lancaster stuck up on a post.

After seeing Dad off, I had a taxi drop me off at a downtown hotel, where I engaged a bed for four or five hours. I left a call for 3 a.m., as next day was Fair Day at Kerrobert, but that's another story.

Trip From Calgary – Fog Layers

I flopped into bed immediately and was awakened as requested. While I settled up for the room, I had the desk man call a taxi. This taxi man doddled a bit so we had to stop at a red light at the first corner – we could easily have gone through on the green. When he stopped, I opened my door and got out and said, "That's it, Buster, you're not going to make an all-day trip out of getting me out to the airport!" He said. "Get in, I'll get you there quick." I got in and we lost not one second getting to the airport after he knew I meant serious business.

Getting my plane out of the hangar was no sweat, even in the dark, and I closed the big doors again, as I'd promised Jim Adie. The only thing that worried me was that even in the darkness, it seemed a bit foggy. I fired up EVO and found a suitable runway. Taking off southwards over the highway, I swung left and headed for home. Some dim dawn light was dubiously increasing but I hadn't gone very far when I knew I was in fog trouble. For how far I didn't know, but it lasted all the way home. I was sure glad my dad wasn't with me. I don't think I ever told him all of the trouble I had that morning.

This was one of the most asinine situations I ever created for myself. I had only the standard (non-sensitive) altimeter for EVO at that time, and no turn-and-bank instrument. I zeroed the altimeter before leaving Kerrobert and when I landed at Calgary, the instrument said I was still 1,400 feet (420 m) in the air.[41] Zeroing at Calgary, I would land at an indicated 1,400 feet underground at Kerrobert. I had zeroed at Calgary.

I hadn't gone far before I ran into heavier fog and elected to go 'up.' Climbing up, I encountered a clear space, but this was merely 'between layers' and I soon ran up into the next layer. The light was still very dim due to the fog blocking out the dawn light, and I was strictly on compass and the seat of my pants. I passed through

---

[41] *Walter's altimeter was either set improperly or malfunctioned along the way. Kerrobert is 2208 feet above sea level and Calgary is 3650 feet above sea level. Temperature also affects altimeter settings.*

layers until I was a mile off the ground, and I was still not 'on top,' clear of fog. I'll admit to being worried. But I eventually saw a hole in the fog and there was the earth. The hole wasn't very large, so I swung around in a spiral, neared ground level, and there was Hanna, Alta.

I continued on my way, but the respite was short and the fog became quite heavy a bit later. I tried for altitude again. Don't remember how high I was this time, but finally found myself out of control and losing altitude – FAST. I tried this and I tried that, but nothing seemed to make the plane level off or lessen my rate of descent. The compass was swinging like crazy, so was useless under the circumstances. I knew I must be near the area of the Hand Hills, and when the altimeter indicated 900 feet below Calgary, I knew it was my time to go. Being half Scotch, I didn't want to miss anything – like covering one's face – and just let it happen.

They have a name for it now – I was in a 'spiral.' This is not a tailspin, but the terminal effect is just the same – you CRASH! I sat there, seeing nothing but the wings, and just knew I'd had it this time. When one emerges from the bottom of a fog, no matter whether it be 1,000 feet from the ground or right on the ground, everything turns brown. Well, I resigned to death at this point, so just waited for it to happen with both eyes wide open – I'd take it.

There is a phenomenon in fog that there can be heavy fog and, from ground or driving level, one encounters a 'clear area' for a mile or two and then you're right back into fog again. I, as a flyer, would perhaps call this a 'bubble.' The fog went brown and I knew this was IT! – and knew I was a dead man.

However, I penetrated a 'bubble' at about 200-feet (60 m) altitude, and EVO was really boring towards the ground at an angle of about 30 degrees. Twitching the controls, the plane instantly corrected to level flight and, I was still living – a quick reversal of my former destination. This 'bubble' may not occur very often, but it was my extreme good fortune to come out of the fog in such an area – about one chance in a million. Below me was a large herd of cattle, and every footprint was full of water, so it was not a good place to land a plane. The water was the result of the storm Dad and I had avoided only a few hours before in the previous afternoon.

My liquid compass was still swinging crazily, and since this bubble seemed to be about two miles across, I started at one side and flew straight for the other side as slowly as possible, but this was not enough time for the compass to stabilize. There were hills all around this clear area. I flew around for a minute or two (there was an old abandoned railway, I remember), and finally trusting my sense of direction, hopped hills in a northeasterly direction. This direction was confirmed later when the compass more or less stabilized.

Well sir, my luck still held, and I eventually hit Compeer, Alta., right on the nose and I was on home ground again. Following along highway or railway, whichever was shortest, I flew to Kerrobert, having to miss grain elevators from memory. The fog was still very heavy. It was a great relief to fly over the hill at the edge of Kerrobert and set EVO down safely on the home field. I should have died that day! It was 8:05 a.m.

It was wet at Kerrobert, too, and I learned that there was to be a meeting about whether we would go through with the fair or not. I revealed that I had flown in from Calgary that morning, but didn't tell anyone about my difficulties. It was decided to go through with the fair. I got the display machinery down to the grounds on the muddy road, and the fair turned out not too badly. We brought our machinery back to the yard that evening, with dust flying.

So, I survived a very serious situation, and told nobody about it, until now...

Return To Calgary – Death Close

Eight days after seeing Dad off at Calgary, we received a telegram to say that he would arrive back at Calgary that afternoon or evening. It was plenty late enough to make it to Calgary that day, but I thought I could make it, stay overnight and fly home in the early morning. Mother threw together some sandwiches, I picked up a six-pack of Cokes on the way to the airport, hurriedly gassed EVO and took off.

It was not a bright day, but the air was smooth and I cruised at about 1,500 feet altitude. After awhile, perhaps near Drumheller, Alta., I dug out my lunch, opened a Coke and began to eat, just taking my time. Not long afterwards, my ears began to act up and this suggested altitude. I had maintained level-flight trim, but when I looked out, I was nearly a mile off the ground and rising rapidly, with the plane in level-flight altitude. I'd noticed some large clouds and realized I was in a severe thermal up-draft. I tried slowing the engine and putting the nose down, but just kept on rising like a feather.

Then I noticed I was getting near the black bottom of a large cloud which, deceptively, looked to be two or three miles across. I could still have done a '180' and got away from it, but I thought, 'What the heck – two or three minutes and I'll be across and into the clear on the other side.' This particular set-up is called a 'thunderhead' among flyers, and pure dynamite to tackle. EVO was just sucked up into that thing. The turbulence was so severe that I have never been able to understand why the plane didn't get its wings yanked off that day.

I knew I was in real trouble, and let out the throttle and hoped I pointed the plane downwards to lose altitude. At one point, the left door slammed me real hard, and the next instant, the right seat came up and slammed me from the other side. Visibility was zero. Cokes and lunch were flying around in the cabin. I was ever so thankful that right from my first lesson, I had decided that since seatbelts were mandatory in flying, I'd always wear mine, and snugly. Some smart alecs loosen the belt after takeoff or take it off in flight, but I just learned to fly all the time with a fairly tight belt, and I'm sure it was this habit that saved my life that day. Otherwise, I would have been tossed around in a helpless position and lost control of the plane. My feet stayed right on the rudder pedals.

Perhaps minutes later (everything had gone brown in heavy rain), I suddenly saw the ground, so close it wasn't funny, and I was heading right for it. I yanked back on the wheel, put on full throttle, and missed crashing by ever so little. From then on, it was a case of maintain contact with the ground without hitting it. This was really a desperate situation, my compass was swinging and useless – the main thing was to not hit the ground – the air was filled with water. I bounced along, missing hills, and eventually saw the Red Deer coulee, crossed it, reached the other side at the confluence of the Rosebud Creek – right on course between Kerrobert and Calgary. Following the Rosebud from the right bank, I eventually flew out of the rain into clear weather and continued on to Calgary. How lucky can one be?

I landed at Calgary OK, just as though the weather had been fine all day, and met my dad. We rented a bed downtown for the rest of the night and left for home early the next morning. The return to Kerrobert was in fine weather, disgustingly smooth, with the bright sun in our eyes. Dad slept most of the way home.

However, the scare of the day before and my appreciation of God's mercy kept me awake. All I told my dad was that I had come through a storm on the way to meet him, but not how serious the trouble was that I'd got myself into. The trip home was uneventful, actually monotonous. All things, then, turned out well after all. Dad had had two good trips to and from Calgary and I, conversely, came near to death on both trips from and to Calgary. I'm ever so thankful that he had the good trips.

Green Lake – Fishing

You were 11 years old, Dave, and on this particular Sunday, we decided to throw our fishing gear into the plane and fly up north for a bit of fishing. We hadn't planned anything special, the main thing was to 'get away' for awhile. About a hundred miles (161 km) north, I asked you, "Where are we going, David?" You didn't know and I didn't know, so we decided to land at Meadow Lake and play it from there.

Remember our fishing equipment of those days? The 3.3 Evinrude motor just fit crosswise behind the seat, weighing 29 pounds, an extra gallon of gas for the outboard, rods, and small tackle box. Those days it was hard to rent a motor but one could usually get a boat. We landed on the Clarks' field west of Meadow Lake and walked the mile or so uptown. At the Avenue Hotel, we caught the three people who were just getting ready to leave by car for Green Lake to do some fishing. We were invited to go along with them.

They drove us out to the plane, where we tied down EVO and put our fishing stuff into the trunk of their car. Away we went for Green Lake. I had never been there – it was about 40 miles of dusty road and the only way in was by car or seaplane. Our friends had set plans and habits about where to fish at Green Lake – there was a point of land sticking out from the east side of the lake where the fish just came to be caught – and that was the way to fish at Green.

Well, we preferred to fish by boat (we had the motor along, didn't we?), so we were let off near a shack and pier, and maybe we could get a boat. The man there said all his boats were out. I asked him about an old tub of a thing lying there, and he said he never rented that. When I asked if we could try it, he said OK, but it isn't much. He was right – it leaked like a straw hat but our motor made it move and we were happily in business, bailing out water most of the time. When we passed the point where our friends were, it was almost covered with people casting their lines and hooks (they must have had to take turns). We were glad to be on our own and not in that crowd.

We moved pretty slowly, lines out, and our score for the day was right – four pickerels for you and four jacks for me. You caught the first fish and all the best ones. Later, we returned to the pier, and walked to where our friends were at the peninsula. They were ready to leave, had caught nothing, and were a bit miffed that we had not done the best thing but caught eight fish.

Back at the hotel, we gave our fish to our hosts, booked in for the night, to rise early next morning and fly home in time for Monday morning work.

The big thrill for me on this trip was what you said, Dave, when we were relaxed in the room and retiring. You had taken off your shirt and were holding it by the neck when you turned to me and said, "Y' know, Dad, we didn't seem to catch very many fish, but we sure had a good time, didn't we?"

I was quite moved, put a hand on your shoulder and said, "David, in the three years we've been fishing, THAT is the lesson I've hoped you'd learn, and I'm really pleased to hear you say that!"

Next morning looked like a good day. We lugged our stuff out to the plane, too, were off about five o'clock and landed on the home field about 8:00 a.m. We were in reasonable time for work and had had a really good weekend.

Humourous Flights

There were many humourous incidents and jokes connected with my flying days. One winter when deep snow and many storms made many more demands on the little plane, I started up the little joke that the trip would cost $1.50 cheaper if I didn't have to stop and let the party out. Nobody wanted to jump out and land on a snowbank, so they all paid the buck-and-a-half.

During a few of those years, the matron of our hospital was Alice Osborne – nee Reynolds. We Williams kids and the Reynolds kids had been friends since early in our youth. Alice used to kid me that the worst patients they got were "the ones Walter flew in." But I did a lot of free ambulance service by truck or Travelall, mostly in summer time, and she'd kid me about those, too.

One day, in passing over a farm, I noted that the man had not built a roof on his outhouse. I didn't see anyone but apparently he was using it at the time, and he must have thought I HAD seen him. Next day, he parked his truck in front of our shop and came in.

I noted that there was lumber sticking out the back of his truck and asked him what he was building. He said, "Doggone it, Walt, privacy is a hard thing to come by anymore with you flyin' around. I'm finally gonna put a roof on the toilet."

A CPR train (mixed) made three round trips a week from Wilkie to Kerrobert, on which there was a village called Tramping Lake. A man from that community had taken that train to Kerrobert one day and nearly a week later he had still not returned home. His wife had expected him back the same day because two to three hours in Kerrobert should have been ample time for any business he had mentioned. So she took the train to Kerrobert to find him and bring him home.

He had been having a pretty good time in the pub and 'around.' A friend of his saw the wife get off the train. He promptly found the fellow in the pub and warned him. The friend and husband quickly left the place via the rear exit and came over to our shop. I told him I couldn't get away right then and that he could return by train, but he wanted to 'meet the wife' when she got off the train at the hometown.

We didn't take off until after the train had left Kerrobert and, in passing the train so nobody would see the plane and remark on it, I flew up the track, raised up enough to fly right over the train, and landed in Tramping Lake in time for him to sweetly greet the wife with a, "Hello, sweetheart, what kept you?" or something like that.

What other troubles developed after that, like a one-way ticket to Hades, was, I thought, strictly their business – not mine.

This was in the days of the old steam engines and I recall inhaling a few stiff whiffs of smoke and steam as we passed over that winter day.

It was summertime and there had been a lot of rains recently, which made the dirt roads still in use on many areas quite muddy. A Tramping Lake man, perhaps the same one who met his wife at the train, explained in the early afternoon that if I could get him to Cochin Beach or even North Battleford right away, he could win bets totalling 96 bottles of beer by being at Cochin Beach in time for dinner.

Roads were so muddy, everybody else thought he couldn't make it. Well, I flew him to the airport at North Battleford and he collected his 96 bottles of beer and had a joke to tell.

So many times, I'd land at the home strip in the dark on my last trip. Numerous people asked me, "How do you know where the ground is?"

I usually told them that "I dragged one foot."

Louis Borschneck was a very sick man in our hospital, a friend of mine. The roads were blocked and a daughter had come as far as North Battleford and wanted to get to see him as soon as possible. It was late in the day when I was asked to go for her, and by the time I landed at the airport there, it was dark.

She was a very cheerful person and readily entered the airplane and we took off. During the flight home, she happened to ask if there was any risk making the flight in the dark. I told her that as long as we didn't 'run out of air,' we didn't have a worry in the world. When I was groping for the ground, making our landing, I jokingly asked her if she'd drag one foot to let me know when the ground was getting close. She took everything well and she and the family were happy that she could see her dad that night. Louis pulled through and was forever grateful.

John Stark was our town cop at one time, a man of occasional but uncertain courage. It took a year or two to talk him into taking a flip in the plane, but the day finally came – a fine winter morning and we were on skis. Soon after our miraculous – to him – takeoff, and when he finally realized we were up in the air, he asked the question so many other people had asked: "What happens if the engine quits?"

I said, "I'll show you," and pulled the throttle right back. Well, poor John. He nearly lost his pants, but swallowed his heart and lived.

I did a steep side-slip on a snow-covered field of Ken Snow's dead ahead and greased 'er on real smooth. Then I opened the throttle again and took right off. I was afraid that if I stopped, he would jump out and walk home. He was scared stiff, but I gave him a nice ride after that and he cooled out a bit. Afterwards, he bought me a cup of coffee at the café and was the bravest man in town. His English was such that he left the 'h' out of the word 'thrill' and kept repeating that his flight has been a "real t'rill."

In those earlier days, roads were narrow and cut-banks through the hills sloped back, and even the best plows we had sometimes took days to open a road. Our government plowman was Joe Suder, and we housed his machine in our shop. Joe's home was near Springwater and he wanted to see his family one weekend. The roads were all open. While he was home there was a storm, the roads filled in and there was Joe, 35 miles (56 km) off base. He called and I flew him in along the road so he could look it over. Mel Morris was his helper then and Mel, just getting up, thought he heard something and looked out the unshaded upstairs window. We got a good glimpse of Mel with his pants at half-mast, and we were so close he thought we were coming right in. He sure came in for some kidding and Joe said, "Mel wasn't ready for work the first time I dropped by."

Precision Drilling – Provost – Czar

One winter, it must have been 1952 in February, I got a call from Ted Oveson of Precision Drilling (who used what they termed 'leaning rigs'), asking me to fly to Provost, Alta., to pick up some drilling rig parts that were on the way by car from Edmonton. Road conditions prevented further progress by car, so would I pick up the parts and fly them to the rig in the Coleville area? I said OK, and though it was late in the short winter day, thought I could make it to Provost and back to Kerrobert. The next morning, I would deliver the parts to the drilling rig.

At Provost, I got word that the car with the parts couldn't get any further than Czar, Alta. I hadn't gassed up for this added mileage but took off for Czar. There, nobody was waiting and I had to walk into town. I found the guy with the parts in the bar. I was boiling mad, for EVO was short of gas and it was getting dark.

I didn't let this individual finish his drink and made him drive the parts out to the plane, in a difficult field. I loaded the parts, about 250 pounds, and headed for home. It was just about dark so I followed roads and highways. It was a moonless night and by the time I reached Luseland, it was snowing as well. Dark, snowing and short of gas – there really are more healthy combinations. It took every trick in the book and luck to succeed. However, I continued, just missing power and telephone lines, to keep in contact with the railway – hard to keep track of under the circumstances – but I finally made Kerrobert. There, I found the ground and ran out of gas just as I landed. Had to walk to the hangar to get gas to taxi in. That night I 'swore off' hairy trips like this one, but it was only one week before the flight when Kasper Herle and I wrecked and were injured.

Next morning, I fired up EVO to deliver the parts to the drilling rig. It was a nice winter morning and in circling to see how close to the rig I could land, I passed over a place where a couple of fellows, Mike Gerlinsky was one of them, were working. I had a rare experience. These fellows were preparing the location for the next drilling operation and they were blasting out a 'mud pit' with dynamite. I felt a big jerk-lift on the wings of the plane, banked the plane to look down and saw big chunks of dirt coming up towards me, then losing their blast-lift, falling back to earth. Some of those chunks came pretty close, so I was glad I wasn't flying lower or I could have been hit by one of them.

Finally, I landed near the drill rig and delivered the parts I had on board. When I next saw Ted Oveson, I told him of my extra difficulties, including the dynamite blast, and he sure paid extra for that trip!

John Herron Flew To Saskatoon

John Herron had been such a dedicated and willing helper that one day when I had a flight to make to Saskatoon on business, I asked if he could manage to go along and it turned out he could. I then asked how he would like to do the flying, and there was only one answer to that one! So, John sat in the left seat and I sat in the off-seat, with both control columns in, of course.

John made the takeoff and away we went. He did all the flying, with teasing and encouragement from me, until we neared Saskatoon. Then I told him that landing was the more difficult part and really, I should be on his side of the plane when we landed at a government airport.

Now, these small planes are pretty tight and with two wheel control columns, tighter still. But we managed to trade places without missing a beat or landing in some small field to affect the change. We did it in flight, and I landed at Saskatoon Airport as though I had been the pilot all the way.

We both got a kick out of that one and I'm sure John won't ever forget the change-over, nor will I. I felt good because John really enjoyed the adventure.

Wedding Cake Takes A Trip

It was that time of the year in late fall when nobody would be surprised if the first snow arrived. Well, it did one cold windy night and EVO was still wearing wheels. There really wasn't enough snow to change to skis, but the high wind accompanying the relatively light snowfall had plugged many weed-lined roads.

A couple of young fellows called at the office the next morning. There was to be a wedding that day at Broadacres, but the wedding cake was north of Major at a certain farm where a really nice elder lady had a reputation for making wedding and Christmas cakes, and she was turning out excellent products. Roads were blocked 'out there,' and could I fly out and get the cake?

I said sure, explaining that I would have to rattle the plane a bit to land on a comparatively rough and frozen summerfallow field, but I'd get the cake alright. Off I went, found the farm and landed on a rough summerfallow field which led right up to the farmyard. I stopped in the yard, only a few yards (metres) from the house.

Before the lady covered the cake for travel, I had to go into the house and admire the cake, which really was a beautiful piece of work. They asked, "Would the cake survive the flight?" I assured these nice people that even a newborn babe wouldn't get hurt in my plane, and urged the lady and husband to not worry on that score. So – she lovingly covered the cake and I carried it out to the plane as solemnly as though it were their dead son or daughter. They came out and I even put the safety belt around it, and again urged them not to worry.

Well, I had to rattle down the rough summerfallow, turn around against the easterly wind and take off right past the farmyard. The elderly couple were standing there, the husband's arm around the lady's shoulders, and I recall thinking that there was a special pride in their breast, to think that an airplane was delivering this cake! What a day – and event – in their lonely winter life.

I don't know what made me do it, but I made a circle around, to gain some altitude, and then did a loop! Of course, the beautiful cake just sat on the passenger seat and suffered no damage. But, (and these people knew me only from reputation), the next spring the old gent was in to see me and said it took 20 minutes or so to get his wife's heart started again, and she really hadn't been the same since then. I was ashamed of that one.

The cake survived the antic and the boys picked it up. It was fit for its original intention and everybody lived happily ever after – except the nice old lady who made the cake…

Picked Up Marion

Marion, my sister, would come from her nursing work in California each year for her holiday visit with her family. Most times I would fly her home from Calgary with little old EVO, but she didn't seem to mind because the 220-mile flight was made with her 'brother' – no matter how small the plane. Most of these flights were just routine, no sweat, but one time I had special adventures which added to the flavour of the trip.

This time a fellow wanted to be flown to Sylvan Lake, Alta., and then I would go on to Calgary to pick up Marion. We started off early from Kerrobert in dull weather, and soon encountered conditions of fog, which were a real worry. On this length of flight I decided to 'fly high,' and soon found myself flying 'between layers' of fog. Eventually, I got down near the ground and wanted to follow the 'iron compass' – the railway. However, this proved to be so twisty and I nearly hit a coal tipple so I elected altitude, which was hazardous at best. We would pass through layers of fog, flying strictly on compass and I was blessed with a passenger who just clasped his hands around one knee and took whatever was happening as matter-of-fact. This was appreciated by me, but didn't lessen my concern for our situation of the moment.

Suddenly, we burst out of the fog area into a clear sky – but where were we? I saw a railway and turned left to follow it, in the hope of finding a town we could recognize, for reference. Well, the first town turned out to be Elnora, Alta., and there was my sister Kay and her husband Bob Cameron waving a towel from where they were both standing in the garden. It was a Sunday. From there, I had only to fly straight west to Sylvan Lake, where I unloaded my passenger as close to the village as I could manage. Then I took off for Calgary to meet Marion.

The fog condition was the penalty for the early flight but the Sylvan Lake passenger was 'paying the freight' because I could never charge my sister Marion for picking her up. I guess this is the difference between business and pleasure.

I picked Marion up at Calgary, and we flew the 220 miles home safely enough, although it was a dull day, fraught with doubts as to what was ahead. But we landed OK and everything turned out well. However, I sure had lots to worry about on the trip as far as Sylvan Lake.

Another time, when our Father was on his deathbed, Marion, who had made a visit home a short time before and had returned to Los Angeles, was phoned to say that Dad was in real trouble after his kidney operation. Marion immediately found out that her quickest flight home would land her at Medicine Hat in the early morning. I said I'd take off at dawn and would pick her up there. We met soon after her arrival and she nursed Dad to his death.

Regina – Barely Cleared Runway

It must have been 1956, when you were at the Boy Scout Jamboree at Niagara-On-The-Lake, Ontario, Dave (the same year Romona went to Korea). Assembly for the Saskatchewan Scouts was at Regina. At that time, a friend or relation of my mother's was visiting at our home, Ursula Rae. Ursula was a widely-travelled lady, not young, who had a charming way and a quite cultured English accent. She must have been bitten with the travel bug, with intent to work here or there for awhile, save money for travel and then blow it on travel to some other part of the world. This was a kind of career I could not understand but it was her way of life.

She thought she had visited long enough with us and was ready to go to Saskatoon and get employment. I told her I would fly her to Saskatoon – on Sunday – the same day you Scouts were assembling in Regina.

For added adventure, Ursula and I flew to Regina first and then on to Saskatoon. At Regina, we got a taxi to take us out to where you guys were assembling – the fairgrounds, I think, and we had a short visit with you there. Back out to the airport by taxi, we prepared for takeoff and I didn't want to take any chances with Ursula along, so went to the extreme west end of the east-west runway and started our takeoff run, straight for the City of Regina.

Well, atmospheric pressure must have been really low that day (I hadn't checked), and we full-throttled down the runway until we were too close to the east end of the runway to do anything but lift off. So I pulled back on the control and EVO was very lazy on the lift. We barely cleared the end of the runway and soon were dodging to miss tall buildings and high chimneys. Thank goodness TV hadn't come to us yet or I would have had antennas to dodge, too. After a bit, I gained a few feet of altitude – enough to clear anything on the ground, and eventually we got into better conditions and acquired reasonable altitude.

It was just like that takeoff from Banff with you and your cousin Alan – fingers and toes all crossed. I should have guessed there would be 'bad' areas when we approached Regina at 7,000 feet (2,100 metres), and something banged on the windshield and the smear suggested a big grasshopper. Now, grasshoppers don't roam around at 7,000-feet altitude, and when a grasshopper hit our windshield then, it should have indicated a severe up-draft.

All the air in the country doesn't up-draft at the same time and to accommodate the up-draft, there must have been a compensating down-draft, and I think we took off in the down-draft area. Afterwards, when we were at a decent altitude at cruising speed, I told Ursula that unintentionally she had had a high view of Regina before landing and a very low look after takeoff. I actually saw gum papers in the streets and wondered if Ursula's future would be terminated then.

Passing Last Mountain Lake, I told her of the time I swam across it years before and how the park authorities wouldn't allow it unless a rowboat went along. Dutch Shields rowed a borrowed boat across to accompany me, and I rowed the boat back. There was no limit to my stamina then, Dave, but there is now!

At Saskatoon Airport, I had many friends and good connections, so we caught or bought a ride downtown. The new City Hall (1956) was a place I showed Ursula, and we took a few slide pictures. Now (in 1978), they're saying that the building has been outgrown with offices in the corridors. Imagine – in 22 years, the facilities are obsolete!

Anyway, allowing myself time to fly home, I left Ursula at lodgings she had arranged for and took off for home. The two big thrills for the day for me were seeing you at the camp in Regina and that dangerous takeoff from Regina.

Dan Boice's Party

Dan Boice came to Kerrobert about the time I was born. His work was digging the ditch from a water main to whatever house was putting in water at the time, and he surely dug a lot of ditches as the town grew. His work was so meticulous that the sides and bottom of the ditch were almost as smooth and square as the walls and floor of a room in a house. He would 'shave' the surfaces smooth with the shovel. Dan had a high sense of propriety and integrity beyond question. His English never reached fluency and on the social register his status was not high, but when someone wanted a good job done, it was 'get Dan.' Dan was also illiterate.

Forty-five years later, when it was time to prepare a pension application, one of our lawyers 'Dutch' Shields, took the matter in hand and it took all of Dutch's wit to get a birth certificate from Vienna for Dan. Dan could help him very little. Pension was finally established and I think Dutch did it all for nothing.

One nice winter Sunday morning, a few of us were at the café and talk turned to the matter of worthy old Dan. Somebody suggested a party for him at the café for that afternoon – a birthday party and to celebrate his pension. Dan had his own little house, with everything (whatever he had) 'just so.' I said, "OK, some of you guys clean him up and dress him in his best (I think the suit came over from Vienna with him) and I will give him a nice ride in the plane just before the party at the café." Jim Lasky, another European (of Jim's Café), laid out a long table. The price was a buck and a half or two, and there must have been 75 or 80 of us there to honour Dan. This whole affair was just a spur-of-the-moment thing.

Dan liked his plane ride, which was quite smooth, and I gave him a full course of information for the 20-minute flip.

At the café, when Dan and I came in, he was accorded a welcome like a standing ovation – hand-clapping and all. He was escorted to the head of the long table, and Dutch Shields sat beside him to act as chairman. There was no liquor at this type of affair in those days – just tea, coffee or water – take it or leave it. Oh, Roy Greer was our mayor at that time and he sat at the other end of the table.

Dutch made a little speech and then we ate. Following that, THERE WERE MANY SPEECHES, and stories about all the years Dan had spent in Kerrobert. Dan would keep wanting to get up to thank us but Dutch kept saying, "Not yet, Dan – you'll get your turn." Well, poor Dan, as stories and time passed, emotion built up so much in his old heart that when it was his 'turn,' he started off but soon broke down with apologies. We all were quite moved that we had affected him so deeply, and we were humbled.

Dan was getting slower and more shaky, and instead of going to a home or on welfare, he took up an offer from Joe Wolfe, who promised to look after him for the rest of his life, but when Dan died, Dan's house would belong to Joe Wolfe. Finally, Dan could not look after himself, and the town had to find a home for him. Kerrobert didn't have a senior citizens' home at that time. Dan was becoming irrational by this time and there was little happiness for either Dan or the people in whatever home he was in. The time came when Dan made his last move. It was the institution at Unity in mid-winter, and it helped him to be co-operative when he was told, "Walter will fly you there."

The flight itself was routine enough and I landed in a little field adjacent to the home. Dan was pretty doddery and I had no wish to wade through the snow, carrying him in my arms. (This would hurt his dignity, too.) I saw a place where I could taxi onto the road to the back door, so that's where we ended up – right at the back door, with the right wing tip about 12 inches (30 cm) from the building. I told Dan what special treatment this was, and it was the last time I saw Dan alive.

Not long after, one night about 10 o'clock, Joe Wolfe, a German with very broken English, came in the shop door and announced "Dandy Boy has died – you gotta be one of de ball-bearings." I said I was sorry, and that I would be honoured to act as a ball-bearing, and thanked him.

Well, I guess Joe slipped a little because in his zeal in obtaining what he regarded as 'the best' for Dan, all six of us were past Masters in the Masonic Lodge, and I'll bet it was the first time our Catholic Church had six Masons for 'ball-bearings.' We didn't know all their kneelings and bowings and hand-clappings, so just sat like statues in the second row, waiting for the service to come to an end. A thing which outraged me was that Dan's body, since he had not given a lot to the Catholic Church, was barely inside the front door, instead of up front, where we put the casket in our funeral services.

What a time, but we all had a lot of respect for poor old Dan Boice…

Jack McNeill – North Battleford

One winter Sunday, lonesome to see you, Dave, I decided to fly to Meadow Lake, have a short visit and give you a ride and fly back home again. Jack McNeill, our postmaster at that time, had once said that sometime if I were going that way, he would go along and visit his father, Dr. McNeill of North Battleford. So I gave Jack a call and he said yes, he would go along.

I didn't check with the weather office at North Battleford and although it seemed to be a really nice day at home, once we gained some altitude we could see what looked like foggy conditions ahead. We did run into fog and I went 'under,' found the old #29 highway and followed that, flying low, until we passed the 400-foot-high (120 m) ridge of hills south of Battleford. Descending a bit, we found a 200 to 300-foot ceiling and slipped onto the North Battleford airport in fine shape. Jack was havin' a good time!

I let Jack off and agreed to pick him up on my way back. Weather people told me I could make Meadow Lake OK but there would be winds which would not speed my trip. Finally made Meadow Lake and you, and we flew and fooled around awhile. Wasn't there an east wind that day? I recall side-slipping to miss a big bluff of trees, squash into the deep snow and hoped to get stopped before hittin' the fence in the Clarks' field. I gave someone else a ride that day – was it Herb Wiese?

At any rate, I finally left for home, flying sideways because of winds aloft. Got to North Battleford about dark. By the time I had gassed up, Jack and I were leaving in the dark. I was not happy that we were so late since conditions could change in 70 miles, but Jack seemed quite cheerful about it and it was an old story for me. So, when we had followed our course in the dark (and it really was dark that night), we finally arrived at Kerrobert.

Our landing, according to the wind direction at that time, put us on the southeast approach, with the lights of Kerrobert to our right. In a case like this, I used to use the CPR fence for reference, which was on Jack's side of the plane. But the lights of Kerrobert were a negative effect, it being so dark. I suggested that Jack should advise me immediately if he saw the fence. He assured me that if he saw anything he would let me know. I didn't know until years afterwards that he had night blindness and couldn't see a thing under the circumstances. We did bounce a couple of times, but finally came to a stop. Then, with Kerrobert lights distracting, we found the hangar, and put EVO to bed for the night.

Well, that was OK for Jack and I, and we were happy that all ends well that goes well. But, in the meantime Jack's wife had phoned the people at North Battleford, learned that he had gone to the airport. They phoned the airport to find that we had left in the darkness for home. By the time Jack and I cheerfully parted at his house, he went inside to face a very uncheerful prospect. Apparently it was tearful, not cheerful, and spoiled his whole day. He told me later that his wife, who nursed at the hospital, sure gave him a lot of hell for flying with that character with the airplane.

As a sideline, she reported for the *Saskatoon Star-Phoenix*, and was very disappointed when Kasper Herle and I had our accident and injury and I told her she would report the incident at the peril of lawsuit on my part, for I forbade publicity of any kind. She was pretty miffed about that and likely took it out on Jack when we got home in the dark. She had to call North Battleford afterwards, and they yakked half the night, Jack said.

Hughenden – Chicken Dinner

One Sunday of a late fall, you and I, Dave, called Jack Fairbairn, who came to us from Birch Hills (same place as Harold Patterson came from). Jack had been a mechanic in our shop, then spent a year on parts with Karl Krips, and back to our shop at Kerrobert. One September (busiest time of the year), he said he was going to farm in the Hughenden district in Alberta. There was no rancour or bitterness – Jack was a decent fellow, trying to get his feet on the ground, but I did wish he had chosen a different time of the year to leave us.

We decided to fly up to see his family that day. It was pretty dull weather and when we landed, I told Jack it would likely be snowing in a short time. We went to the house, where we visited and had a chicken dinner. By then it was snowing alright, and a lot heavier than I would have liked – you know, that large-flake kind and the flakes were elbow-to-elbow, making for very difficult visibility.

We had landed near the buildings but the field was not too large, in a primarily bushy and hilly country. So Jack told us that a field 'over there' was a lot bigger. I flew over alone, with a lot of apprehension about the visibility, and landed. You boys came over and you climbed in, Dave. Away we went, and soon found the railway, which would be our 'iron compass,' all the way home, if necessary.

By the time we passed Provost, Alta., the snow was really thick, we were flying lower and lower, and I was memorizing the more suitable fields for use if needed. We went on towards Hayter and conditions kept getting worse. Had I been alone, I may have taken more chances, but in weighing the responsibility of my son's neck, I suddenly saw a good mark for reference in a quick '180 degree turn,' and we were headed back to Provost. About a mile just east of town, I had seen a decent-sized stubble field bordering the CPR track. When we came to Provost, I made a fairly wide 270-degree turn to the left to line up with that field and there wasn't much of a let-down as we were too low for that. Missed the south fence, shut 'er down, and we were 'on' immediately. Then we had to get stopped before hitting the snow fence, as we were on wheels. The falling snow was dry and fluffy, with no drifting, so we just rolled and rolled. Braking had the effect of making the straight-rib tires slide like skis, but we finally did get stopped, just short of a snow fence along the railway.

We got out, I on my side and you on yours, Dave, and I vividly remember you stamping your young feet on the ground and saying, "Boy, Dad, it sure feels good to have your feet on something SOLID!" So, I guess you were worried, too, and it finally came out.

Safe now, we took our time about screwing in the tie-down pegs and tying EVO down, then walked into downtown Provost (which was no sweat), and went to the hotel. Started to phone Kerrobert for someone to come out and drive us home. Finally, it was Ed Bomersine with the old DS-30 and as we waited at the hotel, it seemed to take forever for him to arrive. Meantime, we read all the free literature for waiting persons. But Ed did get there, and drove us home.

The following Tuesday, weather being fine and my affairs juggled to accommodate my absence, Bert Hill drove me to Provost, where we pulled out the tie-down, and I beat him home. But he must have made pretty good time because by the time I had put EVO away in the hangar, I didn't have long to wait for Bert to drive me to the shop.

I'm glad that we, or I, chickened out on that flight, because the railway winds and twists so much in the Primate area we might not have made it, daylight and all. I guess I did the right thing for once, and didn't hurt my son.

Mother – Red Deer – Thanksgiving

One year at Thanksgiving time after Dad's passing, Mother and I decided to fly to Red Deer to help the Camerons eat a dead turkey they were having for Thanksgiving dinner. Flying to Red Deer from the east, one sees Red Deer only when you're almost there, because of the height of the land. At that time, the Cameron home was on the east boundary of Red Deer and Kay's husband Bob, sitting on the chesterfield facing the big front room east window, saw us approach. The Camerons all got into the car and watched us land in a field east of Red Deer, a little pasture.

They picked us up and took us to the house, where we had a very nice visit and turkey dinner. All was going well except that mother started worrying about getting back to Kerrobert. I had it all figured out re: timing, but she had to worry anyway.

When finally it was the time I decided, we drove out to the field and were ready to leave for home. Any pilot looks his plane over, and I discovered that the Maule tail-wheel tire was flat. Well, this threw my mother into a dither and she thought we were stuck with a flat tire. We were in a pasture and I assured her that all we had to do was take off as usual, and fly home. She worried just the same, but I assured her that it would not affect our takeoff or landing, and I'd repair it tomorrow at Kerrobert.

The weather had dulled, and a south wind had developed so that when I finally got my twilight bearings, I was near Luseland, a bit off course. But we managed Kerrobert before it was too dark, and I made my southward descent. Mother asked if she could hold a strut in the cabin, just to make her feel better. We made a dandy landing, stopping right in front of the hangar. Thus ended a very successful flight to Red Deer and back, and Mother admitted that this had been an adventurous day for us both.

Dr. Palmer – Unity

I attended a hockey game between Kindersley and Kerrobert, and my guest was Ken Barkley, salesman for International Motor Trucks. He had previously been in the Mounties. During the game, a couple of Kindersley fellows were sipping something from soft drink bottles, becoming more obstreperous as time dragged on. Since we were 'Kerrobert' fans (sitting directly behind these fellows) and I was not accepting their insults so easily, I became the target obsession of the meanest of the two.

There was great rivalry between the teams and fans of the neighbouring towns of Kindersley and Kerrobert, and by the time the third period was over, this one guy 'Bill' had it in for me and I wouldn't back down. Bill's friend tried to restrain him and Ken tried to calm me down.

Well, Bill was drunk and I was sober and, being a businessman of middle age, I asked myself how I should react under these circumstances. I pushed him off several times when he tried to obstruct my progress out of the rink, but I managed to get outside the building. Ken and I were still between the parked cars when this Bill tried, forcibly, to bring things to a crisis. I pushed him off and got out into the street with Ken when Bill loudly called me the one name that will start a fight anytime.

By that time I'd really 'had it,' so I went back, grabbed him by the front of his overcoat and started banging his head on a car. By then, I was ashamed of myself but wouldn't let go. I lost my hat and glasses but remained upright and since I'd knocked the starch out of him, I let go, found my hat and glasses and Bill's friend took him away.

Ken and I went to a café for a coffee, and by then I knew that I had a pain in my neck and shoulders from dragging three guys who had their arms around my neck. Next morning, I was really hurting from a spinal dislocation, so I phoned a Dr. Palmer at Unity, a chiropractor, for an adjustment. It was nearly noon and I wanted a one o'clock appointment. I told him I was at Kerrobert and Dr. Palmer said, "Y' can't make it!" I said, "Yes I can – you be there and I'll be there."

I flew up in EVO, and he was there on time and so was I. When we met at his office door, he asked if I'd been fooling. I had him look south past the CNR station where he could see EVO parked in the snow, and I told him that's the way I travel. In his office, he very efficiently eased my spinal distress and I guess it was a 'first' for both of us.

In 1976, Romona and I moved to our present home on Ferguson Avenue, Saskatoon, and we are neighbours of Dr. Palmer's son and family – he is in income tax and his wife is a supervising nurse at University Hospital, and they have a near-lady daughter. We regard them very highly.

One other thing happened the night of the hockey – somebody backed a truck into the back of Earl Haycraft's car and really rumpled up his trunk lid. I came in for some kidding for doing that bending with Bill's head, but it was not Earl's car I had used for Bill's head. However, it made a good story.

That incident made me realize the folly of being a hockey 'nut,' and I haven't seen very much hockey since that date. These games keep occurring, though, and a couple of years later while Harold Patterson and I were having our going-to-bed coffee at the café, the after-game crowd came in. I saw someone point me out and heard him say, "He'll fix you up."

You wouldn't guess it, but it was the Bill I'd had trouble with. His Buick was leaking motor oil like crazy and there was no way he would make it home. So, Harold and I let him into our shop, found the trouble and went all-out to put him safely on the road.

At one time, I was the only one at his car and Bill came over, sober this time, and said he guessed he owed me an apology for the incident at the rink. I told him that all reports I'd heard about him were that he was a really swell fellow until he drank, and then he became a real so-and-so. He admitted that it was a fact and wondered if we couldn't act as friends from here on in. I said sure, we could be friends but if he ever tried that drunk act on me again, I'd work him over real good and it MIGHT be his last time. I've never seen him again. We got his car on the road and I hope he's still going strong.

Lac La Ronge – Dave And I

It was 1956 or 1957, Dave, when you and I decided to fly to Lac La Ronge, just for a weekend trip. To stay one night and fly back home again the next day was our intention. It was nice summer weather and we got to Lac La Ronge in good time, after gassing up at Prince Albert. The La Ronge airport had been improved since the trip I made with Tom.

We parked off to the side and tied down our little plane beside those belonging to millionaires and made our way three miles, into the settlement. We had the slide camera along and took a number of pictures, which I still have, as a record of our trip. For staying overnight, it was October, I think, we took a very bare room in the Lac La Ronge Hotel, with a bare bulb hanging from a cord, price $8 for the night, and someone's friendly young dog stayed in the room overnight with us.

Remember their picture show, pretty old, we saw at their 'theatre' with hard wooden benches for us to sit upon? On our walk back to the hotel afterwards, we heard Indians talking in the bush alongside the road we were walking on, who, from your Meadow Lake experience in your younger years, you identified as Cree, I think.

Having rested overnight, we rose early, and there was frost on the wharf where we took your picture. We walked everywhere – to the small fish plant on a small peninsula, where there was the whitest Indian I ever saw. I remember saying to you that that guy must have T.B. When we walked east where the road made a loop and turned back, we went into the 'powerhouse.' I remember remarking as we approached that the exhaust sound indicated something unusual. We found that the power for the community was furnished by a five-cylinder Vivian diesel engine, manufactured in Vancouver. We studied that engine pretty thoroughly. Did you ever see another 5-cylinder Vivian? I never did.

We wandered around quite a bit. We took a picture of two young Indian girls who came along just as we were looking over an ancient Anglican church built on native grey rock. Another time, walking back from the lake to the only road through Lac La Ronge, we detoured around a team of Husky dogs that were tied to a tree. They looked pretty fierce and we didn't fool around with them.

When it was time that we thought we could still make home that night, we went to the airport, gassed up and took off for home via Prince Albert. When we gassed at P.A., we met two really nice girls who worked for the Royal Bank in P.A. They were sisters and owned a small plane between them. They were both pilots, and I took their picture with you, all standing beside EVO. You, perhaps having not fully developed your appreciation of the opposite sex, stood looking away from them quite casually. I get quite a kick out of that picture. I also recall that one was shorter than the other, the most talkative had 90 hours of flying time, and she was my unlicensed choice of the two.

We took off again, circled for Kerrobert, and in passing nearby took a very good picture of the P.A. Penitentiary. Soon after that, I discovered that we couldn't find the map for an accurate course for home. I remember giving you a pretty bad time over that, which I now admit I shouldn't have. I found it later in the belly of the plane, and it could have been anyone's fault or an accident that we couldn't find it.

However, we did make it home just after the sun had set. We had two shots left in the camera, and I took a lovely sunset shot through the windshield between Biggar and Kerrobert, and the last one after we'd landed at Kerrobert, with you standing beside the plane. In that one, one could barely make you out in silhouette, standing beside the plane.

This is one of my favourite theme sets of films and I recall the whole experience with pleasure. I hope you do, too.

It was on this trip that we bought a bracelet for Romona, then in Korea, made up of all the coats of arms of all the Canadian provinces. She still has it, and it is very dear to her. Guess we scored that time, eh?

Jim Fisk – Gull Lake

For some reason, (I think it must have been 1956, when you were at the Jamboree), I had to fly the plane to Swift Current. You were not around, so at five in the morning I tapped on Jim Fisk's window, wakened him and asked if he would like to fly to Swift Current with his parents' consent. He was cleared and willing and in a few minutes we were on our way to the airport.

The flight to Swift Current was routine and uneventful, and we landed at Al Smith's little field OK – distance 130 air miles (209 km). When we pulled up to the hangar, I noticed that a panel truck was parked out of the way. Well, there weren't too many around at that time, and I noticed an atmosphere of no levity or smiles, as was usual, and sensed gloom.

The reason became clear when Al Smith told me that of all the pilots he had turned out of his flying school, one had finally died at Gull Lake – killing a friend who was with him. (Reminded me of Kasper Herle and I). Al said that this fellow had a very bad habit of turning downwind at low flying speed and he (Smith) had done everything he could to break this man of his dangerous practice, with no apparent success. This was his first student to die due to pilot error, and Al Smith was very depressed.

South of Gull Lake was a little level patch of prairie grass, which airplanes used as a landing field. The fellow and his friend had overshot it and had pulled up with the Luscombe plane they were flying. Sure enough, at near stalling speed, they turned downwind to make a quick return for another landing attempt, absolutely premature. The result was a complete stall at minimum altitude, and the boys piled 'er in, headfirst. They both were killed, here and NOW.

When my business was finished at Smith's, I asked Al if he thought I could go via Gull Lake and see the wreck. It wouldn't add very many miles to my return to Kerrobert. Al said it might not do us much good since a Mountie was on guard there until officials could clear the investigation.

We took our chances and landed on the 'field.' We approached the officer, I introduced Jim as Cpl. Fisk's son and gave my identification. We were allowed to view at close hand the wreck and all that pertained. The engine had piled right back into the cockpit, killing both men. They had to jack the plane apart to get the bodies out.

We flew home after that, in the late afternoon, and had a lot to talk about regarding fellows who will not learn cardinal rules of flying safely. It was quite a day for Jim and for me, too.

Dick Pittaway – Flew Close By

I met Dick and Jean Pittaway at the airport, and their daughter Wendy was just a baby then. We used to hobnob and our friendship strengthened. Dick had been a Second World War flyer, the same as Harold Mitchinson, and a good friendship grew between them, too. This was not too long after the war and Dick was looking for a good plane to set his feet down.

Previously, Dick had joined the R.A.F. in England, been an instructor in Oxfords, Ansons and Wellingtons. Later he flew Mitchell bombers. War over, he went to Normal School and taught for a short time in Canada. Meeting Jean, whose home was a farm near Sylvania, Sask., was one of the best things that ever happened to Dick, and they were married.

He was doing some work for Mitchinson's Flying Service, but eventually obtained a position with International Harvester Company and he and family moved to North Battleford, where Dick's work was at that time. Meantime, I acquired EVO and was at the North Battleford airport many times, either going to or coming from Meadow Lake.

Dick had an uncanny faculty of knowing just about every kind of plane, just by sound. EVO had no muffler, but had two exhaust stacks, emerging from the lower part of the cowling, one left and one right. Timing of the engine made two cylinders exhaust out of one stack, and the next two from the other stack. Dick could easily pick out EVO from all other kinds without looking. He'd say, "I heard you coming, Walter," and I knew he hadn't been out of the house or hangar.

Dick was hit really hard with polio one year and was almost totally paralyzed. He could barely breathe, which kept him out of the artificial lung. If it were not for Jean's heroic care and devoted attention, Dick would never have made it. Early in Dick's illness, he had in some way fallen from a hospital bed onto the floor. Sharp little Jean, sensing something drastic had happened, kept at the hospital people until she learned of the fall. She became a tigress and said she'd have Dick removed from that hospital. They said she didn't have any place to take him. She said, "I'll take him home!" They said there would be nobody to look after him. She said, "I'll look after him!"

Jean had Dick taken to their home and she must have felt quite desperate. Their doctor came to the house and told Jean that their case would be Number One on his list, no matter what or when. Therapists came and courageous Jean was accorded royal consideration and assistance. I learned of Dick's illness and called at the house. Jean told me never to go to or through North Battleford without calling in to see about Dick. This I did, early or late, and I don't know how or when Jean rested, so devoted was her care for her man.

Sometimes I'd make flights to North Battleford in EVO just to see Dick. He heard me every time and would tell Jean, "Walter's coming." I would take something to read and we'd have a visit, and it was time to fly home again. Soon after he had recovered enough to talk, he asked me if I thought there might be a chance that he could fly again. I hardly knew how to reply, but said we'd have to trust in God's mercy and Jean's devoted care, and said that I didn't know of anyone who possessed more determination than he did himself – let's trust – and hope.

It's got to be a funny thing about flyers – for that's the first question I asked Doc James when I was injured in the plane crash. One day recently I sold parts to a man named Fox, six miles west of Landis, who has a landing strip on his farm. He recognized me and said I had once landed my plane on his strip. Fox had a Massey combine, a certain model that had a big flat belt that mangled many a man, including one of the Kissick boys. Well, the belt on Fox's combine tore his right hand clear off. When he saw the handless arm, his first thought was, "There goes my flying days!" But now he wears a hook, still flies the old Piper Cub as well as a Cessna 170. Flyers have just got to be a funny breed.

Dick's recovery was slow, but the determined spirit of Jean and Dick could never be surpassed. They fought out their battle in their own way and won out where many others would have failed. Dick's recovery is a lot less than 100% but he did go flying again, even continued giving instruction to students, conducted 'ground schools,' drives a car and a motorcycle with sidecar. International Harvester reinstated him in office work of managerial status. They are grandparents now, and two really wonderful people.

One day, I had dropped or picked up someone near the CFQC broadcasting towers at Saskatoon. On takeoff, I hadn't attained much altitude when all at once there was another aircraft alongside. I think it was a green Piper, and who should be grinning and waving from the rear seat but Dick Pittaway. He was the instructor and his student was in the front seat. Those days I carried a slide camera, so quickly got it out and took their picture. They were close enough that on the slide, one can recognize Dick and the student. It really wasn't anything special in itself, but the fact that it was Dick meant a lot to me after all the trouble he'd been through.

Peter Foulger – Home Movies

A great friend of mine, an Englishman and civil engineer, was in charge of highway construction in our area about 1960-1961. Peter Foulger would come into town for a coffee break and formed the habit of seeing if I could have coffee with him, half a block from our shop. As the friendship ripened, he became more interested in my flying and yarns about it. He was an amateur home movie fan and had quite a library of his private films. At my suggestion that he should add some that were taken from the plane, he became interested.

We made several flights, and by the time I had run out of ideas, Peter had enriched his library to an extent beyond his first impressions. The first thing we did was to fly alongside a large white cloud so that the bright sun on the other side of the plane would cast a silhouette shadow of the plane on the white cloud surface. The moisture in the cloud provided a circular rainbow all around the dark silhouette of the plane. On the ground, one can see only a one-half circle of the rainbow, only from left horizon to right horizon. But in the air, with no ground surface to get in the way, one sees the remaining, or lower half, and the result is a rainbow in a complete circle. Peter took several of these shots and was quite pleased.

I talked him into taking movies, first out the side window and then through the windshield, while I put the plane through respective loops for each occasion. I advised him to brace himself and the camera well, due mostly to increased 'G-force' on the pullout at the bottom of the loop. The results more than thrilled him and he later claimed that one person had fallen right out of his chair while viewing the films. It was pretty impressive alright, to see the earth's surface gyrate in a complete circle. Other shots were taken through stall-turns, and in low-flying. Anyway, Peter was quite thrilled to add these films to his library, so much so that he lost his terror of our antics in the air.

When I gave rides to his wife and son Peter Jr., they were pretty mild rides, and I didn't fool around like we did when we were taking pictures.

Later, Peter returned the favour by getting his crew, after hours, to survey and blueprint our airport. This was necessary for our town in applying for licensing of the field for a satellite flying school to be conducted at Kerrobert Airport. The town paid the bill and I think the boys charged only a hundred bucks – a bargain.

Near The End Of The Road

During the course of his flying, Walter Williams had many adventures and made many friends. None were as close to him as those who worked with him in the shop of B. Williams & Son IHC, and Walter grieved when those men either left the business or died.

Flying EVO for all those years was a tonic for Walter, helping him through the guilt and pain of a failed marriage and giving him the ability to have a little fun and also help others who were in need.

Although it might not be apparent from his stories, Walter's flying habits changed a little after his huge crash with Kasper Herle in 1952, said his son Dave. "Maybe his goose gyros were jogged a bit or else he didn't want that much trouble anymore, because one winter night we were churning along in thick snow with ice building up on EVO again, about 50 feet (15 m) above the CPR tracks, when Dad cut power and landed at the next town while we could still see the ground. We had supper in the café and waited for a truck to take us to Kerrobert." Before the crash, Walter would have carried on and taken his chances on making a safe landing at home.

For Walter's tombstone in Saskatoon's Woodlawn cemetery, his artist son created a picture of EVO on skis, just barely skimming over a barbed wire fence that was half-buried in the snow in the middle of a field. "Somehow that seems appropriate for a stern but resolutely good guy like Walter Williams," said Dave. "When he is Judged, it will be scary, but I bet he will rise up and pass over the threshold into heaven."

A Tribute To Harold Patterson

In 1952, when Morley Nord, our partsman, had decided to return to RCMP service and been accepted, I had advertised, interviewed and employed Harold Patterson of Birch Hills. When I met and interviewed him in Saskatoon, he turned out to have the build of a gas barrel – 46" at chest (71 cm), waist and hips – quite heavy and very firm. He was cross-eyed from an instrument birth. His parents lived at or near Birch Hills and his sister was secretary at the Birch Hills Hospital.

Over a dinner, we talked things over and made a deal. I brought him back to Kerrobert and found room and board for him at Olive May's place, as Harold was always a bachelor. He loved to play pool and it was always amusing to see him looking 'sideways' to shoot, but he was really good at it. In the evenings, he could always be found at the pool hall until it closed and he had to go home, usually after a coffee with me at the café. Harold was most honest, conscientious and loyal and it came to pass that I loved the guy and I think he loved me, too.

Nearly fours years passed, and one time when he was halfway through his holiday period, he phoned me on a busy Saturday night to say that he had a very good offer in his hometown of Birch Hills and would like to resign. It was quite a shock but I took it 'in stride' when he explained that his folks were really not well and that he would like to be living nearer to them. I thanked him for letting me know as soon as possible and hung up the phone with a very heavy heart.

(For several years, we had been hiring Slim Murdoch who had previously worked in our parts department for six months to fill in during Harold's holidays – Slim's holidays being arranged to coincide with Harold's.)

I always knew that Harold, never being able to eat enough and being built the way he was, would some day 'drop' from heart failure. Well, that's exactly what happened. He was sitting on a Coke machine several years later after his evening game of pool when he just keeled over and was dead when he hit the floor.

The first winter Harold was with me, there came phone calls re: people needing the plane. At first, Harold would get the name but no further details, and it would severely tax me to connect with the party involved. Harold had very tender feelings and when I took up this matter, he really sulked and at first refused to take any further messages of that nature. But I had a good talk with him and he turned out to be a real jewel in ascertaining details which would pinpoint me to a certain spot and time – for instance, "The man on a snowbank 60 miles (96 km) away in the dark."

When I gave Harold his final cheque (we paid monthly those days), he had tears in his eyes when he told me that this was his 47th cheque from me – and I nearly cried, too.

Selling Aviation

All through my flying years, involving thousands of passengers, I sold aviation as a means of travel compatible with flying conditions, making allowances for circumstances which could negate flying. Now, further to that last phrase, I didn't always practice what I preached. My average of good luck under unsuitable conditions was very high but there were times when I did get caught and not charge it to anyone but yours truly. I knew the rules – knew I was breaking them, and therefore had to live with whatever the consequences, 'for better or for worse.' Only once did a passenger become injured. I was injured worse than he was, but this did not diminish my regrets about his getting hurt due to my habit of taking foolish chances.

You see, it's like some other things – one becomes accustomed to the chance good fortune of 'getting away with it' and tends eventually to think that good luck will never let him down. However, sometimes one does encounter the dead end and when there's no way to prevent it, the boom lowers.

I was injured only the one time, but poor faithful EVO took an awful beating sometimes. Through the years, it cost a lot of money and time and travel to make necessary repairs. Despite all these things and being the only aircraft for miles around, that part of my activities was a matter of public observation. Still, I always stoutly defended the principle and practice of aviation, making it clear that my failures were my own fault because, behind it all – I did know better.

Quite a few times the passenger would be a person who had sworn to himself or herself that he or she would never enter an aircraft, let alone fly in one. I recall when Pete Kopp shut his eyes and covered his head with his arms, so great was his terror of flight. After we had gone about halfway to our destination, I persuaded him to take a peek out the window, pointing out that we were at least a thousand feet clear of the snow-covered ground. He did look, and I pointed out Kerrobert and other places he knew.

Finally, we landed at our destination where he was to look at a second-hand machine. We looked over the machine, talked with the owner, Eph Read, who had flown several times with me, before that time, and made a deal (while Pete Kopp was in shock, no doubt). Then we nonchalantly got into the plane and flew home, Pete feeling more relaxed with every passing minute. When I taxied into his yard, only a few yards from his house, Pete didn't want to get out of the plane, but would have preferred to spend the rest of the afternoon right where he was, safety belt on and all, and would fly with me again at any time, if necessary. He was 'sold' on aviation.

Another time a young female schoolteacher from south of Luseland had to get back to her school at Superb this particular Monday morning. Roads had all plugged in while she visited with her folks at home. Her father phoned for me and by the time I arrived she nearly had to be bound and gagged to get into 'that thing!'

We got her in and belted down, I flipped the prop and had to taxi quite a way south, turn around and take off northward between a telephone line and a fence, because of wind direction. Ed Gurhlke, her Dad, was elated. But the girl began to scream and screech orders, and I quietly reminded her that she was not now an order-giving schoolteacher but just another passenger, and that I was the pilot and knew what I was doing. I told her she could put on her show and act up any way she could think up, but I'd get her to school in time and in good shape – just another humdrum flight.

Well, she came to her senses and by the time we got to her school, she hated to get out. Thought she'd pulled off a dandy and would fly with me again any time – Oh, I'd bite my nails sometimes and say I wondered if we'd get this thing down right side up, but everybody knew I'd always made it – with a couple of exceptions. I converted many people from the terror of flying, to liking and believing in it. Quiet explanation and assurance certainly went a long way.

Satellite Flying School

Neil McDonald had come to our shop as a qualified 'pressure welder' with Direct-Current papers. He was an excellent welder, resourceful and inventive, and trade in that field flourished again.

I had had to get a divorce, so to speak, from my welding activities since the death of our father had forced me to spend my time managing and selling. I had to hire men to do the work I'd been doing for years prior to father's passing.

Neil was not only a superlative welder but he had a burning desire to become a mechanic as well. Our welder was a portable unit but furnished AC current, which required a different welding rod in pressure welding. So Neil practised up on that rod and passed his exam, and therefore was doubly qualified as a pressure welder, holding both AC and Direct Current ratings. I helped and encouraged him in his mechanical endeavours, and he had much encouragement from the service department of IHC in Saskatoon. Neil was so versatile and dependable and willing and ready for anything that we became good friends as well, and I really loved the guy.

One day, after a long hot session of welding, he shut down the outfit, came to my office and asked what all would be involved for him to learn to fly. I told him all that I had had to go through to get my private licence, always having to go to Saskatoon, but that new regulations were permitting satellite schools at fields like Kerrobert's, with a government grant. If we could arrange it, he would be only a mile from his lessons and the time would shrink from months, in my case, to days in his case. So, we decided to find out all about it and see if that could come about.

We flew to North Battleford and interviewed Hugh McPhail, my friend, who ran a flying school there. He filled us in on details and he had already conducted satellites at other points. We would have to get a temporary licence on our field, comply with whatever requirements the Department of Transport dictated, and go through a lot of red tape. He would give us all the help he could from his end.

Neil and I went to a meeting of our town council, stated our case, and asked their help. We explained that the school would have to turn out 10 or more new pilots to qualify for the grant, and that the field would have to be formally surveyed and a blueprint sent in, etc., and that government inspectors would have to be satisfied.

The council promised help, wishing to have the school held at our airport, but Neil and I would have to do the legwork. Peter Foulger arranged for the survey, town men made the field markers – the town paying the bills. Neil and I talked a dozen other fellows into taking the course, from as far away as Denzil.

Re: the survey, it was pointed out by the town clerk that one corner of our strip went into some lots that had been sold when Kerrobert was born, owned by people in Ontario who had been 'taken in,' in the original enthusiastic promotion in the early days that Kerrobert would eventually become a great Western Canada metropolis. However, for our purpose, it was a case of keep mum and tread lightly. Eventually, everything passed government requirements, we had enough guys signed up and we were ready to go!

McPhail moved planes and instructors to Kerrobert, we obtained free use of a schoolroom at nights for the ground schooling, the air was full of airplanes (including mine) for several weeks, and we finally had the required 10 new pilots pass their exams. Everybody concerned qualified for the government grant.

From everyone's standpoint, it was a much cheaper deal and the course was conducted 'right at home.' It all took a lot of arranging and hard work, but how glad and happy we all were when all was completed. Of course, EVO's hangar was the focal point of the whole effort and the brome grass didn't get very high on the field that year – it just got worn off! Our crop of new pilots included a doctor, a lawyer, farm fellows and wage-earners like Neil. Flying affects everyone about the same way – it just burns a big hole in you. The new pilots couldn't think of anything else. They just wanted to fly all the time.

I told Neil one day in the shop that he didn't have to buy a plane, as he could fly my EVO any time, just pay the bare expenses, that's all. He was very pleased and did fly EVO a lot but NEVER failed to ask or check with me beforehand. He was on the way to becoming a good pilot when he was killed one night on the highway in his car by a drunk who just drove right into him.

With the loss of my friend Neil and his loss in the business,[42] flying fever diminished somewhat in my own life. EVO was getting old and would soon require a whole new fabric job, so one fall I sold her to help me make my year-end settlement with International Harvester.

This was about the end of my flying years, and I had to swallow a lot to accept that fact. However, I had given much more through flying than I ever recovered monetarily, and I realized that to stop flying was the best thing for me after all from that time forward.

As a relief from the nostalgia caused by relating the former, and to substantiate my faith in Neil, I shall tell of the time when something happened which I think, Dave, that you don't think I observed.

It was early one evening and Neil was going to take you for a ride in EVO. Not long before in the shop, Neil and I had been talking about flying, and I had told him that sometimes things can happen so fast that require a pilot to react so quickly there isn't even time to THINK before making a corrective move. It had to be done instinctively. I recall telling him, jokingly, that there isn't time to write home and ask, 'What'll I do now?' I told him that you have to 'Do it NOW,' without thinking, or lose everything.

Neil and you, Dave, went down to the hangar after supper, got EVO out and were going for a flight. EVO had two gas tanks – one in front, like in a Cub, and the reserve tank was behind the seat, about the same level as the front one, in level flight, perhaps slightly higher. Some way that gas line connecting the two tanks had been left open and all the gas from the front tank ran back into the rear tank, due to the plane tilting down at the back, to rest on the tail wheel. The rear tank showed lots of gas, but the gas would not run into the front tank until the plane was in level flight. You guys thought there would be enough gas in the front tank to start you off and then gas from the rear

---

[42] *Neil McDonald worked for Walter Williams from July 1958 until his accidental death in April 1961.*

tank would run forward and feed the front tank. The front tank was the only one that fed gas to the engine.

Well, something made me watch from the pickup truck down by the elevators, and I saw you two fire up EVO. I didn't know then about the gas situation. You had enough gas in the front tank for the warm-up and then you started to take off. You just got a few feet into the air when the engine quit – out of gas in the front tank. I saw the prop stop.

Well, sir, Neil was right on the bit. He immediately nosed 'er down and you two made a dandy landing – right on takeoff. Then you put gas in the front tank, took off and had your flight. You never mentioned it and I didn't bother to say I'd watched the whole thing. I was pretty proud of Neil's immediate and appropriate reaction.

Jim Young – Compeer, Alta.

It was January 28, 1950, a Saturday. Kindersley was coming up to Kerrobert to play hockey with the Kerrobert Tigers that night and there was great rivalry between the teams from neighbouring towns. Jim Young, a young fella at that time from Compeer, Alta., was in Kerrobert that Saturday afternoon and the Tigers made it plain that if Jim could play with Kerrobert that night, they'd have a better chance against Kindersley.

Jim told them that he would be needed at home to do chores for a bunch of cattle and it wouldn't be fair for the folks at home if he played hockey all over the country. He surely would like to play but that was the way it was for him. Kerrobert coaxed and finally asked if he'd play if Walt Williams flew him home early the next morning.

Well, perhaps he phoned the folks at home, I don't know, but it was agreed that he would play that night under those conditions. The game was played and Kindersley beat Kerrobert – 4 to 2. However, Kerrobert was glad to have Jim playing for them that night.

Next morning, January 29, Jim and I were in the air by 9:30, started out for Compeer and the Young farm. It was Jim's first ride in a plane and his eyes were just sparkling – he didn't miss a thing. I had known the Youngs a long time and it was really easy for Jim to understand anything I could tell him about flying. Perhaps that was the day he got hooked on airplanes. He had already been using a snowplane, but flying was different.

Along about Major, Sask., he wondered if I'd mind making a small detour to fly over a certain farm. I said sure – where is it? Turned out to be the Ferner farm, north of Fusilier. When he pointed out the farm, I asked if he wanted to 'buzz' it and he said yes – so we did. When the skis straddled the chimney, Jim was about ready to get out – there was terrific magnetism about that place for him – Margaret Koneker, teacher of the nearby Warcop School, lived there. Jim was really havin' a good day, but more about that later...

A few minutes after that, we were approaching Jim's home farm, so that Jim wouldn't have too far to walk, I decided to squeeze into a small field just across the road from the Young farmstead. We just nicely missed the telephone line and a fence corner, and touched down on a slight down slope towards a low spot with a few willows in it. With no brakes or wind to slow us down, we were still sliding along briskly when all of a sudden a flock of partridges burst out of the snow, right in front of our idling propeller. That was the day we found out how very agile birds can be in flight. Not one of those birds was touched by any part of the plane. We came to a stop in the low spot and I'm sure he walked on air all the way home.

It didn't seem to be very long afterwards that we heard that Margaret and Jim were married. They started up for themselves on a farm near Jim's home, replacing the old house that had been there by building a new one. They had two nice little girls who are two nice young ladies. Now, after many years, the girls are on their own. Jim has passed on and though Marg lives in Luseland, she still has the farm.

Somewhere along the way, Jim learned to fly, and by all reports he was born to it. There are good flyers and some not-so-good, but Jim was one of the good ones. Many years later his plane crashed in a field. Jim was killed and I choose to think that he went out the way he would have wanted to, and is still flying and will be forever. He was buried beside his father's grave in Dorca Cemetery near Compeer. Marg had a likeness of Jim's favourite plane in flight engraved on the stone. The drawing of the plane was furnished by my son Dave, who among other things, is a flyer and artist. Dave knew Jim well – flew with him and for him, so the drawing was a work of sentiment and accuracy. Also, Dave thinks Marg is one of the finest ladies he ever met.

Just flying a plane didn't satisfy Jim Young, so he and a non-flyer friend, Marion Galloway, went into the crop spraying business. This requires flying finesse to the n'th degree, to the extent that I don't think any insurance company in the world would insure a crop-sprayer. Jim loved it and lived it. Marion's son Neil learned to fly too, and business boomed. They bought another plane one year and hired my son Dave to help out and Dave logged 85 hours of field-spraying time with Young and Galloway.

My Dave is a writer and several years later, wrote quite an

article about the good and bad times of field spraying. This was published without any deletions, complete with drawings and cartoons by Dave, in a Calgary flying magazine – *Wings Limited*. Many were the comical aspects of that venture and Marg wouldn't part with her copy of that issue for anything.

Nick Huckle was station agent for the CPR at Compeer, and he had learned to fly. One day, he got a plane from Young and Galloway to get a bit of flying time and to fly John Ezokites from Kerrobert to Compeer. I took off a few minutes to drive John down to the plane, and then hurried back to the shop before they were to take off. It seemed only a few minutes later that someone burst into the shop with the news that a plane had crashed at our airport. I hurried down and sure enough, it was Nick and John. They had stalled on takeoff and dived onto the field at about an 85-degree angle. Both men were gone, and the plane a total loss. Perhaps it was the last time I saw Jim Young when, that evening, with several friends, Jim came to the shop and we talked it all over. Jim was very upset.

Jim's mother's name was Clarke, and in the past seven years I have known two of her nephews, both United Church ministers, Bill and Harvey. Now, in 1979, Rev. Bill Clarke is serving Grace-Westminster United Church here in Saskatoon and Rev. Harvey Clarke has First United Church in Swift Current. I always regarded Mrs. Ella Young as a very gracious lady who must have commanded extreme respect from everyone who met her. Latest word I had was that she now lives in the Kamloops, B.C. area.

Ed Hopkins – Near Wilkie

Ed Hopkins was a young lad who worked as a mechanic in the Edmonds & Wright G.M. and John Deere dealership in Kerrobert. Everybody called him 'Hoppy,' and he was really a pleasant jolly fellow. His family lived northeast of Wilkie and he wanted to go visit them. I said I'd never landed in that area before but we could look it over and try it or fly home again – whichever we decided.

It was a perfect summer day so we fired up EVO, rolled the wheels a little way and were happily in the air, chatting and joking away like two guys in their right minds. Past Wilkie, he guided me to the farm, which was in a no-no area for airplanes – patchy bush with either hay or hay crop fields between the patches and little knolls all over the place.

Well, fortunately or otherwise, I was not one to back down easily, so I circled and scouted until I saw a very small streak in an area where the hay between the bush had been baled in small stooks of three each. I explained to Hoppy that this little strip in the bush was risky, but the best I could pick out. It meant that we'd put the wheels down on one knoll, roll down and up two or three more knolls, trying not to catch a tree with a wing, using brakes as much as possible, hoping to get stopped without disaster. Well, Hoppy said, "Sure, your neck's here, too," and he'd go along with anything I'd try.

So I circled around, lined up with this little space (with both eyes wide open, of course) and touched down on the first knoll at about 40 miles an hour. Wiggling to miss the bush, two or three knolls later, we were slowed down to where I thought we 'had 'er made.' However, rolling down that last knoll, there was a small stook of three hay bales dead ahead. I had barely enough time to cut the switch and steered right just enough for the prop to miss them. But the left wheel banged into them. We wrecked the stook, busted one bale, and the baler twine was wrapped around the left axle. Sure was lucky and no harm done (except to one bale).

We didn't have far to walk over to Hoppy's farm and his folks. Hoppy had a better time than I did. Just because we'd teased our way into this very impractical field didn't mean that we'd get out of it. So, during part of our stay there, I went over the field on foot, clearing this and that, pacing distance, praying all the while that Lady Luck would let us be airborne again, on our way back home.

Eventually, it was time to head for home, and Hoppy and I strapped ourselves in. I told him the risks, but he agreed to take whatever happened and I let my 65 small horses out of the barn – full throttle, and prayin' a little. Y' know, we roared over a few knolls and were finally in the air, and hadn't hit a thing! We got away with a lot of sins that day, but made it!

Through the intervening years, I've remembered Hoppy, but today, March 26, 1979, something happened which made this whole incident flash back.

I had been visiting my sister Marion at City Hospital on the third floor and, at the elevator, a lady was coming along the hall. When the door opened, I held it open until she entered and on the way down to the main floor and walking down the hall, I learned that she was concerned about missing the bus out to Wilkie (her husband had been in City for five weeks). At the door, I put on my rubbers and she was standing at the door, wondering if she should call a taxi.

Society has changed in the past few years, and I guess I have a little bit, too, so I didn't offer to drive her to the bus – realizing that she could be suspicious of me, too. I recognized her Kerrobert-Wilkie-Unity-German accent, and this took me 'way back to my younger days. This lady might be my own age.

I paused outside the door but started to walk to the car. Halfway to the car, I couldn't stand it any more, so I walked back and asked her if she'd mind if I drove her to the bus depot to catch her bus. She hesitated but I said, "Come on, I think I know your people – my home town is Kerrobert." So she came, and my conscience quit bothering me.

Making small talk in the car, her name turned out to be Heiland, and did I know an Ed Hopkins who lived only a mile or so from Heilands – used to work in Kerrobert?

Well, this whole incident flashed back and I told her about it. She said, yes, that's him, because visiting is never dull when Ed is around.

She said Ed is farming the home farm and has a bunch of kids (he was always a hard, conscientious worker). I dropped her off at the depot, to her great relief.

The world gets small sometimes, doesn't it?

Going To Sleep In Flight

Many times, I would be so tired and played out that I should have gone to bed for some rest instead of taking off on a flight for someone. I'd have to work all night in the shop to keep promises there in order to make a flight I'd promised somebody 'first thing in the morning.' This meant that a very tired boy would take off on a flight. It was not so bad as long as I had someone to talk to but coming back alone, I'd get pretty sleepy. This was worst when it was a smooth flight, with no bucking or rocking to correct (which would help keep me awake) – also a hot sun didn't help me very much.

The first time I dropped off to sleep in flight, it was not long before the left wing and nose of the plane dropped a bit, the engine speeded up a bit, too, and I was headed into a dive, would soon run out of air and – Bingo – hit the ground. I quickly came to, twitched the plane back into level flight and was alarmed enough to make the rest of the flight OK. This was the only time this happened to me. All other times, and there were many, I unconsciously maintained level flight, and always gained altitude. One time, on a flight home from Saskatoon, I was right on course, but passed over Biggar a mile high. By that time a fellow feels pretty foolish and, having rested a little, finishes the flight successfully.

There was the time when Mrs. Gust wanted in the worst way to get to Drayton Valley as soon as possible because the eldest daughter surely needed her. I don't know if it was illness or lonesomeness, but Mrs. Gust agreed on the price and made a date for dawn the next morning. I was dead tired and worked the rest of the night because I'd be away for a large part of the next day.

It was slow going, against a breeze from the west, so by the time I reached Camrose, Alta., I didn't want to get lower on gas than I already was, so we landed in a field with about a hundred head of cattle in it – it was a dairy farm and the cattle were Holsteins. Leaving Mrs. Gust in the plane, I walked to the buildings and bought five gallons of car gas. When I got back to the plane it was surrounded by curious cattle. Poured in the gas, walked back with the can, came back and had quite a time herding the cattle all over to one side of the field that I might have enough room to escape from the field or pasture.

We flew west, following the highway to Wetaskiwin, where we landed and gassed up. Lloyd Johnson's wife looked after us (Lloyd had checked me out in a G-3 Cub several years before at North Battleford, when I was dismantling the heat plant which is now the Kerrobert Rink) and she told me where Drayton Valley was – just about 70 miles – straight west over real bush country. Boy, was I tired! But I toughed it out (there was nowhere to land anyway along the way), and I finally reached Drayton Valley, which was completely serviced by trucks, as there was no railway. I remember being disappointed to find that their fine strip was gravelled at the time, which meant that on takeoff, the prop and parts of the plane would be chipped by small stones picked up by the prop blast.

We landed OK, and a passing truck took us right to the trailer where Mrs. Gust's daughter lived. I didn't go in and the man drove me out to the plane again – no charge, glad to help. Well, well, no dinner and nearly dead with fatigue, I started out for Wetaskiwin. Sure, it was foolish, but I started out anyway.

I must have gone to sleep soon after I got into the air. The next thing I knew was when I wakened, wondering where I was. There was so much bush and some waters here and there. I had missed seeing Pigeon Lake, which really wasn't small. I had about a mile of altitude and finally identified Edmonton to my left and a town that could be Wetaskiwin to my right, 40 miles south of Edmonton, and sure enough, I was soon approaching the highway. I was about 12 miles off course, north of Wetaskiwin.

So, I just flew down the highway, throttled back a bit to lose that altitude and gassed 'er full at Wetaskiwin. Then I was in the air again, realizing that I had had more than my share of good luck for the day, and reached Kerrobert without going to sleep again. Oh, I'd hit myself real hard, and used all the tricks I knew, but kept awake, landed OK, put the plane away, and went back to work in the shop.

Another time, the day after the Len Ward boy drowned in the Kerrobert Dam (he was 10 and so were you, Dave, at that time, so it would be 1950). After we pulled the body out of the water, I flew

Mrs. Andy Hamm to a field near her home farm because her father was deathly ill. Andy, being a druggist, gave her an anti-sickness pill before we left (she was prone to motion sickness), so she took the rough flight pretty well. There were big white clouds all over the sky and the flight was rough. At one time, the plane nearly turned upside down and she took that in her usual cheerful style. On the way back, about Viscount (I'd been up nearly all night and was very tired) I thought of landing a short snooze to refresh me. I landed but the wind buffeted the plane so much I just gunned 'er off. I was a pretty tired boy when I landed at home.

These things I've kept quiet about all these years, but now that I've joined the seniors, it doesn't matter any more to the government boys, and I'm still glad to be alive, and well enough to recount these experiences. I find myself living them all over again as I write.

Bill Hellofs – Cattle Buying

Throughout my flying years, I flew Bill Hellofs many times. I'd land him near a designated farm, walk in with him to the cattle pen and finally to the house. Haggling and chiselling for a carload of cattle would get down to the difference between $10,500 and $11,000 and a deal would finally develop or not develop, depending on who won the argument. Then it was time to fly on to the next call on his list.

Bill was in the butcher shop and cattle-shipping business, and had been at it so long that I remember my father in his farming days (which ended when I was eight years old), told me that he always seemed to get a better deal from Bill Hellofs, whether it was a few head or a carload. Bill seldom paid me on the spot, so I would have to catch him when he was in town and show him he owed me so much for specified trips, and I'd get a cheque up-to-date, no argument. Bill must have trusted me and was a stoic passenger, usually with both hands clasped around one knee. Sometimes I'd made quick turns and twists, examining a landing area. He'd sit there like a statue and I could fly as though I were alone. I was ever grateful that he never complained.

Many times he told me of the more unconventional aspects of his life, knowing that I would never tell. One thing he hated was the 'rope,' especially in the administration of capital punishment. After we'd landed, I would ask him, "How's that, Bill?" and he always replied, "Just fine," grabbed his bag and we'd start wading through the snow.

One day in the Broadacres area, the 65-HP engine of EVO petered out and I couldn't get off the snow with Bill aboard. EVO was hitting on three cylinders. That first engine had given me many more hours than was recommended by D.O.T. I had to leave Bill at the farm and limp home, alone on three cylinders, promising that I would get another flyer to pick him up. I was ashamed and pretty well disappointed but a fact is a fact, isn't it?

I phoned Tony Hoiland at Kindersley, who had a Cessna 120, asked him to fly Bill for the rest of the day, giving him detailed instructions for pickup. Tony complied and Bill got back OK. I had to pay Tony for his trouble.

My next phone call was to McDonald Bros. Aircraft in Winnipeg. Yes, they had an overhauled and guaranteed 65-HP Continental engine, and if I would ship them my worn-out engine, they would take $650 difference. I accepted the terms and said, "Ship it." They took my word that I would ship the old engine to them, so when the overhauled engine arrived, the C.O.D. bill was only the $650.

I got in touch with my airport buddies in Saskatoon and, instead of having to hire them to fly out and install the replacement engine, they said that if I made the engine change and flew in to Saskatoon, they would check it all over and sign it out as though they had done it themselves. I took out the old engine and installed the replacement in winter weather. I shipped the old one back to Winnipeg in the crate the new one had come in. Then I flew EVO to Saskatoon, where my friends checked everything out and signed out the engine logbook. Sure nice to have good friends, isn't it?

So, with the fresh start of an overhauled and guaranteed engine, I continued cheating death time after time, postponing the time when I'd have to meet my Maker.

Bill Hellofs continued to be my customer. In retrospect, I'm reminded of something someone wrote: 'Our life is God's gift to us. What we do with it is our gift to Him.'

Throughout all the chances I took, and the close shaves I had, I tried very hard to extend my future, but I was never unaware of the possibility that God's tolerance had let me get away with it. Sure, I damaged my plane several times and suffered injury once, but I was always able to get the plane repaired, and in the one instance, myself. I was able to go on flying until I decided to sell the plane, and quit flying.

Air In My Hair

In the years of my flying, I worked practically night and day and flew the rest of the time, after 1948 September. The first year I had EVO, I logged over 350 hours and ended somewhere between 3,000 and 4,000 hours because there are few log books which are a true record for engine, aircraft and pilot (and there's a log book for each of these) because of one reason or another.

Mostly in the summertime, I'd be on the road, in shop or office and some days were pretty hectic. There were many times when I would take a break between working all day and working nearly all night and go flying for an hour. With EVO, its 65-HP engine using a little over 2½ gallons per hour, I used to refresh myself and get 'air in my hair.' I'd horse around, doing all kinds of things like high-flying, stunts, low-flying buzzing, feinting a crash – anything to relax for awhile.

'Toilet paper' was a great game and, at first, I'd use one roll. The idea being that at 2,000 to 3,000 feet (900 m) altitude you threw out the roll, having unrolled a 'tail' to start it unrolling, and then you would fly back and forth and cut the streamer that was unrolling on its way to the ground. A wing cut was best, because then no paper fouled anything. I hit it dead centre one time and was digging toilet paper out of the engine cowling where it had got trapped. Got pretty good with one roll so tried two rolls, and then it was a bigger trick to get lined up and cut both streamers. Took some good figuring to turn around quickly and be lined up with the two rolls, but I got so I could handle that, too.

I found a place where, due to lower ground level, if I flew there, I was level with a country road. That road had a culvert. I could have won many a bet because when I flew by, I could see right through the culvert, just for a fraction of a second. I did this for some friends and justified the statement that I could see through a culvert from my aircraft.

It's a fact that if a pilot idles his engine and opens his window, he can shout out to a person directly below. Of course, he can't hear an answer, but many a time I have startled someone by calling out a message or a joke and used his or her name. Similarly, a student at a parachute school can receive instructions from an instructor on the ground because he doesn't have an engine to drown out the instructor's voice.

Now that I'm older and bald, and mentioning that I used to get relaxation from getting 'air in my hair,' I say that I must have overdone it because now there's more air than hair, but there are advantages to having an air-cooled head. One can think as hard as one can and his head won't heat up and burn out like the guys with hair all over their heads.

Frank Beatty ran our theatre and, on a summer evening, he had just finished his dinner and it was too early to go down to the theatre. So he went out to the front lawn to relax in a reclining lawn chair he had there. Then I appeared in the blue and he watched me. That night I decided to do a dozen or two loops without stopping and finish up with some small turns, and stall-and-dive diversions. Frank told me afterwards that he fell out of the chair and became ill – just watching. We had a good laugh over that. I invited him to come along next time, and he said, "No way!"

Flying became a great passion, relaxer and a field of experimentation with me. Calculating risks became the common thing, and success the reward. EVO should have kicked me out but, having no brains of her own, did as I controlled. Many other pilots wouldn't tackle or even think of doing the things I pulled off with EVO. I got a kick out of it (once in the face), but it did put colour into my life and did wonders for more than 25 years of marital separation. What Old Smokey did in her turn, EVO did for the rest of that period of my life.

I knew, through Old Smokey and EVO, that I was branded the most harebrained fool in the country, but it held me together morally and in regard to flying, if it could be done with an airplane, people said, "Get Walter Williams." I didn't resent the harebrained bit one iota, but I did receive great reward from the confidence people exhibited when the chips were down and they needed me. I couldn't have helped as much as I did it if were not that EVO and I became as compatible as thumb and forefinger, and everyone knew that my neck was there as well as theirs.

I did what servicing was allowed for a private pilot, got a 'hundred-hour check' every several hundred hours, and hired the experts to look after the things which were beyond my licence in keeping the plane in reliable running order. It is absolutely wonderful the confidence a man can place in his machine. Never once did EVO let me down. Any unfortunate events were my fault, not EVO's.

Acknowledgements

The publisher gratefully acknowledges the financial assistance of: the Saskatchewan Publishers Group through the Cultural Industries Development Fund; St. Paul's United Church Women in Kindersley, Sask., and all those who pre-ordered a book.

Thank you: to Dave and Miriam Williams, Walter's son and daughter-in-law, for providing family photos, documents, memories and detailed information on Walter's life and flying days; to Walter's niece Faye Climenhaga for providing family photos and memories; to Walter's brother-in-law Esmond Allcock and sister-in-law Ferne Vincent for sharing memories of Walter and Jean in their younger years; to Walter's niece Brenda Lawrence for assisting with photo identification and memories; to Lyle Busch for Kerrobert details; and to Harv Heeg for explaining many aircraft terms footnoted in this book.

Thank you to Richard Anderson and Kerrobert Paint & Auto Body, as well as Lorne Janzen and the Town of Kindersley for supporting this book within their communities.

Thank you to Al Driver for his 'backup' editing and constant support.

Finally, a special thank you to the late Rev. Romona Underwood Williams for recognizing the importance of publishing Walter's stories, and to Rev. Joyce Sasse for acting on the wishes of her friend Romona and finding a publisher for ***Prairie Pilot: Lady Luck was on My Side***.

A fascinating and important piece of Saskatchewan history has now been preserved because of all of you.

To order more copies of

PRAIRIE PILOT

LADY LUCK WAS ON MY SIDE

THE STORIES OF WALTER D. WILLIAMS
Compiled and Edited by Deana J. Driver

Contact

DriverWorks Ink
110 McCarthy Blvd. N., Regina, Saskatchewan S4R 6A4
306-545-5293
www.driverworks.ca